PRAISE FOR *THE FOOTBALL GAME THAT CHANGED AMERICA*

"Dennis is a bona fide expert on anything and everything connected to the Super Bowl. He has tracked the impact of this colossal sporting event from the very start and has his finger on the pulse of what it will look like in the years to come. This book takes you behind the scenes to see what has made the game and all that surrounds it the phenomenon it is today."

—IAN EAGLE, CBS Sports commentator

"Nobody is more qualified to discuss the Super Bowl and its influence on the American culture. Dennis combines a career as a TV professional with academia and 'fandom' to cover all the bases! Bravo!"

—DREW ESOCOFF, directed seven Super Bowl telecasts, Sports Broadcasting Hall of Fame 2022

"If there was ever a topic worthy of complete inspection, the Super Bowl is it. From its history to every aspect of the spectacle, Dennis Deninger details every angle in a thorough and entertaining style."

—FRED GAUDELLI, produced seven Super Bowl telecasts, Sports Broadcasting Hall of Fame 2020

"The Super Bowl has grown to almost supernatural significance since it was first played before a less than capacity crowd in the Los Angeles Coliseum in January 1967. Dennis Deninger has done a marvelous job documenting what it has come to mean for all of us who love the sport of football. I highly recommend this book."

—VERNE LUNDQUIST, CBS Sports commentator, Sports Emmy Lifetime Achievement Award 2016, former TV voice of the Dallas Cowboys

"In a little over a half century, the Super Bowl has evolved from a game that didn't sell out into a national holiday—by far the most-watched television program in the United States annually. Dennis Deninger takes the readers on a journey covering all aspects of the football game that changed America . . . championship prose at its finest!"

—KENNY ALBERT, FOX/TNT/MSG/NBC sportscaster, author of
A Mic for All Seasons

"In the United States, the Super Bowl has become the preeminent sporting event, eclipsing even the World Cup and the Olympics. It captures the passion Americans have for their favorite teams in their favorite sport. *The Football Game That Changed America* is a captivating story of how the Super Bowl was created and how it grew into a colossal event that transcends sport. Dennis Deninger, an Emmy Award-winning television producer and professor of sport media, takes you behind the scenes to feel the power, the magic, and the magnetism of America's premier sporting event. Don't miss it!"

—DAVID FALK, legendary sports agent

"It used to be 'just' a game. It's hard to remember that now. But thanks to this amazing book by Dennis Deninger, we all get to see exactly how that changed—thanks to Joe Namath, Vegas, all those commercials, your buddy who runs your Super Bowl pool, and the largest collection of TV cameras in America. Dennis is a great storyteller whose exceptional attention to detail weaves this improbable tale together in a way no one ever has. I'm so grateful he wrote this book!"

—JAYSON STARK, senior writer at *The Athletic*, Baseball Hall of
Fame Career Excellence Award 2019

"Some of the most entertaining and educational hours I spent at Syracuse University came in Professor Deninger's classroom. His energy, passion, and deep knowledge of the material kept it fun—and memorable. Years later, I can still recite the stories of Johnny Unitas playing hero in 'The Greatest Game Ever Played,' Rep. Hale Boggs cutting a deal to enable the NFL merger, and Joe Namath guaranteeing a win—and that was all before 1970! When it comes to the intersection of sports and business, there's no one I'd rather learn from than Dennis Deninger."

—DREW CARTER, TV voice of the Boston Celtics

"From the network board room to the university lecture hall, Dennis's experiences and relationships offer the perfect foundation for telling the story of America's yearly greatest day in sports. Sure, there is the game, but going beyond the field of play and doing a deeper dive into the culture around the event before and after is where the true scope of the Super Bowl is revealed in this book."

—RICH FEINBERG, Penske Entertainment senior vice president, Indianapolis Motor Speedway executive producer

"Super Bowl. Such a simple name, that has grown to have complex qualities. It is the pinnacle of all things in sports, and while others try to create their own version, Dennis Deninger shows why the NFL will always be the envy of the athletic world."

—ROB STONE, FOX Sports host and commentator

"The Super Bowl is so much more than a game. It's a superlative. The biggest and most important version of anything you can name is that thing's Super Bowl. Professor Deninger's book explores how America's unofficial holiday has combined sport, entertainment, business, and culture to influence and reflect the heart and soul of a nation."

—FRANK SUPOVITZ, former NFL senior vice president of events, president & CEO of Fast Traffic Events and Entertainment

The Football Game That Changed America

THE FOOTBALL GAME THAT CHANGED AMERICA

How the NFL Created a National Holiday

DENNIS DENINGER

ROWMAN & LITTLEFIELD
Lanham • Boulder • New York • London

Published by Rowman & Littlefield
An imprint of The Rowman & Littlefield Publishing Group, Inc.
4501 Forbes Boulevard, Suite 200, Lanham, Maryland 20706
www.rowman.com

86-90 Paul Street, London EC2A 4NE, United Kingdom

British Library Cataloguing in Publication Information Available

Library of Congress Cataloging-in-Publication Data
Names: Deninger, Dennis, author.
Title: The football game that changed America : how the NFL created a national holiday / Dennis Deninger.
Description: Lanham, Maryland : Rowman & Littlefield, [2024] | Includes index. | Summary: "The Football Game That Changed America is the first book to chronicle the entire history of the Super Bowl and examine the social, cultural, economic, and political impact of this colossal event, bringing to life the colorful characters, bold rivals, and twists of fate that played a role in the creation and explosive growth of the Big Game"—Provided by publisher.
Identifiers: LCCN 2024005908 (print) | LCCN 2024005909 (ebook) | ISBN 9781538196786 (cloth) | ISBN 9781538196793 (epub)
Subjects: LCSH: Super Bowl—History. | Popular culture—United States. Classification: LCC GV956.2.S8 D46 2024 (print) | LCC GV956.2.S8 (ebook) | DDC 796.332/64809—dc23/eng/20240215
LC record available at https://lccn.loc.gov/2024005908
LC ebook record available at https://lccn.loc.gov/2024005909

♾™ The paper used in this publication meets the minimum requirements of American National Standard for Information Sciences—Permanence of Paper for Printed Library Materials, ANSI/NISO Z39.48-1992.

To my MVPs

Gail, Matthew, and Kevin

Contents

CONTENTS

FOREWORD

On that long-ago Sunday afternoon, it was all about the Green Bay Packers and a big bowl of M&Ms. Mostly the M&Ms. My brother and I had been dropped at our grandparents' apartment to watch the last football game of the season. My beloved Packers were facing the champions of the AFL (whatever that was), the Kansas City Chiefs. My Nana, the sports fan, told me it was something new and a really big deal. She had no idea.

I smile in wonder at how that distant afternoon was the birth of what has mushroomed into a mega-event and the most vivid annual expression of American culture.

The Super Bowl stands apart. For scale and scope, there is nothing that even comes close to this convergence of sport, entertainment, and business.

In a splintered society, with endless sources of input diffusing our focus and pulling us apart, Super Sunday brings a hundred million of us together in a way nothing else can, whether it's the on-field action, the halftime performance, or the imaginative commercials.

As we've witnessed, a football game can unite us after tragedy and connect us during a pandemic.

In *The Football Game That Changed America*, Dennis Deninger has created the definitive book on the Super Bowl's many facets. He brings to life countless rich anecdotes and hard-to-believe (but true) tales of the game's humble origins. Readers are taken into the backseat of a car parked at a Texas airport, where the negotiations that led to the game's creation first started. Deninger then details the bold choices, backroom deals, and sheer financial muscle that led to the Super Bowl's astonishing growth.

I have always been impressed by Dennis's keen instincts and insight. And that isn't merely because he is the one who "discovered" me as a twenty-three-year-old with a fresh broadcasting degree and got me hired to host a brand-new ESPN show he was producing, *Scholastic Sports America*. His patient guidance and the trust he showed were crucial to my professional growth. In the same ways, he has continued to mold more generations of young media talent.

Dennis approached this book with the same gifts of curiosity and enthusiasm I have seen him bring to all his various endeavors. His typical diligence and thoroughness helped create a book that is masterfully structured. The distinct chapters work together to create a rich portrait of the Super Bowl that will surprise and entertain you. Insight gained from his decades in media shape a closing chapter that imagines and forecasts the game's future.

Like me, you will come away realizing how much you *didn't* know about our country's biggest annual event. After all, Deninger does teach the definitive college course on the Super Bowl at his alma mater, Syracuse University.

Thanks to Dennis's passion for the topic, exhaustive research, and skillful storytelling, you will never again watch the Super Bowl the same way.

Chris Fowler
ESPN/ABC Sports commentator

Acknowledgments

My friend Michael Veley, the founding chair of the Department of Sport Management at Syracuse University, set me on the path that led to this book when he pitched the idea of creating a course about the Super Bowl and its impact on American life. It was at my first faculty meeting before I had taught a single session of any class in the department. The research I have done and the contacts I have made from teaching our Super Bowl and Society class during the past fourteen years made this book possible.

I want to thank everyone who contributed to this project and who generously shared their time with me and my students, providing us invaluable insights and answers to our questions. Special thanks to Bill Fitts, Bob Rauscher, and David Plaut for their great stories and historical materials. Bill started producing NFL games for CBS in 1961 and was the executive producer for Super Bowls I, II, IV, VI, and VIII. Bob produced ESPN's Super Bowl week coverage from its inception in 1986 well into the twenty-first century, winning sixteen Emmy Awards. David first learned about my class when his son Jonathan enrolled as a student at Syracuse. David won seven Emmy Awards over the course of his forty-two-year career as a producer, director, and writer at NFL Films. My thanks also to Rich Cimini and Dave Walsh for reading my chapters and making valuable suggestions that improved the finished work.

I am grateful for the enthusiasm and guidance of my literary agent, Gary Krebs, the dedication of my editorial assistant, Bradley Trust, and most of all, for the support and encouragement of my family and friends.

INTRODUCTION

Through many unlikely turns, the Super Bowl became the most important sports event in the history of America. Its story is filled with colorful characters, bold rivals, and twists of fate that played a role in the creation of a colossus. The Super Bowl has changed what was once just another wintry Sunday into America's unofficial holiday, bigger than most of our official holidays. Super Bowl Sunday, Christmas Day, and Thanksgiving are days when the majority of Americans gather for a common purpose, to share time together and break bread. In fact, more food is consumed on Super Bowl Sunday than on any other American holiday, with the exception of Thanksgiving.

It's also the biggest media consumption day of the year. In a universe that is increasingly splintered with hundreds of streaming services and niche channels, two hundred million Americans tune in to watch at least a portion of the Super Bowl, and social media usage spikes on that Sunday evening. This all combines to make the Super Bowl the largest shared American experience of the year. More of us watch this game than vote in presidential elections.

The biggest entertainment event of the year, the Super Bowl halftime show has a larger audience than any other musical or cultural event on any channel. The halftime show featuring Usher in February 2024 was the most-watched entertainment show in the history of the United States, averaging more than 129 million viewers per minute as measured by Nielsen. That is a larger audience than watched the final episodes of *M*A*S*H* or *Seinfeld*, the Beatles on *The Ed Sullivan Show*, or the annual Academy Awards.

It's also the most important advertising event of the year—the only program for which millions of people tune in to see the commercials, not the content of the show. Advertising campaigns that will continue for months or even years launch during the Super Bowl. Because of its massive reach across all demographics, advertisers introduce new products and promote new movies and video programming on Super Bowl Sunday. Online and social media distribution of the most-talked-about commercials doubles that audience in many cases. The television network that airs the Super Bowl reaps more than half a billion dollars in advertising revenue on that one day alone.

It is the biggest gambling event of the year. The spread of legalized sports gambling to a majority of American states has geometrically increased the amount of money wagered annually on the Super Bowl. It's estimated that more than a quarter of the American adult population now bets on the game. And those bets are placed on far more than the outcome of the game. Thousands of "prop bets" are offered, including who will win the coin toss, which kicker will score first, and what color Gatorade will be dumped on the winning coach.

The economic impact of the Super Bowl surpasses the annual gross domestic product of many nations, having soared past $40 billion. When you add the billions of dollars wagered on the game to the billions more that people spend on food, drink, team merchandise, new televisions, furniture, and decorations for Super Bowl parties, plus the cost of travel and accommodations for the thousands of media covering the event and the thousands more attending the game, the sky-high price of tickets and television advertising, the economic impact of this one game on its unofficial holiday is staggering.

The Super Bowl has changed the outcome of elections. A prime example was in 1990, when voters in Arizona rejected a referendum to adopt the federal Martin Luther King Jr. holiday. The NFL responded by moving the Super Bowl that had been awarded to Phoenix for 1993 to the Rose Bowl in Pasadena. Apparently hosting a Super Bowl proved to be more important to Arizona citizens than taking a stand against the new holiday, because two years after the failed referendum, 62 percent of Arizona voters approved the endorsement of MLK Jr. Day.

The game has been the subject of a papal message. That has never happened for the World Series, the NBA Finals, or any other sports event in the United States. Pope Francis delivered his special Super Bowl Sunday message in 2017, saying that "Great sporting events like today's Super Bowl are highly symbolic, showing that it is possible to build a culture of encounter and a world of peace." The pontiff called sports "a privileged place to learn virtue and practice fraternity." It isn't hard to see the parallels that exist between football and religion in their rituals, their narratives, and their ability to bring people together and to stir the emotions.

The Super Bowl has dramatically changed its host cities, which have invested in and benefited from upgrades in infrastructure, airports, social programs, and prestige. Every year dozens of local charities receive an influx of money from the NFL Foundation and the local host committee. When Indianapolis hosted its one and only Super Bowl in 2012, local corporations used $1 million dollars in NFL seed money to raise more than $150 million, transforming an entire neighborhood and building a new community center. The Super Bowl hasn't returned but its beneficial impact remains.

America has changed socially and culturally because of the Super Bowl. The game has come to serve as a symbol of America to the rest of the world. Former NFL Commissioner Paul Tagliabue called the Super Bowl "winter's 4th of July." It celebrates the American virtues of hard work, perseverance, teamwork, courage, and reward based on merit, regardless of race, creed, or humble beginnings. In no small measure, it also trumpets the success of American business and of the United States as a powerful nation. The Super Bowl's overt patriotism has been part of the overall design of the game from its inception.

How did all of this happen?

To begin answering that question, we need to go back more than a century to a warm Friday evening in September at an automobile show-room in Canton, Ohio. The owners of a handful of Midwestern semipro teams got together over a few cold beers to discuss organizing a football league. The success of their venture would be fueled by star power, as has been the case throughout the history of the NFL. Joining the team owners for beers that night was the most famous American athlete of his day, hailed as one of the greatest of the twentieth century—Jim Thorpe.

The Pre–Super Bowl NFL:
Humble Beginnings

IT WAS SEPTEMBER 17, 1920. RALPH HAY, THE OWNER OF THE CANTON Bulldogs, had invited the representatives of eleven teams from mostly midsized Midwestern factory towns to meet at his Hupmobile showroom on the first floor of the Odd Fellows Hall at the corner of Cleveland Avenue and Second Street SW in Canton, Ohio. With them was the most celebrated American athlete of the era and the star of the Bulldogs, Jim Thorpe.

George "Papa Bear" Halas, who represented his Decatur, Illinois, "Staleys," remembered the meeting in his autobiography. "Chairs were few," he said. "I sat on a running board."[1] The team owners who gathered among the four new cars on the showroom floor that night were from Ohio, Indiana, Illinois, plus one from Rochester, New York. Ralph Hay hoped that Halas and the others would be interested in helping him launch a new American Professional Football Association. His goal for the APFA was "to raise the standard of professional football in every way possible, to eliminate bidding for players between rival clubs and to secure cooperation in the formation of schedules."

Halas, who was then twenty-five years old, had started the previous year as the player-coach of the Decatur team, which was organized by workers at the A. E. Staley Company, a manufacturer of agricultural products. He was joined by representatives from the Chicago Cardinals, Akron (OH) Pros, Cleveland Indians, Dayton (OH) Triangles, Massillon

(OH) Tigers, Hammond (IN) Pros, Muncie (IN) Flyers, Rock Island (IL) Independents, and the Rochester (NY) Jeffersons. The Staleys moved to Wrigley Field in 1921 and played their first season as the Chicago Bears in 1922. By the time professional football started to attract millions of diehard fans and generate billions of dollars in revenue, most of these teams had either moved or disbanded. In fact, thirty-five different franchises in the league, which renamed itself the National Football League in 1922, failed in the first ten years. Even the Hupp Motor Company of Detroit, Michigan, stopped making Hupmobiles in 1939.

After grabbing cold bottles of beer from ice buckets in the room, the men settled down to business at 8:15 p.m., sitting on running boards and a few chairs or leaning against fenders. Their first item of business was the withdrawal from the league of the Massillon Tigers, which immediately reduced the number of original teams to ten. As the organizer of the session, Ralph Hay was the favorite to be elected the first president of the American Professional Football Association, but Hay declined, saying that the new league needed a public face to attract attention from the press and fans. He turned to Thorpe.[2]

The League's First Star

Eight years earlier, Jim Thorpe had won gold medals for the United States in the decathlon and pentathlon at the 1912 Olympic Games in Stockholm, Sweden, despite never before competing in the decathlon. At the medal presentation ceremony, the king of Sweden told Thorpe, "You, sir, are the greatest athlete in the world." Thorpe returned to the states as a hero, heralded by an adoring public with a ticker-tape parade in New York City.[3]

Jim Thorpe was born in Indian Territory (now Oklahoma) near Prague, in 1887. His father was half Irish, half Sac and Fox Indian. His mother was half French and half Potawatomi. Thorpe's athletic prowess started to gain broad attention after he was enrolled in the Carlisle Indian Industrial School in Carlisle, Pennsylvania, in 1907. It was an experimental college that sought to educate and assimilate Native Americans into American society. At Carlisle, Thorpe competed in football, track and field, baseball, and lacrosse. His football coach was the legendary Glenn

Scobey "Pop" Warner, who was credited with introducing the single wing and double wing formations to the sport. With Thorpe in the backfield, kicking, and playing defense, Carlisle beat the college football powers of the era, including Harvard in 1911 and West Point in 1912.

Thorpe signed to play Major League Baseball with the New York Giants in 1913, playing a total of six seasons with the Giants, the Cincinnati Reds, and the Boston Braves. He played his first professional football game in 1915, earning $250 per game for Ralph Hay's Canton Bulldogs.

At age thirty-two, still acclaimed as "the world's greatest athlete," Jim Thorpe was the unanimous choice as president of the new APFA. He served in that role for only one year, and in 1922 he left the Canton Bulldogs to join the league's Cleveland team and the following year gathered a group of fellow Native American players for two years as player-coach of the Oorang Indians in La Rue, Ohio.[4] The Indians were organized as a barnstorming team by the owner of the Oorang dog kennels, Walter Lingo, with the sole purpose of promoting the sale of the Airedale terriers that he bred. In his 1923 promotional publication, Lingo wrote, "You know Jim Thorpe, don't you, the Sac and Fox Indian, the world's greatest athlete, who won the all-around championship at the Olympic Games in Sweden in 1912? Well, Thorpe is in our organization." Thorpe assembled an all–Native American team, but they won only four of the twenty games they played in their two NFL seasons, 1922 and 1923. That didn't generate the excitement or sales that Walter Lingo had hoped for, so the team disbanded. Thorpe moved on to other teams, playing his last game in the NFL at age forty-one for the Chicago Cardinals in 1928.

Succeeding Thorpe as president in 1921 was the owner of the Columbus Panhandles, Joe Carr, who would lead the league through its name change to the National Football League in 1922 until his death in 1939. During his tenure, Carr created the NFL constitution and bylaws, developed the standard player contract, and oversaw the first postseason league championship. Carr's Columbus team was one of four that had joined the APFA immediately after the initial organizing meeting, just in time to start play during that inaugural 1920 season. The Panhandles, named for the Pennsylvania Railroad "Panhandle" shops in Columbus, lasted only three seasons, folding in 1923. In addition to Columbus, the other new members that first season of 1920 were the Buffalo All-Americans, the Chicago Tigers, and the Detroit Heralds.

The First Game, the First Season

In the first APFA game in history, on October 3, 1920, the Columbus Panhandles lost to the Dayton Triangles 14–0, at Dayton's Triangle Park. Dayton finished its season with a record of five wins, two losses, and two ties. The Akron Pros held the best record during the fourteen-team league's inaugural season, going undefeated, 8–0–3. The Pros star tailback was Frederick Douglas "Fritz" Pollard, the first Black star in American professional football history. Pollard had grown up in a German neighborhood of Rogers Park, Illinois, outside Chicago, hence the nickname "Fritz." As a freshman at Brown University, the five-feet-nine, 165-pound Pollard led the Ivy League team to the 1916 Rose Bowl, becoming the first African American ever to play in the "granddaddy of them all." Pollard, along with Bobby Marshall, who played for the Rock Island Independents in 1920, were the first two Black players in the APFA. Pollard was inducted into the Pro Football Hall of Fame in 2005, twenty-nine years after his death in 1986 at age ninety-two.[5]

The team that would win the first Super Bowl forty-seven years later, the Green Bay Packers, had a similarly inauspicious beginning. They were organized in 1919 when Earl "Curly" Lambeau, fresh from playing on Knute Rockne's first Notre Dame team, worked at the Indian Meat Packing Plant in Green Bay, Wisconsin. The twenty-one-year-old Lambeau asked his employers to sponsor a football team. He told them he would need $500 for equipment and uniforms and asked to use the company field for practices. Curly Lambeau was the Packers captain and featured back who ran and threw the football. His cofounder of the Packers was George Whitney Calhoun, the news editor and sports columnist for the *Green Bay Press-Gazette*. Calhoun helped publicize the new team, and on game days, he circulated through the crowd to pass the hat, collecting donations to help pay the bills.

The Green Bay Packers joined the now one-year-old APFA for the 1921 season in which the league expanded to a total of twenty-two teams. Calhoun's collections just weren't enough to offset low attendance and Wisconsin's bad weather. The team went broke, but Curly Lambeau refused to let it die. He visited local merchants, pitching the value of keeping a football team alive in Green Bay. He cajoled them into making loans that totaled $2,500, which he used to set up a nonprofit trust that would own and run the Packers, with him as the coach and manager.[6] That trust exists to this day, making the Green Bay Packers the only publicly owned NFL franchise. Curly Lambeau played for the Packers until 1929 and continued as head coach until 1949, winning six NFL championships. Inducted into the Pro Football Hall of Fame in 1963, he passed away two years later at the age of sixty-seven.

Credibility Arrives with the Galloping Ghost

During its early years, professional football was barely a flicker compared to the bright light that was college football. The sport's success was strengthened by the increase in college enrollment that followed World War I, the rapidly expanding circulation of newspapers, which saw increased daily sales when they devoted more space to sports, and broadcasts by radio stations that were building towers in cities all over America following the successful launch in 1920 of the nation's first licensed station, KDKA in Pittsburgh. The enthusiasm for college football fed a stadium building boom that included construction of the Yale Bowl in 1914 with 70,896 seats, the Rose Bowl in 1922 with a capacity of 57,000 at the time, and Ohio Stadium in Columbus in 1923, which held 61,210 fans. In the 1920s, Michigan, Illinois, Minnesota, Pittsburgh, Washington, Vanderbilt, and Northwestern also built stadiums that could accommodate more than fifty thousand fans. More people gathered to watch a single college football game on a Saturday afternoon than attended an entire season of games in the newborn NFL.

The heroes of college football became national celebrities, and none shone brighter than Harold "Red" Grange, the three-time All American from the University of Illinois. In the 1924 game against the Michigan Wolverines, Grange rushed for 262 yards and four touchdowns in the first twelve minutes. Grantland Rice, a newspaper columnist and nationally broadcast radio sports commentator, nicknamed Grange "the Galloping Ghost." Damon Runyon, whose work appeared in the Hearst newspapers for thirty years, wrote, "On the field he is the equal of three football players and a horse."[7]

It is safe to say that anyone who followed sports in America in the 1920s knew the name Red Grange. When he signed a contract with the Chicago Bears in the fall of 1925, less than a week after his last game as a senior at Illinois, the National Football League of mostly Midwestern semipro teams immediately benefited from the spotlight of national star power and the increased recognition and credibility that came with it. The Galloping Ghost became the face of the NFL and its number-one drawing card. When Grange played his first game for the Bears against the Chicago Cardinals at Wrigley Field on Thanksgiving Day in 1925, a standing-room-only crowd of thirty-six thousand people turned out, the largest ever to see a professional football game up to that point. They saw Grange total ninety-two yards from scrimmage, add fifty-six yards on punt returns, throw six passes, and pull down an interception that broke up the Cardinals' only real scoring threat of the day. The game ended in a 0–0 tie, but it was just the beginning.

The Bears organized a sixty-seven-day barnstorming tour that included a game on December 6, 1925, against the New York Giants at the Polo Grounds, which broke the NFL attendance record set at Wrigley just weeks earlier. A crowd estimated at close to seventy thousand saw Grange and the Bears win 19–7, making headlines and generating the kind of promotional publicity that the struggling NFL never could have afforded to buy. Part of the deal for the tour, negotiated by Grange's agent C. C. "Cash and Carry" Pyle, gave his client a share of the gate receipts at every stop. Red Grange left New York with a check for $30,000, and by the end of the barnstorming trip, Pyle had negotiated endorsement contracts for cigarettes, clothing, a candy bar, a doll, socks, shoes, a fountain pen, and even a recipe for meat loaf. Every time somebody bought one of these items or saw one advertised in a store, the beneficiaries were Red Grange, the Chicago Bears, and the NFL. Decades later, George Halas would refer to Red Grange as "the eternal light of the National Football League" due to the impact of his star power on a league that was struggling to survive before the "Galloping Ghost" arrived.[8]

The Postseason Began by Accident

The increased attendance, media coverage, and revenue-generating potential that could be found in larger cities helped bring the early era of the NFL to a close in the 1930s. Those factors, along with the reduced buying power of the American public due to the Great Depression, which began in October 1929, forced the NFL to abandon its small-city roots, except in Green Bay, Wisconsin. The Packers were thriving on the success of the team on the field. They finished at the top of the standings in 1929, 1930, and 1931, claiming the NFL championship before there was any playoff structure. The only other small-market team remaining in the league in 1932 was the Portsmouth Spartans from Ohio, which finished that season with only one loss, tying them with the Chicago Bears. The league office organized an additional regular season game between the Spartans and the Bears to be held December 18, 1932, in Chicago to determine which team would be crowned NFL champion. Bitter cold and heavy snow that day forced the game to move indoors to Chicago Stadium. The arena could accommodate only an eighty-yard field, which ended at the walls; the goal posts had to be moved from the end lines to the goal lines. In a game that foreshadowed the future of NFL postseason play, the Bears won 9–0, scoring the winning touchdown on a two-yard pass from Bronko Nagurski to Red Grange.

The league scheduled its first NFL Championship game to be played the next year, following the 1933 season. With the addition of teams in Pittsburgh, Philadelphia, and Cincinnati that year, the league split itself into two divisions. The champion of the Eastern Division would play the Western Division champion, alternating as hosts each year. The Chicago Bears of the Western Division ended their 1933 campaign with ten wins, two losses, and one tie, and the New York Giants won the East with eleven wins and three losses. They met in the NFL's first championship postseason game at Wrigley Field on December 17, 1933, before an estimated crowd of twenty-six thousand. The Bears scored the first points of the contest with two field goals by Jack Manders. Giants tailback Harry Newman threw the first touchdown pass in NFL Championship game history when he connected with left end Morris "Red" Badgro for twenty-nine yards, making the score at halftime 7–6 Giants.[9]

The Associated Press described the game as "a thrilling combat of forward passing skill, desperate line plunging and gridiron strategy that kept the chilled spectators on their feet in constant excitement. The lead changed hands six times during the furious sixty minutes of play."[10] Four players from that Giants team and five who were on the field for the Bears would later be inducted into the Pro Football Hall of Fame along with Bears coach George Halas, Giants owner Tim Mara, and his coach, Steve Owen. One of those future Hall of Famers, fullback Bronko Nagurski, led the Bears to victory. Nagurski gained sixty-five yards rushing on the day, and in the closing minutes with the Giants leading 21–16, he threw fourteen yards downfield to fellow Hall of Famer Bill Hewitt, who then lateraled the ball to right end Billy Karr. Karr raced into the end zone to give the Bears a 23–21 victory. Each member of the champion Chicago Bears received a ten-karat gold ring and a check for $210.34. The payout for each member of the Giants was $140.22.

Fittingly, the year of the first NFL Championship game closed the book on the small-town history of the APFA. The Portsmouth Spartans

1920 APFA Teams	1934 NFL Teams
Akron Pros	New York Giants
Decatur (IL) Staleys	Boston Redskins
Buffalo All-Americans	Brooklyn Dodgers
Rock Island (IL) Independents	Philadelphia Eagles
Chicago Cardinals	Chicago Cardinals
Dayton Triangles	Chicago Bears
Rochester Jeffersons	Detroit Lions
Canton Bulldogs	Green Bay Packers
Detroit Heralds	Pittsburgh Pirates
Cleveland Tigers	St. Louis Gunners
Hammond (IN) Pros	Cincinnati Reds
Chicago Tigers	
Columbus Panhandles	
Muncie (IN) Flyers	

played their last season in Ohio in 1933 then were sold and moved to Detroit, where they were renamed the Lions. The league in 1934 had matured and expanded to reach larger population centers. At this point, the only team remaining from the inaugural 1920 season was the Chicago Cardinals.

The NFL's TV Era Begins in 1939

At the end of its second decade, the NFL comprised ten teams. The St. Louis and Cincinnati teams had folded, the Redskins had moved from Boston to Washington, DC, and the Cleveland Rams had played their third NFL season. The league recorded two momentous milestones in 1939 that propelled it toward the modern Super Bowl era. The first was the NFL surpassing one million fans for the first time, with a total of 1,071,200 paying fans attending games during that eleven-game regular season. The second was the NFL's television debut. Scheduled television programming in the United States began in 1939, following its introduction at the RCA pavilion of the World's Fair in New York that April. The first televised sporting event in the United States was a college baseball game on May 17, 1939, between Princeton and Columbia at Baker Field in New York, broadcast by NBC's experimental station W2XBS and seen locally on only a few hundred television sets. NBC, which was owned by RCA and whose purpose was to create shows that would entice consumers to buy RCA televisions, spent the year experimenting with which sports best suited the new technological innovation. The first major league baseball game ever televised occurred that summer from Ebbets Field in Brooklyn, where the Dodgers hosted Cincinnati on August 26. The NFL's Brooklyn Dodgers also called Ebbets Field home, and that's where the NFL made its television debut on October 22, 1939: the Dodgers and the Philadelphia Eagles played to a 0–0 tie, with more fans sitting in the stands than watching on television, because only about a thousand TV sets had been sold at that point. The station broadcasting each of these early games was the only station on the air at the time, W2XBS, which would later become WNBC-TV.[11]

The sports that worked best on television in its first decade were boxing and wrestling, which took place indoors in small arenas with their own lighting and could be covered with just one or two cameras. The return of millions of American servicemen and women after the end of World War II in 1945, the stability and growth of a peacetime economy, and the Fair Labor Standards Act, which had established a standard forty-hour workweek in 1940, provided the leisure time and money that created demand for millions of television sets in the late 1940s and throughout the 1950s. The first baseball World Series was televised in 1947 (the New York Yankees won four games to three against the Brooklyn Dodgers and their rookie infielder Jackie Robinson).

In 1950, the Los Angeles Rams became the first NFL team to have all their games televised in a single season. As part of a promotional campaign to sell their TV sets, the manufacturer of Admiral television sets partnered with the Rams to televise every home and away game. Admiral agreed to compensate the Rams for lost revenue due to reduced attendance at their home games resulting from televised games. Despite a winning season, the Rams saw a nearly 50-percent drop in the size of their crowds at Los Angeles Memorial Coliseum. Admiral reportedly paid the Rams $307,000 in compensation, and the deal was not renewed. The NFL took preventive action in 1951 by instituting its first blackout rule, prohibiting any TV station or network from televising any game within seventy-five miles of the stadium in which it was being played.

The first NFL Championship game broadcast on television was at the end of the 1951 season, when the Rams defeated the Cleveland Browns 24–17 at the Coliseum. It was a dramatic matchup: the Rams had left Cleveland in 1946 and now faced the team that had supplanted them in Ohio. The DuMont Network had televised five regular season games in 1951, then paid the NFL $75,000 for the rights to televise the championship game on December 23. Like RCA, DuMont was primarily in the business of building and selling televisions, so it hoped to attract new buyers in the booming peacetime economy by offering sports programming on its stations. The DuMont network followed up its telecast of the 1951 NFL Championship game with full two full seasons of weekly televised games in 1953 and 1954. They all originated from New York, Philadelphia, Pittsburgh, or Washington, DC, cities in which DuMont owned TV stations and had negotiated separate rights contracts with the

Giants, Eagles, Steelers, and Redskins. After 1954, DuMont started to cut back its programming schedule, and it went out of business in 1956.

The Reintegration of the NFL

The Rams' move from Cleveland to Los Angeles played a crucial role in changing the face of the NFL that we recognize today. Just two years after the Rams had shut down operations for a season during World War II, they won the 1945 NFL Championship, defeating the Washington Redskins 15–14 at Cleveland Municipal Stadium. A new professional football league, the All-America Football Conference (AAFC), had announced plans for a Cleveland team to begin play in the fall of 1946. The Browns, led by Coach Paul Brown, would also call the seventy-eight-thousand-seat Municipal Stadium home. Rather than share the stadium with the Browns, Rams owner Dan Reeves announced that he would move his team to Los Angeles less than one month after winning the NFL title.

During the 1945 season, every player on the Rams roster was white—as was every player on every NFL roster. In its early years, a number of NFL teams had Black players. Among them was Fritz Pollard, the player-coach for the Akron Pros. But there had been no players of color since the end of the 1933 season, when Joe Lillard played his last game for the Chicago Cardinals. A "gentlemen's agreement" among NFL owners, effectively segregated professional football beginning in 1934. Initiated by Redskins owner George Preston Marshall, the agreement contended that "white players, especially those from the South, would go to extremes to physically disable" Black players. His argument was that by preventing African Americans from playing in the NFL, he was protecting them from harm. Segregation remained the custom and the law in much of the United States in 1945, but with Black soldiers having fought heroically and died on foreign battlefields during World War II, the winds of change began to intensify. (President Harry S. Truman ordered a formal ban on racial discrimination in the US armed forces in 1948.)

Against this backdrop, the Rams owner proposed that his all-white team move to the publicly owned Los Angeles Memorial Coliseum to play games against the rest of the NFL's all-white teams. Rams General

Manager Charles "Chile" Walsh made the formal presentation at a public meeting of the LA Coliseum Commission on January 15, 1946. After his presentation, Walsh agreed to take questions from the public. Halley Harding, the sports editor of the *Los Angeles Tribune* and an African American, took the floor, delivering an impassioned, impromptu speech about the history of Black players such as "Fritz" Pollard. Harding's short speech—less than five minutes long—also pointed to the sacrifices that Black soldiers had made during World War II and the contributions of Black workers and their tax dollars, which went into the construction and upkeep of the Coliseum itself. He called it "singularly strange" that the NFL had not signed any Black college football standouts like Kenny Washington, a former UCLA star who, at the time, played for the Hollywood Bears of the integrated Pacific Coast Professional Football League.[12]

In response, the Rams GM said his team would "take any player of ability we can get," singling out Buddy Young of the University of Illinois (who would end up with the New York Yankees of the All-America Football Conference), adding that "Kenny Washington is welcome to try out for our team anytime he likes." The Rams did sign Washington and fellow UCLA star Woody Strode for their inaugural seasons in Los Angeles, bringing the era of segregated NFL football to a close and opening the league to the merit-based selection of players that successive generations have all come to know and expect. It does bear mentioning that the last team to add an African American player to its roster was George Preston Marshall's Redskins, which had no players of color until 1962, a full sixteen years after Washington and Strode took the field for the Rams. The integrated NFL had left the all-white Redskins in the dust of their segregated past. During the combined 1959, 1960, and 1961 seasons, Marshall's team won a total of only five games, lost thirty, and tied three times.

The Challenge of a New League
A second professional football league began play in 1946 with eight teams. The AAFC, the All-America Football Conference, had been the brainchild of *Chicago Tribune* sports editor Arch Ward, who

in 1944 reasoned that the thousands of men returning home after World War II would provide a new crop of football players. The league fielded eight teams for its first season, five in NFL cities: New York, Brooklyn, Chicago, Los Angeles, and Cleveland, plus three in cities that were not part of the NFL: Buffalo, San Francisco, and Miami. There was no "gentlemen's agreement" segregating the AAFC, so it opened its doors to the best players, including future Hall of Fame running back Marion Motley. Paul Brown signed the twenty-six-year-old Motley to play for Cleveland, having coached against him when Brown was at Washington High School and Motley starred for McKinley High in Massillon, Ohio. At six feet one and 232 pounds, Motley was a bruising running back who averaged 5.7 yards per carry for his nine-year career.[13]

1946 All-America Football Conference

Eastern Division	Western Division
New York Yankees	Cleveland Browns
Brooklyn Dodgers	San Francisco 49ers
Buffalo Bisons	Los Angeles Dons
Miami Seahawks	Chicago Rockets

A crowd of 60,135 turned out on September 6, 1946, for the AAFC debut at Cleveland Municipal Stadium. With Motley in the backfield and another future Hall of Famer, Otto Graham, at quarterback, the Browns crushed the Miami Seahawks 44–0. Paul Brown's team went on to win the championship all four years of the league's existence. The team was so successful that some skeptics said AAFC must stand for "all about football in Cleveland." The Miami team folded after one season and was replaced in 1947 by the Baltimore Colts.

The All-America Football Conference presented the NFL with a viable competitor for the services of the best college players, which led to a signing war that the AAFC owners were not equipped to handle for long. The Cleveland Browns won their fourth consecutive AAFC championship game, defeating the San Francisco 49ers 21–7 in December 1949. A merger agreement had been announced two days earlier by NFL Commissioner Bert Bell that would move the Browns, the 49ers, and the Colts to the NFL for the 1950 season and beyond. The other teams left in the AAFC folded, but many of their players were picked up by NFL teams. Paul Brown continued coaching the Browns until 1962. If the All-America Football Conference had been successful long term, a season-ending championship game between the best team from the AAFC and the best from the NFL might have given us a "Super Bowl" years before the game was first played in 1967.

The Greatest Game Ever Played

At the beginning of the 1950s, fewer than 9 percent of American homes had a television set. By the end of the decade, 95 percent of American homes had at least one TV. The nation's population had grown from 150 million in 1950 to 179 million ten years later. The power to simultaneously reach so many people with the same content, whether it be entertainment, news, or sports events, irreversibly changed communications and American society. The National Football League was a prime beneficiary of increased television exposure on local stations in each team's home region and on three national networks: DuMont, NBC, and CBS.

The DuMont Network televised the annual NFL Championship game nationally from 1951 until 1954. NBC took over in 1955, paying the NFL a $100,000 rights fee for the game. After the collapse of the Dumont Network, CBS reached an agreement with NFL Commissioner Bert Bell in 1956 to begin televising a full regular season of games for a rights fee of approximately $1 million. Because each team controlled its own regional broadcast distribution, CBS also had to negotiate agreements with all twelve teams, which it did.

The 1958 NFL season ended with the New York Giants and Cleveland Browns tied atop the Eastern Conference with identical 9–3 records. A divisional playoff game would be needed to determine which team would go on to play the Baltimore Colts, winners of the Western Conference. The Giants defeated the Browns 10–0 at Yankee Stadium, which set up the NFL Championship the following Sunday, December 28, 1958, to be played on the Giants' home field. The Colts had also finished regular season play with nine wins and three losses, led by twenty-five-year-old quarterback Johnny Unitas. The unplanned divisional playoff game provided an additional week of suspense and promotion in the news media, which helped draw a large nationwide television audience for the title game on NBC.

The Giants opened the scoring in the first quarter with a thirty-six-yard field goal by Pat Summerall, who later became one of the most respected sports broadcasters in American history. The Colts surged in the second quarter with a two-yard touchdown run by Alan Ameche and a fifteen-yard touchdown pass from Unitas to Raymond Berry to take a 14–3 halftime lead. The Giants held Baltimore scoreless while running in a touchdown in the third quarter and then took the lead on a fourth quarter pass from their thirty-seven-year-old quarterback Charlie Conerly to Frank Gifford, also destined to join the ranks of elite American broadcasters. The back-and-forth nature of the game helped steadily build the audience on NBC to an estimated forty million people, fully one-quarter of the entire US population.

After Gifford's touchdown, the Colts put the ball in play with only one minute and fifty-six seconds left, trailing 17–14, at their own fourteen yard line. Unitas engineered a remarkable drive that included passes to Berry of twenty-five, twenty-one, and sixteen yards. With seven seconds left in regulation, Colts kicker Steve Myhra booted a twenty-yard field goal to tie the game at 17–17 as time expired. In 1958, NFL regular season games that ended in a tie score remained just that, a tie. Sudden death was so rare that Frank Gifford said later that most of the players on the field had no idea how the game would be decided.

The Giants won the coin toss to receive possession as the overtime period began, but they failed to make a first down and were forced to punt. Baltimore started from their own twenty-yard line, where Johnny Unitas began another dramatic drive. The Colts relentlessly made their way to the Giants' eight yard line, when NBC lost its feed from Yankee Stadium, and the millions of viewers watching history unfold before their eyes saw their TV screens turn to electronic hash. In the stadium excitement and feverish activity that accompanied the final drive, one of the main television cables at field level became disconnected. NBC's director had to find a way to delay the game to give his network technicians time enough to restore the broadcast signal before the final plays could be run.

He reached an NBC business manager who was helping out with statistics on the sidelines, and that's when Stan Rotkiewicz took matters into his own hands. Rotkiewicz stumbled onto the field feigning inebriation, grabbed the game ball, and wrestled it away from the umpire. He then ran down the sideline in the opposite direction. The radio announcers thought they were seeing the antics of a drunken fan, but Stan Rotkiewicz saved the day for NBC's viewers. The cable was reconnected, and the television signal was restored in time for all to see the Colts win 23–17 on Alan Ameche's one-yard plunge into the end zone.[14]

In the next morning's *New York Times*, Louis Effrat wrote, "In a sudden-death overtime period, the Baltimore team coached by Weeb Ewbank fashioned the winning touchdown after 8 minutes 15 seconds. The excitement generated by football's longest game left most of the 64,185 spectators limp. Aside from an experimental exhibition contest, it was the first sudden-death game (with victory going instantly to the first team to score) in the league."[15]

The Rise of the American Football League

This epic title game attracted the attention and captured the imagination of the American public. It quickly became known as the "greatest game ever played" and triggered an upward surge in the popularity of professional football in the United States. On the field that day were seventeen players who would go on to be inducted into the Pro Football Hall of Fame. Watching the game in a Houston, Texas, hotel room was Lamar Hunt, a twenty-six-year-old former backup receiver for Southern Methodist University and, more importantly, the son of oil billionaire H. L. Hunt. In Houston to attend the Southwest Conference Holiday Basketball Tournament that December, Hunt had spent a good portion of 1958 exploring the possibility of investing in either a professional baseball or football team for his hometown of Dallas, which at the time had neither.

In the spring of 1958, Lamar Hunt contacted NFL Commissioner Bert Bell and told him that he would be interested in bringing an NFL franchise to Dallas. At the time, the NFL was a twelve-team league, and Bell explained that his owners were not interested in expansion until they could sort out their problems in Chicago, where the league had two teams, the Bears and the Cardinals. The problem was that the Cardinals were perennial losers on the field (averaging ten losses per season in the 1950s), and they were losing money. Bell suggested that Hunt contact Cardinals owners Walter Wolfner and his wife, Violet Bidwill Wolfner, to see if they might be interested in selling the team to Hunt, who could then move it to Dallas. As it turned out, Commissioner Bell also had directed a number of other wealthy investors interested in expansion teams to contact the Wolfners.

Lamar Hunt traveled to New York in the fall of 1958 to hear Branch Rickey talk about his plans to launch a third professional baseball league. Rickey was the former president and general manager of the Dodgers, the man who had signed Jackie Robinson in 1947, breaking the color barrier in major league baseball. Lamar Hunt never invested in a baseball team, but he came away from those New York meetings with one very important concept: revenue sharing. Bill Veeck, owner of the Chicago White Sox and before that the Cleveland Indians and St. Louis Browns, told the group that any new league should pool its earnings, including all television rights payments, and divide the total equally among its clubs to keep them all profitable. That idea would resonate in Hunt's head and pay dividends in the very near future.

After watching the "greatest game ever played" on a black-and-white TV in his hotel room that Sunday afternoon in December, Hunt realized that his mind was made up. "My interest emotionally was always more in football," he said, "but clearly the '58 Colts–Giants game, sort of in my mind made me say, 'Well that's it. This sport has everything, and it televises well.'" Lamar Hunt had a good sense of how important "televising well" would be for any American sport in the years to come. Television had been the key ingredient that the AAFC lacked a decade earlier.

Hunt set up a meeting with Walter Wolfner in February 1959 to discuss buying the Cardinals and moving them to Texas. The meeting was in Florida, where the Wolfners had a winter home. Wolfner refused to sell the team and boasted that a number of other wealthy investors, including Kenneth Stanley "Bud" Adams from Houston, had approached him about buying the Cardinals, but he had turned them all down.

On his flight from Miami back to Dallas, Hunt said, "A light bulb came on!" If there were all these investors who wanted to buy NFL teams for their home cities but whose overtures had been denied, why not contact each of them and together start a new football league to serve cities that didn't have NFL teams? He said he asked a flight attendant for some paper, and before the plane landed in Dallas, he had sketched out a business plan on three pages of American Airlines stationery that he titled "Original 6 and First Year's Operations." It was the plan that would launch the American Football League (AFL). Hunt, the son of a billionaire with millions to spend on a professional football team, was flying near the back of the plane in coach.

Though he now had a plan for a new league on paper, Lamar Hunt reached out one last time to NFL Commissioner Bell. Bell recommended that Hunt call Chicago Bears founder and owner George Halas, who was part of the league owners' expansion committee. In 1956, Halas had predicted that the NFL would enlarge to sixteen teams through successive grants of franchises to four additional cities between 1960 and 1965, but there was resistance from other owners who feared that new teams in neighboring regions would cut into their profits. When Hunt called, Halas told him that expanding the NFL beyond twelve teams was "probably a long way off."[16]

The Foolish Club

At that point Lamar Hunt started calling the list of investors he called his "Original 6" to say that if they couldn't get NFL franchises, they should consider forming a new league. He convinced Bud Adams and four others to join him in what Hunt called the "Foolish Club"—foolish for going up against the long-established NFL. The six original cities would be Dallas, where Hunt would finally get his professional team, plus Houston, Denver, Los Angeles, New York, and Minneapolis. The only two of these cities that had NFL franchises at the time were Los Angeles and New York. The Los Angeles owner was Barron Hilton of the Hilton Hotel chain, who named his team the Chargers partly because Hilton owned the Carte Blanche charge card company. The Chargers played just one season in Los Angeles before moving to San Diego in 1961.

Hunt had hoped that his new league could cooperate with the NFL. At the end of June 1959, Hunt visited Commissioner Bell at his home near Atlantic City, New Jersey. Hunt told Bell that the new league wanted to maintain a friendly relationship with the NFL. He proposed that Bell serve as a common commissioner of the AFL and the NFL, that the two leagues hold a common player draft, and that arrangements be made to black out television during home games in both leagues. Bell rejected these offers but gave Hunt advice and information about television, drafting players, and other details about operating a league.

The original six AFL owners held their first meeting in Chicago on August 14, 1959, and a week later christened their new venture the "American Football League." Ralph Wilson of Buffalo was extended the league's seventh franchise on October 28, 1959, and William Sullivan of Boston became the league's eighth owner on November 22, 1958, the date of the AFL's first player draft. When the NFL saw that Hunt was serious about his plans for a rival league, they offered him an expansion franchise for Dallas. However, by that time, late in 1959, Hunt respectfully declined because he had "sunk too much money into this" and had made too many commitments to his fellow "Foolish Club" owners to consider accepting an NFL offer. Unable to derail Hunt from moving ahead with the American Football League, the NFL granted a new Dallas franchise to Clint Murchison Jr. and Bedford Wynne, who founded the Cowboys to compete directly with Lamar Hunt's Dallas Texans beginning in the fall of 1960. From zero pro football teams, Dallas would soon have two.

The NFL also enticed the AFL ownership group in Minneapolis to take an NFL franchise instead. On January 27, 1960, the Minnesota group backed out of the AFL and, one day later at the NFL owners meeting in Miami, was granted their charter as the Minnesota Vikings. It didn't take the AFL long to find a replacement: on January 30, 1960, a group from Oakland, California, headed by cement contractor Y. Charles "Chet" Soda signed up. The original team name chosen in a Junior Chamber of Commerce contest in the *Oakland Tribune* was the Señors, and their team colors were to be orange and black. Helen Davis, an Oakland Police Department employee, won the contest, writing a letter supporting the "Señors" as the mascot. (Helen Davis was no relation to

Al Davis, who joined the Raiders three years later as head coach and general manager and became the team owner in 1972.) The Señors nickname was quickly dropped, as reported in the *Oakland Tribune* in March 1960. "Sombreros and serapes were tossed aside today as Oakland's embryo pro football team discarded the name 'Señors.' Give 'em a knife and a gun and turn 'em loose. They're officially the Raiders."[17]

Pro Football Becomes a National TV Product

The most important factor in making the AFL's inaugural 1960 season successful was its agreement with the ABC television network. Signed on June 9, 1960, it granted ABC five years of exclusive rights to air games on Sundays, plus the AFL Championship game and an AFL all-star game. ABC contracted to pay a total of $8.5 million over five years to the AFL, which divided the revenue equally among its eight clubs in accordance with the revenue-sharing concept Lamar Hunt began considering after his baseball meeting back in 1958. That came to just $1.7 million dollars per year for the league. Divided eight ways, each team received $212,500 per season—enough when combined with ticket sales and other revenue to help move the AFL toward solvency. The attorney whom Lamar Hunt hired to negotiate this first television contract was Jay Michaels, from entertainment giant MCA. Decades later, his son Al Michaels became identified with the NFL as one of its premiere play-by-play voices. "When I was in high school, I remember that original contract sat on our kitchen table for my perusal," said Al.[18]

At that point in time, each NFL team negotiated its own local, regional, and national television packages, some in concert with one or two other teams. For example, the New York Giants, in the NFL's largest market, were making $350,000 per year in television revenue, ten times the $35,000 that the Green Bay Packers earned in the league's smallest market.

The NFL's new commissioner, Alvin "Pete" Rozelle, had been hired by the NFL owners in January 1960, three months after previous commissioner Bert Bell had died. Rozelle had been the Los Angeles Rams public relations director and at age thirty-three was serving as the team's general manager when he was selected to lead the league. One of his first and most important tasks was to convince the owners of the wisdom of revenue sharing. "He said that for the strength of the league, they had to share the money equally or the league would go to hell," remembered Jim Kensil,[19] one of Rozelle's aides in 1961. Using the AFL as an example, the young commissioner won agreement from the owners and proceeded to negotiate a two-year, $9.3 million television contract with CBS that would share television rights revenue equally among each of the fourteen NFL franchises beginning in 1962. However, that contract signed in 1961 was later nullified by US District Court Judge Allan K. Grim, who deemed it a violation of the Sherman Antitrust Act. In his decision dated July 20, 1961, Judge Grim ruled that the contract between the NFL and CBS was the product of an agreement among the NFL clubs to eliminate economic competition among themselves for the sale of television rights to home games. He found that the contract gave CBS the sole right and discretion to determine which games would be telecast and where, which restricted the rights of the individual clubs from deciding which of their games should be aired. Serving the Pennsylvania district, Judge Grim concluded, "I am therefore obliged to construe the Final Judgment as prohibiting the execution and performance of [this] contract."[20]

Under the law, each team was an independent company not owned by the NFL, so if these separate companies were to combine into a bloc for the purpose of negotiating a contract with CBS that would exclude any other television competitors, it could be interpreted as a violation of antitrust law. An NFL contract with CBS would have the effect of preventing non-CBS stations from buying rights to air any games played by their local NFL teams and profiting from any commercials that could be sold in what had become popular Sunday afternoon programming.

Judge Grim told Commissioner Rozelle that to make a contract with CBS acceptable in the courts, the NFL would need an exemption from the Sherman Antitrust Act to cover all television rights agreements. Rozelle immediately began a concerted effort to lobby Congress for that exemption. Backed by the considerable political clout of his powerful team owners and with some advice from his old University of San Francisco college buddy Pierre Salinger, who worked in the White House as President John F. Kennedy's press secretary, Rozelle's mission to Washington was successful. Less than three months after he started his lobbying efforts, both the House and Senate approved Public Law 87–331 and sent it to President Kennedy for his signature in September 1961.

The Sports Broadcasting Act of 1961, as it came to be known, exempted any professional football, baseball, basketball, or hockey league in the United States from antitrust regulation in any contracts for the "sponsored telecasting" of their games. The legendary Vince Lombardi said that the Sports Broadcasting Act "probably saved football in Green Bay." The sharing of television rights revenue that followed put the small-market teams on equal footing with the big-city franchises. After the Sports Broadcasting Act became law, the NFL and CBS renegotiated the two-year rights contract that had been nullified, making it a three-year agreement. CBS paid the NFL slightly more than $5 million for the rights to nationally televise games in 1962, and that figure swelled to more than $14 million for the 1964 season, the third year of the deal. In 1966, the Sports Broadcasting Act was amended to also cover any mergers of two or more professional football leagues as long as the combination of their operations would increase and not decrease the total number of clubs operating. This legislation helped pave the way for the merger of the NFL and AFL, which made the Super Bowl possible.

In a *New York Times* article following Rozelle's death in 1996, Cleveland Browns/Baltimore Ravens owner Art Modell said, "Congress sanctioning the single network deal is the most significant thing Pete ever did."[21]

CHAPTER 2

The Creation of the Super Bowl

THE AMERICAN FOOTBALL LEAGUE (AFL) MADE ITS DEBUT ON A FRIday evening, September 9, 1960, at Nickerson Field in Boston, the home field of the Boston University Terriers. A little more than twenty-one thousand fans watched the Boston Patriots lose to the Denver Broncos 13–10. Tickets cost $5, and you could buy a program for 50 cents. The game was not televised, but ABC's broadcast schedule of AFL games would begin two days later on Sunday, September 11. Whereas the All-America Football Conference met failure in the era just before the proliferation of televised sports, the AFL's cumulative television exposure during the next several seasons, its deft leadership by Lamar Hunt, and the deep pockets of its owners helped it to successfully challenge the NFL.

The NFL inadvertently gave the AFL an early advantage with its own blackout rule. The NFL did not allow CBS stations in any market where a home game was being played to televise any NFL games on those Sundays for fear that fans might stay home to watch an out-of-town game instead of going to the local stadium to see the home team play. The ABC network was free to broadcast AFL games on their stations in every NFL market, which meant that fans who did choose to stay home on Sunday afternoons could sample the AFL product on television. What they saw was a wide-open game with more passing, great athletes selected from the best college players regardless of their race, and innovative TV coverage. "We were selling excitement and entertainment," said Hunt. "We had to be different. We couldn't afford to be dull." Hunt's longtime aide Jack Steadman said, "Lamar had the vision that pro football would grow dramatically because of the way it televised. He also took note that the NFL was only in a few cities, most of them in the East. He saw the game's growth potential when so many other people did not."[1]

The AFL Had to Be Different to Survive

From its inception in 1960, the AFL played a fourteen-game season as compared to the NFL's twelve-game schedule. That meant that for two additional weekends in September—before the NFL started its season on the fourth Sunday of the month—the AFL was the only game in town and, more importantly, the only professional game on television. The NFL responded in 1961 by expanding its season to fourteen games. Adding another element of interest and excitement to their games— especially those in which the difference in the score was eight points or less—the AFL innovated the option for a two-point conversion after a touchdown. The league was the first to put players' names on their jerseys to foster greater fan identification with men whose faces were usually obscured by helmets, helping to promote their new stars. Hunt and his fellow AFL owners were fortunate that ABC entrusted the production of their games to Roone Arledge, the twenty-nine-year-old visionary who created ABC's *Wide World of Sports* series, made ABC the network of the Olympics in the 1960s, and later launched *NFL Monday Night Football*. In his December 2002 *New York Times* obituary, Arledge was called, "The most important behind the scenes figure in the television coverage of major events in the last half of the 20th century."

Arledge initiated what came to be known as "AFL coverage." ABC cameras purposely avoided showing any shots of the stands, which, in the early years, very often were sparsely populated. On kickoffs, for example, instead of a wide shot of the whole field that followed the flight of the ball across an expanse of empty seats on the far side of the field, ABC showed a closer shot of the kicker approaching the ball on its tee, then cut to a similar close shot of the returner as he received the ball and began to run. Neither shot showed empty stands. Viewers at home who see empty seats at any venue immediately assume—regardless of the sport—that "it can't be important if no one is there." That's the message that ABC avoided sending with its AFL coverage strategy. Arledge also increased fan interest and added storylines with "hero graphics" that identified players who had just scored or made a significant play and displayed information such as how many touchdowns or pass receptions they had that season. ABC production crews added videotape of previous games to show a team's past highlights and successes, and at halftime they played highlights from the first half. Instant replays during game coverage would not be seen until December 1963, when they were introduced on CBS by director Tony Verna at the Army–Navy football game.

Arledge said that "in order to make it successful, we had to develop some production techniques that made people want to watch it. One of the things we did was we showed the names of the players when they caught a pass or were running off a field or something. Because we wanted people to remember the next time the guy caught the pass; we wanted them to say, 'Oh, that's the same guy who did that before.' And we also experimented with slow motion and stop action and all that kind of stuff." Working with the AFL, a league with no prior history or traditions, Arledge had the leeway to try new ideas that hadn't been used on television before. "We were able with the AFL—because it was brand new and they were willing to almost let us do anything—to do some things that we probably couldn't have done if we had had the NFL," he said. "It was a period in which the NFL announcers treated the games kind of like a religion. It was kind of like you were in a cathedral. We decided that we wanted to have more fun than that. So we loosened up the announcing, and we loosened up the production . . . all of which later became staples in this industry."[2]

The AFL and ABC innovations marked a turning point in the coverage of football as a television spectator sport. The televised AFL games that Americans began to see in 1960 foreshadowed where live broadcasting would take the sport as it moved toward the beginning of the Super Bowl era. It's a prime example of how competition in any endeavor improves the product and in so doing raises the expectations of those who consume that product.

Hunt Says No, and the NFL Says Game On

When the NFL finally offered Lamar Hunt a Dallas franchise in late 1959, the league expected him to happily accept what he had so fervently sought and to drop his plans for a rival league. When he did not, the NFL immediately classified Hunt and his fellow AFL owners as true rivals to be dealt with as opponents on the gridiron. The first move to undercut Hunt had been to award a Dallas franchise to Clint Murchison Jr. and Bedford Wynne that would begin play in 1960, would share the Cotton Bowl as home field with Hunt's Dallas Texans, and would compete for the loyalties of fans in Texas and throughout the South. During that first season, Cowboys fans saw zero victories, eleven losses, and one tie. By contrast, the Texans had a winning season in their first year competing in a league composed exclusively of first-year teams, compiling a record of eight wins and six losses.

The NFL, which only one year earlier had shown itself resistant to change, now made several moves designed to strengthen its position against the AFL. In addition to establishing the Dallas Cowboys, the NFL uprooted the long troubled, underperforming Chicago Cardinals team that Lamar Hunt and so many others had sought to buy, relocating the franchise to St. Louis. The NFL expanded to a third new market in 1961 with the Minnesota Vikings ownership, which had originally signed with the AFL.

The AFL's response was to file suit in June 1960 in Maryland federal district court against the NFL and most of its owners, alleging that they were guilty of "monopolization, attempted monopolization and conspiracy to monopolize major league professional football" in the United States. This court action—more than any other factor—made enemies of the two leagues, and the idea that later in the decade the two could sit in the same room and talk about cooperation and merging into one organization was the furthest thing from any NFL owner's mind.

In their antitrust suit, the AFL owners claimed that the granting of NFL franchises to Dallas and Minneapolis-St. Paul "constituted an exercise of monopoly power, and that those acts were done as part of an attempt or a conspiracy to monopolize." Monopoly, in legal precedents, is defined as "the power to control prices or exclude competition." A business organization could be found "guilty of monopolization if it undertakes a course of action the consequence of which would be to exclude competitors or prevent competition." The NFL and its owners as the defendants contended that the award of those two franchises was "made pursuant to a policy of expansion adopted by the NFL before the AFL was organized, and that the timing was at most an effort by the NFL and its members to compete more effectively with proposed AFL teams in the particular cities."[3]

In its decision announced on May 21, 1962, the US District Court found in favor of the NFL, stating that neither the NFL nor its owners, acting separately or in concert, had attempted or conspired to monopolize professional football. The AFL lost in court, but beginning its third full season, the league had begun to develop a fan base and was optimistic about the future. So despite the animosity that arose from the antitrust suit, Lamar Hunt in 1962 started proposing to the NFL that the two leagues hold a title game between their respective champions. The NFL rejected the idea outright, knowing that if it allowed an AFL team to take the field with an NFL team, it would automatically "give the upstarts instant credibility at the very moment the NFL was waiting for the upstarts to fold their tents and disappear." But that wasn't going to happen, and the "upstart" league was beginning to have an impact on the NFL where the owners would feel it most: in their wallets. After the 1962 season, Hunt stopped competing with the NFL in Dallas and moved his team to Kansas City, renaming it the "Chiefs."

The Big Money Battle for the Best Players
A clear example of this was Billy Cannon, the Louisiana State University (LSU) halfback who was the number-one draft pick in the 1960 NFL draft held on November 30, 1959, at the Warwick Hotel in Philadelphia. The NFL timed its annual draft to coincide with the end of the college football regular season. The Los Angeles Rams had the first pick that year, and their general manager Pete Rozelle, who had not yet been elected commissioner, signed Cannon to a $50,000 three-year contract before his college season was over. Rozelle told Cannon to keep the

signing quiet until after the Sugar Bowl game that LSU would play on New Year's Day 1960.

The AFL scheduled its inaugural draft for one week before the NFL's player selection meeting in November. It was held in secret in Minneapolis, which at that time was still going to be part of the AFL. Each of the eight teams got thirty-three picks, one as a territorial pick to select a top college player from their area as a drawing card for local ticket-buying fans, plus thirty-two more, whom they would attempt to sign to fill out their opening day rosters. In the AFL draft, the Houston Oilers also chose Billy Cannon, who won the Heisman Trophy as the outstanding college football player of 1959. Despite already having signed with the Rams, Cannon also inked a contract with the Texans, who had offered him double: $100,000. He signed the Oilers contract after the Sugar Bowl game was played on January 1, 1960, in New Orleans. (LSU lost to Ole Miss 21–0.)

Two days before that game, Cannon sent a letter to Pete Rozelle saying that he no longer wanted to play for the Rams, and he enclosed two uncashed checks that the Rams had given him totaling $10,500. Rozelle and the Rams took Cannon to court, claiming that their contract, having been signed first, should be enforced. But a US District Court judge in California found that execution of the Rams contract had been contingent on "approval by the Commissioner" of the NFL. Commissioner Bert Bell had died in October, and NFL treasurer Austin Gunsel was serving as president in the office of the commissioner until a successor to Bell was named at the end of January 1960. Therefore, the Rams contract did not have a commissioner's approval and was found to be null and void. Billy Cannon got his $100,000, and in its first year, the AFL scored an early victory over the NFL, stealing away its number-one draft pick. It was the first round of what would become a heated, expensive battle for players, and it showed the AFL to be a serious competitor that could suit up top-quality players and attract fan loyalty.[4]

The NFL felt compelled to adopt a strategy of "babysitting" the players they wanted most during successive AFL drafts. NFL teams sent coaches, ex-players, and team representatives to convince their player prospects that signing with an AFL team would be a mistake and that they should join the older established league instead. Occasionally that strategy backfired, as it did with Abner Haynes, who signed with the Dallas Texans in his rookie year of 1960 and became the AFL's first player of the year. The Pittsburgh Steelers planned to draft Haynes, so head coach Raymond "Buddy" Parker and quarterback Bobby Layne went to Haynes's home in Denton, Texas, to "babysit" him. Haynes remembered the two out on the front porch of his home early on the morning of the NFL draft. Haynes said, "They was on my front porch about 5:30. Woke me up. Said, 'we gonna draft you this morning.' They were so drunk they were holding each other up in front of my house saying, 'The hell with that AFL.' I don't think they knew my dad was a minister. He went out front, and he said, 'you won't be going to Pittsburgh.' I said, 'Yes sir.'"[5] Despite these predraft tactics, the two leagues managed to maintain an informal agreement that no team would try to sign players away from rival league teams *after* their contracts had been signed.

When the Minneapolis franchise agreed to join the NFL, all thirty-three players that the team had chosen in the inaugural AFL draft transferred to the AFL's new Oakland franchise. Unable to select any of their own players in the first AFL draft put the Raiders at a disadvantage, but one of the Minneapolis draft picks was center Jim Otto from the University of Miami, who played his entire fifteen-year Hall of Fame career with Oakland. Billy Cannon himself would be traded to Oakland before the 1964 season, and he played in Super Bowl II for the Raiders against the Green Bay Packers. The new Minnesota Vikings were left without a roster, a primary reason why their NFL debut did not come until 1961.

The $400,000 Quarterback

The spending war among owners of the two rival leagues escalated each year until it reached its tipping point in 1965 with the signing of Joe Namath by the New York Jets. The 1965 NFL draft was held at the Summit Hotel in New York City on Saturday, November 28, 1964. The AFL draft was held on the same day via telephone conference call, the only draft in professional football history to be held without a central location. The New York Giants had the first pick in the NFL, and the New York

Jets acquired the first pick in the AFL in a trade with the Houston Oilers. The Giants needed a running back to fill the void left by the retirement of future Hall of Famer Frank Gifford, so they passed on Namath at number one and instead selected Auburn's Tucker Fredrickson. Namath was chosen twelfth by the NFL's St. Louis Cardinals. The New York Jets made Namath the first overall pick in the AFL.

Alabama head coach Paul "Bear" Bryant told his senior quarterback that he should ask the Cardinals for $200,000, double what Namath had originally hoped for. Two representatives from the Cardinals reluctantly agreed to that number in talks with Namath in the days following the drafts, but nothing was signed. Namath then met with one of the Jets owners, David A. "Sonny" Werblin, whose first offer was $300,000 for three years. Namath's lawyer Mike Bite used that number as a starting point, negotiating a three-year package for his client worth $427,000, the largest contract in history for a professional athlete at the time. The money didn't all go into Namath's pocket: the total included $30,000 each for Namath's two brothers and his brother-in-law to serve as "scouts" for the Jets for three years, plus $7,000 for a Jet-green Lincoln Continental.

Where did the money come from? Sonny Werblin had made his fortune building the television division of MCA, the Music Corporation of America, into a dominant force that packaged hit shows like *Ed Sullivan* and *The Jackie Gleason Show* and represented clients such as Frank Sinatra, Dean Martin, Elizabeth Taylor, Johnny Carson, and Ronald Reagan. But the reason the Jets were able to offer Namath such a generous deal was at least in part because they and their fellow AFL teams had just received a windfall of television money.

From 1960 through 1963, NBC watched CBS and ABC dominate Sunday TV viewing in America with their telecasts of NFL and AFL games that attracted more advertising dollars each year. When ABC's contract with the American Football League concluded its fourth season, with only one year remaining, NBC executives saw an opportunity. NBC initiated talks with the AFL, which was represented by Commissioner Joe Foss and the Jets' Sonny Werblin, who had decades of television negotiating experience. In January 1964, an agreement was reached for NBC to pay the AFL $36 million for the rights to five years of regular season and playoff games beginning in 1965—$26.5 million more than ABC had paid for the first five years of AFL coverage. ABC had the right of first refusal on any new contract, but the network declined to renew its deal at what would have been a 423% increase. Rather than serve as the lame-duck broadcaster of AFL games in the fall of 1964, effectively promoting what would become the property of a rival network, ABC ceded its rights to NBC. The new rights deal with NBC guaranteed each of the eight AFL teams $4.5 million in television revenue over the life of the contract, just under $1 million per year per team. Cleveland Browns owner Art Modell said later that when he heard about the NBC deal with the AFL, he knew that the new league "had made it" and that a merger was now inevitable.

Joe Namath's signing by the Jets was announced on January 2, 1965, the day after he had been named the Orange Bowl's most valuable player, despite his top-ranked Crimson Tide's loss to Texas 21–17. Namath almost immediately became known as the "$400,000 quarterback." Reaction was swift, particularly from veteran NFL quarterbacks like Frank Ryan, who had just led the Cleveland Browns to the NFL championship. "If a fellow who hasn't even pulled on his cleats in pro ball is worth $400,000," said Ryan, "then I must be worth a million dollars."[6]

A Merger Meant to Save Money

Competition for their services from two professional leagues obviously gave players coming out of college tremendous bargaining power and put the owners at a disadvantage. They would either meet the demands of star players or lose them to well-financed owners in the rival league. Merging the AFL and the NFL into one league would not be in the players' best interest financially, but it became apparent that despite the animosity between the leagues, a merger would be the only way for team owners to stop salaries from escalating higher and cutting deeper into their profits.

Just a year after the Namath signing, Dallas Cowboys general manager Earnest "Tex" Schramm was on the phone with Los Angeles Rams owner Dan Reeves. Schramm had many times repeated, "I hate the AFL," but he and Reeves began discussing the need for a merger of the two leagues that day in February 1966. Schramm followed up by briefing

Commissioner Pete Rozelle, who encouraged him to put together a small group of league executives, including the owners of the two teams that shared markets with AFL teams: the San Francisco 49ers and the New York Giants, to begin considering how a merger could be achieved.

In early March, Schramm and Rozelle outlined a merger proposal to the group that included a stipulation that the Jets move out of New York and the Raiders relocate to either Seattle or Portland. After consulting the NFL's attorneys in Washington, DC, Covington and Burling, it was time for Tex Schramm to call Lamar Hunt. On April 4, 1966, he called Hunt and asked if he "might be able to come to Dallas to discuss a matter of mutual importance." Two days later, on April 6, the two men met at the Texas Ranger statue that stood in the Love Field terminal, then went out to the parking lot where they sat in Schramm's Oldsmobile and talked for forty-five minutes.

Schramm said that he told Hunt, "I think the time has come to talk about a merger if you'd be interested in that." He recalled Hunt saying, "Fine, I'm interested." They went on to discuss the conditions of Schramm's proposal: Pete Rozelle would be commissioner of the new unified league, and all existing franchises would be admitted into the NFL, but the Jets would have to move out of New York to avoid competing with the Giants, and the Raiders would be forced to leave the Bay Area in order to eliminate competition for the 49ers. Hunt responded that neither the Jets nor Raiders would depart their home cities, part of the reason being the huge popularity of "the $400,000 quarterback" in New York, who had by now been fondly nicknamed "Broadway Joe."[7]

Lamar Hunt did not tell his fellow AFL owners about his exploratory talks with the NFL when they held their annual meeting forty-eight hours later on April 8, 1966, in Houston. At that owners meeting, the AFL's first and only commissioner, Joe Foss, a World War II fighter pilot who had won the Congressional Medal of Honor and been a two-term governor of South Dakota, submitted his resignation. As his successor, the owners elected Al Davis of the Oakland Raiders, who yearned to take on the NFL head-to-head.

Lamar Hunt also kept his merger talks secret from the new AFL commissioner until he could present a well-thought-out plan that his fellow owners could discuss and then accept or reject. On May 3, Hunt heard back from Tex Schramm, who informed him that the price tag for admission to the NFL would be $18 million, a fee of $2 million for each of the AFL's original eight teams and the league's ninth team, the expansion Miami Dolphins, which was set to begin play in the 1966 season. A week later, Hunt responded to Schramm, saying that in his opinion an agreement on the terms they had discussed could be reached.

That same week, there was a breach in the unwritten agreement not to raid players from the rival league. New York Giants owner Wellington Mara had played golf at Winged Foot Golf Club in Westchester County, New York, with the agent for Buffalo Bills placekicker Pete Gogolak, the first soccer-style kicker in the history of pro football. Gogolak's twenty-eight field goals in 1965 helped propel the Bills to their second straight AFL championship. Mara's Giants had a rookie placekicker in 1965, Bob Timberlake, who made only one field goal in his fifteen attempts. The Giants were assured that Gogolak was a free agent and available, so they signed him to a three-year contract worth $96,000.

News of the signing, which won approval from Commissioner Pete Rozelle, came out at the NFL owners meeting May 16 in Washington, DC. Owners and team executives feared that the Giants acquisition of the Bills kicker could trigger massive player raids by AFL teams in retribution. Vince Lombardi of the Green Bay Packers, reportedly red in the face, yelled at Mara: "I can't believe you would do something like this to put us all in jeopardy."[8]

The AFL's new commissioner Al Davis heard news of the Gogolak signing during a visit with Bills owner Ralph Wilson. "We just got our merger!" he said. "If we go out and sign their players, we'll destroy them, and they'll have to come to the table." Davis had a plan to target the NFL's top ten players, including his Oakland Raiders signing Los Angeles Rams starting quarterback Roman Gabriel for the 1967 season and the Houston Oilers signing San Francisco 49ers star quarterback John Brodie, each for sums far in excess of their NFL contracts. Tex Schramm met with Pete Rozelle after the tumultuous NFL owners meeting had adjourned for the day, telling Rozelle that his subcommittee of owners was resolved to move forward with the merger of the two leagues as the only way to shift the economic climate of professional football back in their favor. Schramm remembered that Rozelle looked him in the eye and said, "All right, let's go." Schramm then called Lamar Hunt to reassure him that despite all the bluster, the merger plans were on track. NFL owners would meet again a few weeks later in New York, where the merger plan would be laid out.[9]

From Two Leagues, One

When the formal presentation to merge the leagues was made to the NFL owners, San Francisco and New York—the teams in markets competing directly against AFL franchises—voiced their opposition. However, when the other ten owners offered to forfeit their shares of the AFL's $18 million entry fee and give $10 million to the Giants and the remaining $8 million to the 49ers, the vote to move forward with the merger was unanimous.

At the same time, Lamar Hunt had flown to New York to reveal the plan to his fellow AFL owners. They initially balked at paying $2 million each to join the NFL, but Hunt had anticipated their resistance and had worked out a twenty-year payment schedule, meaning that each owner would have to pay only $100,000 each year. It took the better part of the next five days for representatives from both leagues to hammer out details and make compromises. On the night of June 7, 1966, in a suite at the Sheraton-Carlton Hotel in Washington, DC, registered to a fictitious "Ralph Pittman," Hunt, Schramm, Rozelle, and his assistant Jim Kensil worked out the wording of the merger announcement that would be made the following day. It took them until 3:00 a.m.

Joint Statement
National and American Football Leagues

The NFL and AFL today announced plans to join in an expanded major professional football league. It will consist of 26 teams in 25 cities, with expectation of additional teams in the near future.

The main points of the plan include:

- Pete Rozelle will be the commissioner.
- A world championship game this season.
- All existing franchises retained.
- No franchises transferred from present locations.
- Two new franchises no later than 1968.
- Two more teams as soon thereafter as practical.
- Inter-league pre-season games in 1967.
- Single league schedule in 1970.
- A common draft next January.
- Continued two-network TV coverage.

With this announcement on June 8, 1966, the Super Bowl was born. It would be played between the champions of the National Football League and the American Football League on January 15, 1967, at a neutral site to be determined. Neither CBS—which held the exclusive rights to televise NFL games including its championship—nor NBC— with its rights to televise all AFL games including that league's championship—had been party to the merger discussions, and neither network was happy. CBS in particular saw its valuable NFL championship game now reduced to the status of a "semifinal." Commissioner Rozelle worked out a formula that would allow both CBS and NBC to televise the first AFL–NFL world championship game for an additional $1 million rights fee each.[10]

Making a merger announcement was one thing. Turning two leagues into one unified entity would be quite something else, considering the many ways in which the AFL and NFL operated differently. For example:

- The NFL had fifteen teams in 1966. The AFL had nine, bringing their combined total to twenty-four clubs. The plan was to add one new team to each league by 1968, bringing the total to twenty-six, which was written into the merger announcement press release.
- The leagues had different playoff structures.
- Each conducted separate drafts in November.
- The leagues had different roster sizes: the NFL had forty players, the AFL thirty-eight.

- The NFL had a $5,000 minimum salary. The AFL had no minimum.
- The leagues had different officials.
- The AFL had the two-point conversion, which was eliminated when the merger took effect and did not return until the 1994 season.
- There were legal and tax issues to sort out.
- Each league had a separate, exclusive television contract.
- They even used different footballs: the NFL used Wilson, the AFL Spalding.

A joint committee of three representatives from each league, chaired by Rozelle, would hold its first meeting on July 20, 1966, and work until the summer of 1969 to sort out these details and unite the two leagues as one with a single set of rules and procedures. Rozelle was joined by AFL owners Lamar Hunt of the Kansas City Chiefs, William Sullivan of the Boston Patriots, and Buffalo Bills owner Ralph Wilson. The NFL representatives who were part of this "transition team" included Dallas Cowboys general manager Tex Schramm, Baltimore Colts owner Carroll Rosenbloom, and Dan Reeves, owner of the Los Angeles Rams.

All these differences needed to be resolved, but they were minor when compared to what the AFL–NFL merger had achieved: a single championship game for professional football in the United States, which could be planned and promoted well in advance to build interest and excitement and to generate huge television audiences and revenues. By uniting as one league, the team owners eliminated the costly competition for players and took back control of their finances. The days of the "$400,000 quarterback" were over, at least for the short term.

That became abundantly clear during the first unified draft in March 1967. Syracuse All-American running back Floyd Little, a future Hall of Fame inductee, was the sixth player selected. (Michigan State defensive lineman Bubba Smith was the first pick, selected by the Baltimore Colts.) Little said that the previous year he had been courted by the New York Jets, who told him that they wanted him in the backfield with

Joe Namath and that they were prepared to pay him "Namath money." Instead, with competition at an end between the leagues, the Denver Broncos selected Little, and his first contract was for three years, starting at only $25,000 and increasing $1,000 per year after that. For years afterward, Floyd Little joked about complaining to his parents that "if he had just been born a year earlier," he could have made a lot more money in his career.[11]

CHAPTER 3

Super Bowl I Was a Scramble—and Don't Call It the Super Bowl

LAMAR HUNT HAD THREE YOUNG CHILDREN WHEN THE AFL AND NFL announced their merger in the summer of 1966. Lamar Junior was nine years old, daughter Sharon was eight, and Clark, now the chairman and chief executive officer of the Kansas City Chiefs, had recently celebrated his first birthday. One of the toys that the Hunt kids enjoyed playing with at home was the Superball made by Wham-O. Watching his children play with their Superball, Lamar Hunt thought that the new championship game between the two football leagues could be called the "Super Bowl." When he offhandedly used that name at the first meeting of the joint merger committee in July 1966, he remembered getting some smiles and a few chuckles. "But nobody ever said, 'let's make that the name of the game,'" he recalled. "Far from it. We all agreed that it was far too corny to be the name of the new title game." Hunt followed up a few days later with a letter to Commissioner Pete Rozelle saying, "If possible, I believe we should coin a phrase for the championship game. . . . I have kiddingly called it the 'Super Bowl,' which obviously can be improved upon."[1]

The language of popular culture in America during the 1960s was liberally seasoned with empty superlatives like "super," "cool," "neat," and "wild," which were used by almost everyone who thought of themselves as "hip" to describe almost everything. Pete Rozelle hated the sobriquet, thinking that "super" was an inappropriate, common word that cheapened the status of an elite, world championship game. He reportedly preferred "Pro Bowl," but that title was already attached to the NFL's annual all-star game. The members of the joint committee couldn't come up with a name that adequately described and promoted the game, so Rozelle announced that it would be officially named the "AFL–NFL World Championship Game."[2]

Regardless of its official title, the Super Bowl—an annual fixture on our collective calendars for decades—was in jeopardy of not happening at all. To protect the merger of the two football leagues from claims that the NFL had become an illegal monopoly, existing federal antitrust law needed to be changed, which required passage by both houses of Congress and a signature from President Lyndon B. Johnson. Without an exemption from antitrust statutes, the commissioner believed that opportunists would have a "hunting license" to come after the newly combined league to seek compensation for damages.

In fact, a suit was filed that summer by a man who claimed that the AFL had promised him an expansion franchise in Chicago and that the merger had torpedoed his plans and anticipated profits. Another suit was filed in Washington, DC, by the would-be founder of a third league; he too claimed that he deserved damages because a merger of the NFL and AFL would subvert his plans and cause him monetary loss. Plus, there was the question of the merger monopolizing the selection of professional football games that would be aired on television and the coverage and profit therefrom. The Sports Broadcasting Act of 1961 had been passed to exempt individual leagues from antitrust laws in the execution of their national television contracts, but the act did not address how protection might extend to league mergers.

Playing Football Required Playing Politics

Pete Rozelle and his communications team responded by developing a lobbying strategy that he would take to Washington in an effort to win approval for a new set of antitrust exemptions. The NFL would stress to lawmakers that merging the two leagues would result in (1) more jobs, since rosters would increase to forty players and new teams would create more job opportunities; (2) higher player salaries, because the minimum would increase to $12,000 per year for every player; (3) greater economic stability for teams in small cities; and, for the fans, (4) new playoff attractions and more spirited competition. The league thought it had a convincing argument, but the chairman of the House Judiciary Committee, which would have to approve any changes in antitrust law, wasn't buying it. Congressman Emmanuel Celler from Brooklyn had served in the House of Representatives since 1923, and he was still upset that the Brooklyn Dodgers abandoned his district in 1958, which he blamed on the antitrust exemption that Major League Baseball won in the 1920s as a result of the US Supreme Court's decision in the Federal League case. Congressman Celler did not want to extend the same monopoly status to professional football.

With support from Democrats and Republicans, the US Senate approved legislation that would expand the antitrust exemptions. But in the House, Congressman Celler allowed it to sit in his committee until the NFL's 1966 season was already underway. The league was planning a new championship game at the end of that season, but without legislative changes, it risked lawsuits or running afoul of the law. The House Judiciary Committee did start hearings on October 11, 1966, but Chairman Celler refused to let the exemptions clear his committee. The pressure was on the NFL to clear this roadblock.[3]

Pete Rozelle reached out to David Dixon in Louisiana, who had promoted NFL exhibition games at Tulane Stadium in the 1960s. Dixon later became the prime mover behind construction of the New Orleans Superdome. One of Dixon's fraternity brothers from his days at Tulane was Hale Boggs, who had been elected to Congress in the 1940s and served as the House majority whip in 1966. In exchange for his help in bypassing the Judiciary Committee, the NFL—through Dixon—told Boggs that the league would award New Orleans its next expansion franchise. Boggs saw this as an opportunity to champion his home state and win back some of the political support that he lost after he had voted in favor of the Voting Rights Act of 1965. Congressman Boggs had seen his electoral majority in a district that was still very much part of the Old South fall from 67 percent in the previous election to only 55 percent.

Boggs enlisted the aid of Senator Everett Dirksen, the Republican minority leader from Illinois, and Senator Russell Long, the Louisiana Democrat who was chairman of the Senate Finance Committee. They attached the NFL's antitrust exemptions to an investment tax credit bill that had already passed the House. That bill would not have to go through Congressman Celler's House Judiciary Committee, and it was on President Johnson's priority list, so his signature was assured.

The amended bill came up for final approval in the full House of Representatives on October 21, 1966, less than three months before the NFL hoped to hold its first "AFL–NFL World Championship Game." In his remarkable book *America's Game*, Michael MacCambridge recounted that, on the way to the House chamber for that day's vote with Hale Boggs, Commissioner Rozelle had said, "Congressman Boggs, I don't know how I can ever thank you enough for this. This is a terrific thing you've done." Boggs responded sharply, "What do you mean you don't know how to thank me? New Orleans gets an immediate franchise in the NFL." When Rozelle assured the congressman that he would "do everything I can to make that happen," Boggs reportedly stopped and turned as if heading back to the committee room. "Well, we can always call off the vote," he said. With his choice clearly laid out before him, Pete Rozelle's response was, "It's a deal, Congressman. You'll get your franchise." The birth of the Super Bowl and of the New Orleans Saints were both guaranteed that day at the US Capitol.[4]

Pete Rozelle's Vision

Pete Rozelle had a vision for what the championship game, which members of the press were already referring to as the "Super Bowl," should be. Since its scheduling placed it in January, he thought it should be staged each year at a neutral site, in a warm weather city, and in as large a stadium as possible, just like annual college football bowl games such as the Rose Bowl, Cotton Bowl, and Orange Bowl. The NFL and AFL championship games had previously all been played at one of the two team's home stadiums. To this day, that remains the case for all other professional league sports in the United States. The NBA Finals, the World Series, and the NHL's Stanley Cup Finals are all home-and-home series, meaning that the sites for their championships are not known until a week or less before they begin. Since the elimination process in the other leagues is not complete until the end of the conference final series that decide which two teams will play for the title, there is very little time in which to mount a promotional campaign or plan ancillary events. The selection of a neutral site for the Super Bowl well before the NFL's ultimate game gave the league the opportunity to attract the largest crowds possible by doing months of promotion, selling tickets far in advance, and capitalizing on how the warm weather site of the game would appeal to fans seeking escape from the cold of winter.

The Los Angeles City Council passed a resolution in late September 1966, offering the Los Angeles Memorial Coliseum as the site for the historic first meeting of NFL and AFL champions. It would be the first bid ever made by any city to host a Super Bowl. The city had just outfitted the Coliseum with 67,378 theater-style seats, and by declaring Los Angeles "the sports capital of the world," city council members hoped to generate fresh revenue to help offset the cost of this renovation. Having worked so many years with the Rams, Rozelle was familiar with the Coliseum, but he held off on the stadium selection process until after his efforts on Capitol Hill in Washington proved successful. In November, Rozelle identified a list of potential sites: the LA Coliseum, the Orange Bowl in Miami, Houston's Astrodome, and Tulane Stadium in New Orleans, annual host of the Sugar Bowl. On November 17, 1966, the *Los Angeles Times* reported that the Coliseum had been selected as the site of the inaugural Super Bowl because of its seating capacity of ninety-three thousand (including bleachers and theater seats) and Southern California's "ideal weather." The Coliseum Authority would keep all concession revenue from the game and 10 percent of the gate up to $50,000.[5]

Rozelle knew that everything about the NFL's season-ending game had to be first class. From the game's infancy, he wanted the media and the public to consider it in the same category as elite sporting events like the World Series and the Kentucky Derby, which had attracted national attention every year for decades. (The Kentucky Derby first run in 1875; the first World Series was played in 1903.) From his years of public relations for the Los Angeles Rams before becoming their general manager,

Rozelle knew that to get positive publicity from the news media, you had to impress them and treat them royally. As part of the NFL's budget for staging the first "Super Bowl," Rozelle allotted $250,000 for media relations, which included free trips for any of the 338 credentialed members of the press who wanted to go to Santa Anita Park for horse racing or to Disneyland in Anaheim, plus free meals with open bars. The commissioner wanted to leave the media with the impression that the "AFL–NFL World Championship Game" was an exceptional event to cover because he knew that positive impression would be reflected in the stories they wrote.

Super Bowl I

With less than two months to prepare for this first championship game, Rozelle's lofty goals would be difficult to achieve. There was precious little time for promotion of an event that had never happened before, for pro football fans to make Los Angeles their mid-January vacation destination, or for any corporate outings to be planned. The game would not be a sellout. Tickets were priced at $6, $10, and $12, but thousands remained unsold at kickoff. (Adjusted for inflation, $12 in 1967 is the equivalent of more than $100 today.) Ninety-three-thousand seats were available, but the official attendance for the first Super Bowl on January 15, 1967, was 61,946. There had been rumors that the NFL might lift its customary seventy-five-mile radius home game television blackout for the Los Angeles area, which might have led some people to hope they could watch the game at home on TV. Blacked out on both the CBS and NBC stations in Los Angeles, the game sent many fans who were unwilling to part with $6 to $12 for a ticket onto the highways headed south toward San Diego to watch in motels or wherever they could find a television.[6]

As fans filed in on the day of the game, it quickly became apparent to league officials that the cavernous Coliseum would appear to be half-empty, with roughly sixty thousand fans spread out across its ninety-three thousand seats. Approximately forty-five minutes before kickoff, the public address announcer invited fans to move into the empty seats near the center of the field. Hundreds of people moved en masse to fill the spaces that would have been embarrassing to the NFL had they been seen on television.

The 1966 season ended with two championship games, as it had every year since 1960. The Packers defeated the Cowboys 34–27, deciding the NFL championship on New Year's Day 1967 at the Cotton Bowl in Dallas. The Kansas City Chiefs traveled to Buffalo, where they beat the Bills 31–7 on the same day at War Memorial Stadium in what would be the biggest game to date in the AFL. The victors won the right to, for the first time, play an NFL team, and that historic game two weeks later would determine the "world champion."

The Chiefs flew home to Kansas City, and, in what would appear to be eager anticipation, flew to Los Angeles on January 4, 1967, arriving a full eleven days before the game was to be played. Commissioner Rozelle wanted both teams to get to LA as early as possible so that they could generate publicity and promote the new event. That was a major reason behind providing a two-week gap between the league championship games and the Super Bowl, instead of the one week that had always separated conference title games and the respective league championships.[7]

Green Bay's coach Vince Lombardi had other plans. He wanted to prepare his players as seriously as possible without the distraction of promotional appearances or news conferences. Lombardi felt the pressure of representing the NFL and defending its reputation as the long-established, superior league. His original plan was to wait until January 14, the day before the game, to fly his team to the site. With the events and media coverage that now dominate the week of the Super Bowl, a team flying in the day before the game would be unimaginable. Rozelle insisted however that the Packers arrive at least a week in advance, so the NFL champions left Wisconsin and arrived in Southern California on Sunday, January 8. Teams traveling one week before the game has become a longstanding Super Bowl tradition.

Vince Lombardi's sense of the NFL's superiority was underscored by gamblers. The Las Vegas betting line on the first "AFL–NFL World Championship" opened with the Packers as an eight-point favorite. That quickly increased to a thirteen-point spread for Green Bay over Kansas City. Because the two teams had used different footballs during their respective seasons, it was decided that when the Packers were on offense, they would use the Wilson "Duke" football to which they were accustomed. When the Chiefs were on offense, they would use a Spalding JV-5 ball, which had a slightly narrower profile than the Wilson ball. Game officials would keep track of which ball they sent in for each set of downs.

One Game, Two TV Networks

The CBS and NBC television crews also arrived in Los Angeles several days early to work out the details as to how they would simultaneously broadcast the game. CBS, as the network that televised the NFL games each week, was designated the "host broadcaster." CBS planned to cover the game much the same way that they had produced the regular season and conference playoff games. Bill Fitts, executive producer for CBS Sports at the time, said that they did add a couple cameras, including an extra handheld camera to get shots of the teams entering the field and one for each of the locker rooms for postgame interviews. But the eleven cameras CBS used in 1967 were bare bones compared with the sixty to ninety cameras that networks now use to cover Super Bowls.

The two-network "split" would have the CBS director calling the shots. NBC would take that feed into its separate production truck without any of the CBS commentary or production elements, add its own commentators, roll in its own instant replays, and insert NBC graphics to the broadcast, which it fed back to New York for distribution nationwide. NBC also had one discrete camera of its own to show their talent: play-by-play man Curt Gowdy, analyst Paul Christman, and reporters Charlie Jones and Jim Simpson. The announcers for the CBS telecast included Ray Scott, Jack Whitaker, Frank Gifford, and Pat Summerall.

NBC executive producer Chet Simmons, who went on to become ESPN's president when the network debuted in 1979, wasn't happy playing second fiddle to CBS. His network had been producing the AFL games for three full seasons beginning in 1964, but he knew the CBS producers well enough, so they all got along. That couldn't be said for the engineers and technicians working for the two networks. The

CBS crew was represented by one union, NBC's by a different union. Back-and-forth taunts escalated to some scuffles, which forced the networks to erect a hurricane fence between their respective production trucks, which were parked outside the Coliseum.[8]

Commissioner Rozelle wanted pageantry to make the world championship a spectacle that would long be remembered. Hundreds of doves would be released along with ten thousand balloons, and two jetpack pilots—one with "NFL" emblazoned on his chest, the other with "AFL"—would emerge from two giant footballs, lift off and fly in a circle, then land and shake hands at the fifty-yard line, symbolically joining the two leagues. At halftime, two college marching bands from Florida A&M University and the University of Arizona performed with a two-hundred-member chorus and jazz trumpeter Al Hirt, a recording artist who was a regular on variety shows of the era. Although a far cry from the rock concerts that have been the staple of Super Bowl halftimes since 1993, the entire presentation had been assembled in only a few weeks' time.

CBS executive producer Fitts remembered being "sidetracked by all of this extra stuff" taking his focus away from the actual game. On the day before the game, Fitts traditionally did his rehearsals, and because he had no idea how high or in which direction the doves would fly, he insisted on rehearsing them. That did not make the "dove wrangler" very happy. He told Fitts, "They're not homing pigeons. I'm going to have to go get a whole new 'pile' of doves!" for the game the next day. Fitts got his way, but it didn't wind up making him happy, either. "I was standing down on the field communicating with our director Bill Daly back in the CBS truck," he said. "When the birds took off, they all pooped! And I was covered in bird shit. I won't ever rehearse doves again in my life."[9]

The NFL's operations staff had been working with an engineer from Dallas on a new remote-control system to allow the officials on the field to control the stadium clock, a huge analog timepiece with wrought-iron hands several feet long that was mounted on the tower at the peristyle end of the Coliseum. The league's press office proudly announced that the official time displayed on the stadium clock would be a historic first. Installed the week preceding the game and tested extensively—including the Saturday before the game during CBS's "doves rehearsal" and one final time on the morning of the game—the system worked perfectly. But when the Kansas City Chiefs kicked off to begin the game, the field judge pushed the button to start the clock and watched in disbelief as the massive minute hand broke off and plummeted to the ground.

Luckily no fans were under the clock tower when the metal hand fell. Their time would have been up, and the NFL would have been haunted by the bad publicity of a tragedy at its inaugural event. The league's long-time public relations director Dick Weiss said that before the broken hand "even hit the ground," the phone next to him rang. "I picked it up on the first ring to hear Rozelle asking, 'What the hell happened to the goddamn clock?'" The cause was later established as "metal fatigue" due to all the starting and stopping during the tests that week. For the rest of the game, the official time was kept by referee Norm Schachter on the field, and the field judge used hand signals to let each team know how much time remained in each quarter.[10]

Halftime arrived with Green Bay leading Kansas City 14–10. In keeping with the plan for requisite "pageantry," this would be the first twenty-minute halftime in NFL history. Halftime had always been fifteen minutes, and the NFL's supervisor of officials Mark Duncan didn't like the change. Before the game he told Bill Fitts, "Halftime is going to be exactly twenty minutes, then I'm kicking off." Fitts said he knew Duncan, a former defensive coach for the San Francisco 49ers, was a "hard ass," so he scheduled his halftime commercials on CBS early to be sure that they would be finished with a few minutes to spare before the second-half kick. NBC's producer Lou Kusserow did not follow suit. At the twenty-minute mark, NBC was still airing its last halftime commercial, but Mark Duncan signaled for play to begin regardless. Viewers watching CBS saw the kickoff, but those watching NBC did not. A sideline TV stage manager began flailing his arms wildly, and the kick was whistled dead before it was touched. That led to confusion in the CBS and NBC television booths and in the stands as to whether a penalty had been called. Curt Gowdy, who was calling the game for NBC, said, "I didn't know what was happening until it was explained to me after the game." By the time the kickoff was set up again, NBC's commercial break had ended, so, in addition to all of the other "firsts" accomplished that January day in 1967, the NFL endured its first and only "Super Bowl do-over." Gowdy said the re-kick clearly demonstrated how important television was to the NFL. "The writers, for years, had proclaimed that TV was running sports, and they're about right. They brought the ball back and kicked it off again. The second half was underway, but it was important to them to get that game on TV and run it the way TV wanted to."[11]

The Green Bay Packers won the game 35–10, and Coach Vince Lombardi celebrated by holding aloft the new silver Tiffany trophy that would later bear his name. Each of Lombardi's Packers received winners' checks of $15,000. Each of the Chiefs got a check for $7,500. (Compare that to the winner's share of $169,000 for Super Bowl LVIII, and the loser's share of $89,000 per man.) William N. Wallace of the *New York Times* wrote, "The final score was an honest one, meaning it correctly reflected what went on during the game. The great interest had led to naming the event the Super Bowl, but the contest was more ordinary than super."[12]

Considering the many problems that the NFL experienced while staging its first "AFL–NFL World Championship Game," Pete Rozelle would have liked to "do over" any number of things. However, the game did yield the "super" impact for which he and the teams from both leagues had hoped: more than fifty million viewers watched the game live. Nielsen reported that 79 percent of all American televisions in use that Sunday, January 15, 1967, were tuned to the Super Bowl. The CBS telecast received a 22.6 Nielsen rating, with a 43 percent share of that afternoon's TV viewing audience, and NBC got an 18.5 rating, which represented an additional 36 percent of the audience.

CHAPTER 4

The Super Bowl Starts Making History

THE MOST IMPORTANT LEGACY OF SUPER BOWL II (WHICH WAS STILL officially the "AFL–NFL World Championship Game") at the Orange Bowl in Miami in January 1968 was that the Green Bay Packers won again. Their victims were the Oakland Raiders, whom they dispatched with a score of 33–14, giving the Packers and the NFL an aura of invincibility.

After the first Super Bowl, Commissioner Pete Rozelle swore that the game would never again be played to less than a full house. The league reduced ticket prices for Super Bowl II in January 1968, and as a result there were no empty stands for television viewers to see. What they did see convinced many that watching a title game between the best team in the NFL and the best team in the AFL was like watching the best major league team play the best minor league team. Claims by many that the best NFL teams were superior to most or all of the AFL teams were emphatically reinforced. Packers' Coach Vince Lombardi himself fanned the flames after Super Bowl I when reporters asked his assessment of the Kansas City Chiefs. "They're a good team with fine speed," he replied, "but I'd have to say NFL football is tougher. Dallas is a better team, and so are several others."[1]

After two consecutive convincing victories for the NFL, interest in hosting the next Super Bowl dwindled. It would stay at the Orange Bowl for a second straight year. The only other city to make an offer was New Orleans, and its bid was reported to be neither enthusiastic nor comprehensive. Fan interest declined after the novelty of the first championship game between the two leagues wore off. The first Super Bowl in 1967 averaged more than 51 million viewers per minute of the broadcast. For Super Bowl II—with the Packers again representing the NFL and going into the matchup as an overwhelming favorite—that figure fell to 39.1 million.

The Super Bowl in Jeopardy

The third Super Bowl appeared to be yet another mismatch: the NFL champion Baltimore Colts compiled a 13–1 regular season record in 1968 and then embarrassed the Cleveland Browns 34–0 in the NFL Championship game. The Colts had lost quarterback Johnny Unitas, the league's MVP in 1967, for the entire 1968 regular season due to an elbow injury. A decade earlier, Unitas led the Colts to the 1958 NFL championship, the "greatest game ever played." His replacement was thirty-four-year-old Earl Morrall, who stepped in and led the league in touchdown passes with twenty-six, winning the Most Valuable Player award for 1968. Even without Unitas, the Colts were installed as an eighteen-point favorite over the New York Jets.

The AFL champs were led by Joe Namath, who, in his fourth year playing in New York, was a national sensation. "Broadway Joe" represented the younger generation that wasn't interested in following their parents' rules or modestly deferring to others. Namath was brash, flamboyant, entertaining, and he produced on the field. During Unitas's 1967 MVP season, Namath had thrown for more yards, becoming the first professional quarterback to surpass four thousand yards in a season. (Unitas was the 1967 MVP with 3,428 passing yards and twenty touchdown passes. Namath threw for 4,007 yards and twenty-six touchdown—offset by twenty-eight interceptions that season.) With his unique presence and outspoken reputation, Joe Namath could attract an audience, though few serious observers gave his Jets a chance against the Colts. In a poll of fifty-five sportswriters taken before Super Bowl III, forty-nine picked the Colts to win. NFL Hall of Fame quarterback Norm Van Brocklin, who had just completed his first year coaching the new Atlanta Falcons team, made his feelings about the competition in the NFL compared to that of the AFL clear the week of the game. "On Sunday," he said, "Joe Namath will play his first professional football game."[2]

On the Friday before the Super Bowl, the commissioner began a tradition of delivering an update on the league's status, achievements, and challenges as it concluded another year of professional football. Popularly—though never officially—known as the "State of the NFL" address, it was followed by a news conference in which the commissioner fielded questions from the media. The headlines the morning after his address on Friday, January 10, 1969, read: "Rozelle Indicates Tomorrow's Super Bowl Contest Could Be Next to Last." He had said that a one-league structure was being considered, which would mix the NFL and AFL teams into new divisions. That could mean reverting to a simple NFL championship playoff structure once the merger was completed, which would allow two NFL teams to meet in the season-ending game, instead of the Super Bowl's format of an NFL team playing a team from the AFL.[3] The league's joint merger committee had been considering how to realign the twenty-six teams into a National Football Conference and an American Football Conference for the beginning of the planned single-league schedule in 1970. A vote on any structural changes would be taken at the owners meeting set for March 17, 1969, in Palm Springs, California. The one-league concept had powerful supporters, including Buffalo Bills owner Ralph Wilson and Paul Brown of the Cincinnati Bengals, which had joined the NFL for the 1968 season.

At that same Friday news conference, Rozelle also announced that, starting in 1970, the "AFL–NFL World Championship Game" officially would become known as the Super Bowl. Although he never liked the term, it had become almost universally accepted by the media and the public. Roman numerals would not be added to the game titles until Super Bowl V in 1971. Because the Super Bowl, played annually in January, crowned the champion of the season that had ended in December of the previous year, identifying Super Bowls by year would have been confusing. A means of distinguishing one Super Bowl from another—other than by the year in which it was played—was needed. Kansas City Chiefs owner Lamar Hunt proposed using Roman numerals, which would lend a greater sense of importance and permanence that Rozelle originally had envisioned for the championship event. Hunt's proposal was accepted by the NFL owners, and Roman numerals were retroactively added to the official titles of Super Bowls III and IV. With the exception of Super Bowl 50 in 2016, every Super Bowl since 1971 has been identified using *L*'s, *V*'s, *X*'s, and *I*'s. Translating them into common numbers eventually started to become a challenge for most fans as the game aged, especially years like 2004, in which Super Bowl XXXVIII (38 in our modern Arabic numerals) was played.

Joe Namath's Guaranteed Victory Saves the Super Bowl

Miami's Orange Bowl was sold out for the Jets versus the Colts in Super Bowl III on January 12, 1969, with 75,377 fans in attendance. In the opening segment of NBC's live telecast, host Curt Gowdy said, "They could have sold 150,000 tickets for this game."[4] The Baltimore Colts were still a huge favorite, and most people expected them to easily deliver a third consecutive title to the NFL. Despite the lack of suspense regarding the game's outcome, Joe Namath was the major drawing card who helped fill the stadium. People either wanted to see the young, long-haired quarterback with the rebel image eat his words and get pounded into the turf by the vaunted Colts defense or back up his prediction of victory.

Namath guaranteed a Jets win at the Miami Touchdown Club's annual awards dinner the Thursday night preceding the game. The club presented Namath its award as pro football's player of the year, the first time a player from an AFL team had been so honored. A victory guarantee was not in his planned remarks that night at the Miami Springs Villas. When he accepted the award, Namath started by thanking his family, his coaches at Alabama and with the Jets, plus the Jets ownership and his teammates. Somewhere in the crowd of about six hundred, a heckler who was clearly a Colts fan shouted, "Sit down." Namath had no idea who the guy was, but he didn't like the sound of authority in the older man's voice, and he had heard too many voices questioning the merits of his team. He responded with confidence, "The Jets will win Sunday. I guarantee it." That guarantee became the story of Super Bowl III. It was headline news the next morning, which helped generate greater interest in a game that didn't appear to be a competitive matchup. Jets' coach Weeb Ewbank was not happy at all. Baltimore's coach Don Shula had played for Ewbank when he was the Colts head coach from 1954 to 1962. He knew that Shula read every news report, looking for fuel that could fire up his team.[5]

Less than a minute into NBC's Super Bowl show, Curt Gowdy said, "I think one big sidelight has been Joe Namath. Joe Namath of course is the man that the Colts have to stop. Namath has not been bashful this week. He's come down here to Miami, and he has said that the Jets are going to win. He doesn't even *predict* it. He says, 'I guarantee a Jets victory.'" Gowdy concluded, "Joe Namath has been on a spot, but he's even more on a spot now."

The Jets followed through on Namath's promise that cloudy Sunday afternoon in Miami. Their dominating 16–7 victory guaranteed the future of the Super Bowl. *New York Times* sportswriter William N. Wallace made that point in his account of the game published the following morning. He wrote, "Namath put competition, anticipation and equality into an extravaganza that needed justification for its continued existence."[6] Any plans that the NFL owners considered for discontinuing the Super Bowl and its league-versus-league playoff structure were permanently shelved. Television ratings for the game began a steady climb the following year, growing by more than 2.6 million viewers per minute to a total of 44.2 million for Super Bowl IV in 1970 and reaching a stratospheric 76 million by 1980. Along with a larger audience came greater interest from advertisers. The price for a thirty-second commercial on NBC during Super Bowl III had been only $55,000. That rate soared by 42 percent to $78,000 for each commercial in the CBS telecast of Super Bowl IV.

With the Jets stunning upset, the Super Bowl had in only three years achieved the lofty status of the World Series, the Kentucky Derby, and the Masters in the lexicon of American sports championships. More cities started to express serious interest in hosting the game, which created a bidding competition that favored the NFL. Starting with Super Bowl IV in New Orleans, the event would begin to attract major sponsorships and establish itself as a destination for corporate entertainment. It was the first time that there were noticeably more fans attending who weren't just from the host city. In light of the progress and change fathered by

Super Bowl III, the argument can be convincingly made that it was the most crucial game with the greatest impact of any Super Bowl other than perhaps only Super Bowl I.

The Super Bowl and Cultural Change

The most significant legacy of Super Bowl III, however, may well be measured in its cultural impact. In leading the Jets to victory, Joe Namath not only increased the NFL's appeal to younger Americans, but, through the media, he validated the values and aspirations of the generation that grew up after World War II. "Broadway Joe is the folk hero of the new generation," wrote Tex Maule in *Sports Illustrated* the week after the game was played.[7]

Johnny Unitas and Earl Morrall had grown up only a decade earlier but before the war and in an entirely different moral universe. Theirs was an era of self-effacement in which the good of the community was always stressed, and people who worked on teams, sports or otherwise, put the team first and tended to avoid the spotlight. During the Great Depression and then the struggle to prevail in World War II, it was of the utmost importance to be loyal to your organization, your unit, and your teammates. Unitas, who like Namath grew up in western Pennsylvania, was deliberately unglamorous. He was a star for the Colts, but when the team traveled, not one man wanted to stand out in the crowd. They all dressed like 1950s insurance agents, and all sported the same short haircuts. "I always figured being a little dull was part of being a pro," said Unitas. "Win or lose I never walked off a football field without first thinking of something boring to say to the press."[8]

When World War II had come to an end, so too did the era of self-restraint that was the product of sixteen long years of deprivation beginning with the Great Depression in 1929. Sacrifice had been essential for survival, and it was the bedrock of the Greatest Generation. But in 1946, when Joe Namath turned three years old, millions of Americans were ready to let loose, relax, and enjoy life. A book that was a milepost on society's road from self-restraint to an era of self-esteem was *Peace of Mind* by Rabbi Joshua L. Liebman, which spent fifty-eight weeks on the bestsellers list. It urged people to set aside the idea that they should repress any part of themselves or be ashamed of any hidden impulses. Rabbi Liebman's message was to respect and trust yourself because every man had infinite potential.

The humanistic psychology movement of the mid-twentieth century that helped shape schools and human resources departments, gave rise to hundreds of self-help books and argued that people did not love themselves enough. They needed to open themselves up and realize that self-love and self-acceptance were valid paths to self-enhancement. Joe Namath emerged as an apostle of self-esteem. He was anxious to leave the self-restraint and sacrifice of his immigrant family behind and enjoy life. Instead of shunning the bright lights, he made himself the center of attention off the field as well as on it. He understood the entertainment value of sports, and with his flamboyant dress, which included wearing a fur coat on the Jets bench, and his most-eligible-bachelor night moves, he cultivated the persona of a lifestyle celebrity, not merely a football star. In a 1969 *New Yorker* article entitled "Namath All Night," he told writer Jimmy Breslin, "Some people don't like this image I got myself, being a swinger. But I'm not institutional. If it's good or bad I don't know, but it's what I like."[9] The year of his Super Bowl success, Namath wrote an autobiography with generous assistance from Dick Schaap that was titled *I Can't Wait until Tomorrow 'Cause I Get Better Looking Every Day*. It is unlikely that Johnny Unitas or Earl Morrall would have ever written or spoken those words in their lifetimes.

A Color Change

The quarterbacks who led their teams to the Super Bowl during the first twenty-one years of the game came from different generations with different life stories and levels of experience, but they had one thing in common: they were all white. No man of color had ever started a game throughout the history of modern professional football until 1968, when rookie Marlin Briscoe took the field for the Denver Broncos in the second game of the season. Briscoe was selected by Denver in the fourteenth round of the second unified NFL–AFL draft. He had been called upon to replace injured starter Jim LeClair with ten minutes left in the opening game of the season. Briscoe directed an eighty-yard drive against the Boston Patriots, running the ball in for a touchdown from twelve yards out. The Broncos didn't win that day, falling short 20–17, but Briscoe had won the starting job for game two and the remainder of the 1968 season.[10]

The Chicago Bears had a Black quarterback on their bench thirty-five years earlier, a man with perhaps the best name ever for that position, Willie Thrower. He had been the backup quarterback for Michigan State when the Spartans won the national collegiate championship in 1952, and he made the Bears roster as an undrafted rookie in 1953. The Bears starter was future Hall of Fame quarterback and placekicker George Blanda. In their game against the San Francisco 49ers on October 18, Coach George Halas was not happy with Blanda's performance, so in the third quarter he sent in Willie Thrower with the Bears on their own forty yard line. The crowd at Soldier Field saw Thrower start a drive that took the Bears to the 49ers fifteen yard line, completing three of his eight passes. Then, as the Bears were threatening to score, Halas abruptly took Thrower out and sent Blanda back in. In an interview with William C. Rhoden, Thrower remembered hearing fans chant, "'Leave Willie in! Leave Willie in!' But that was it; the end of the game for me."[11] The Bears released Thrower at the end of the season. He played four more years in Canada before a shoulder injury brought his football career to an end. Willie Thrower died in 2002 at the age of seventy-one.

For Thrower and countless other talented young Black men, the lack of opportunity undoubtedly resulted from the persistent myth, fueled by racism and ignorance, that a Black man could not be a successful quarterback. "People of color were only expected to reach certain heights in life," said Briscoe in an interview with the Associated Press in 2018 for the fiftieth anniversary of his historic start.[12] A Black man could excel as an athlete, but when it came to the job of quarterback, which required intelligence, leadership, the ability to handle complexity, and the application of split-second decisions, the myth discounted any candidate who wasn't white.

Marlin Briscoe threw 224 passes for the Broncos in 1968, completing fourteen for touchdowns. He was runner-up for AFL Rookie of the Year, but Denver didn't give him a chance to compete at quarterback the following year, so he asked for his release and gave the Canadian Football League a try. When that didn't work out, the Buffalo Bills picked him up in 1969 but converted him to a wide receiver. Marlin Briscoe threw only eleven passes in the final eight years of his pro football career. It would be another twenty years before the quarterback color barrier was broken in the Super Bowl.

During those two decades, however, with the door cracked open by Briscoe and the Broncos, a handful of Black men stepped over the obstacles laid before them and onto NFL fields as quarterbacks, the leaders of their teams. James Harris, who had played for legendary coach Eddie Robinson at Grambling State in Louisiana, was selected in the eighth round of the 1969 NFL draft by the Buffalo Bills. He started one game for the Bills in the 1969 campaign and was used sparingly the next three years. But with the Los Angeles Rams in 1974, he started nine games and threw eleven touchdown passes, earning All-Pro honors. During his ten-year NFL career, James Harris started forty-one games at quarterback.

The first African American to be named his team's starting quarterback for the opening game of an NFL season was Joe Gilliam, who made history when he and the Pittsburgh Steelers took the field September 15, 1974, to play the Baltimore Colts at Three Rivers Stadium. Gilliam (pronounced Gill-um) was an eleventh round pick out of Tennessee State who was beginning his third season with the Steelers. He had been Terry Bradshaw's backup, but in training camp the summer of 1974, he beat out the four-year veteran to become Coach Chuck Noll's starter. Bradshaw remembered that "Joe Gilliam had a phenomenal preseason. He won the starting job, and I lost it."[13] Noll looked like a genius when Gilliam hit perennial All-Pro receiver Lynn Swann on a fifty-four-yard touchdown pass in the second quarter of the Steelers home opener. Gilliam finished the day having completed seventeen of his thirty-one passing attempts for 257 yards and two touchdowns as Pittsburgh crushed the Colts 30–0. His production tailed off in his next five starts, and Bradshaw reclaimed his starting job in game seven, never to relinquish it again.

The Black QB Becomes MVP

These trailblazing quarterbacks—Briscoe, Gilliam, and Harris—had begun the process of destroying the "myth of the Black quarterback." And they did it the hard way, coming out of small colleges and being drafted in the fourteenth, eleventh, and eighth rounds respectively. The first quarterback of color chosen with a first-round pick by an NFL team would also become the man who would later break the Super Bowl's QB color barrier, Doug Williams. The Tampa Bay Buccaneers used the seventeenth pick of the first round in the 1978 NFL draft to select Williams, who like James Harris ten years earlier, had played college football at Grambling. If ever there were a team in need of help, it was the Buccaneers. In the year of their birth, 1976, they did not win a single game. And they started their second season losing twelve in a row, which ran their winless streak to twenty-six before they won their last two games in 1977. At one point during the disheartening string of losses, Coach John McKay was asked by a sportswriter what he thought of his team's execution, and he replied, "I think it's a good idea." When asked when his team would win a game, he said, "Only God knows, and I'm not too close to God now." Heading into the 1978 NFL draft and their third year in the league, Tampa Bay was a franchise with an overall record of two wins and twenty-six losses.[14]

Doug Williams was an impressive six-feet-four, 220-pound quarterback who had been a four-year starter at Grambling. As a senior in 1977, he was the leader among all NCAA quarterbacks with thirty-eight touchdown passes and 3,286 passing yards. Williams was named to the AP All America team, the first time a Black quarterback from a historically Black college had been so honored. Regardless of the color of his skin, Doug Williams was just what the Tampa Bay Buccaneers needed.

It was rare at that point of the NFL's history for any rookie quarterback to be named the starter in the first game of his first year. The prevailing wisdom was that young quarterbacks needed to spend at least their first year learning and observing from the sidelines. Therefore, when Tampa Bay hosted the New York Giants in game one of the 1978 season, Gary Huff was the starter, and Doug Williams was on the bench. The Bucs lost that game 19–13, and with Huff again at the helm, they lost at home again in week two, falling to the Detroit Lions 15–7. After thirty regular season games, Tampa Bay's record was now a dismal two wins and twenty-eight losses. That was more than Coach McKay could stomach. The teams he had coached at the University of Southern California had won their conference title nine times, and in four of those years USC had been declared national champions of college football. McKay liked winning a lot more than losing. When he and the Bucs traveled to Minnesota for a date with the Vikings in week three, McKay handed the ball to Doug Williams and made him the Bucs new starting quarterback. And they won. The Buccaneers won a total of five games in 1978, which for them was unprecedented, and Doug Williams was named the top rookie quarterback by the Pro Football Writers Association.

Williams had proven he could lead and win. The Bucs made it to the NFL playoffs three times with him as their starter. However, he remained the lowest-paid starting quarterback in the NFL, making less per year than forty-five other quarterbacks, including many who weren't starters. After the strike-shortened 1982 season ended with a wild card loss to the Dallas Cowboys, Williams asked for a salary increase from $125,000 to $600,000 per year. Tampa Bay team owner Hugh Culverhouse reportedly refused to go higher than $400,000 despite the protestations of his coach, John McKay. Doug Williams jumped to the rival United States Football League (USFL), and the Buccaneers went back to their losing ways, failing to make the NFL playoffs again for fourteen years.

The USFL ceased operations after its 1985 season, which left thirty-one-year-old Doug Williams unemployed. The man who had scouted Williams for Tampa Bay and served as the team's offensive coordinator was now the head coach of the Washington Redskins: Joe Gibbs. He needed a strong backup for his young quarterback Jay Schroeder (pronounced SHRAY-der), who was going into just his second season. Williams said Gibbs gave him a call and asked if he'd be interested in being his backup quarterback. Williams said his response was, "Coach I don't have a job. I can be 'any up.'" His concerns at the time were those facing any unemployed single parent. Williams's wife Janice had died in 1983 at the age of twenty-six, following surgery for a brain tumor ten days short of their first wedding anniversary. Doug's mom was raising their two-year-old daughter Ashley Monique back in his hometown of Zachary, Louisiana. During their years together in Tampa, Williams and Gibbs had developed a strong connection. Coach Gibbs said that he and his wife Pat had regularly invited Doug to their home for dinner. "Pat thought the world of Doug," said Gibbs. "He used to play around with my kids. They kinda looked up to him." Williams explained that "every night in training camp when everybody else was going to their hotel rooms, I would go home with Joe Gibbs."[15]

Coach Gibbs's plan appeared to be working well in 1987. Now in his third year, Jay Schroeder had led the team to an 11–4 record going into the final game of the season against the Minnesota Vikings at the Hubert H. Humphrey Metrodome. But after Schroeder threw two interceptions, bringing his season total to twenty-two, Gibbs decided to send him to the bench and bring in his thirty-two-year-old backup. Washington was trailing 14–7 in the third quarter when Doug Williams threw a forty-six-yard touchdown pass to Ricky Sanders. Then he hit Sanders again on a fifty-one-yard scoring strike in the fourth quarter. Washington had come from behind to win on the road 27–24, and Gibbs decided to stick with Williams at starting quarterback as the team headed into the playoffs.

Playoff victories over the Chicago Bears and then the Vikings put Doug Williams and Washington into Super Bowl XXII, which was scheduled to be played January 31, 1988, at San Diego's Jack Murphy Stadium. That's when millions of Americans realized that the twenty-one-year string of white quarterbacks in the Super Bowl was about to end. The media frenzy that ensued about the first Black quarterback bordered on the surreal. But Williams appeared to take it in stride. "My whole life, whatever I was, I was the first of," he said. "It was destined. It was in the cards."[16]

The night the Washington team arrived in San Diego for Super Bowl XXII, Doug Williams was met at the airport by twenty reporters, most of them asking him about the historical significance of being the first Black quarterback to start in the Super Bowl. Williams and his teammates had flown cross-country, and he was getting tired of the same questions. So Butch John of the Jackson, Mississippi, *Clarion-Ledger* decided to approach the topic from a different angle. He recalled something Williams had said earlier in the season about how being a Black quarterback had never been an issue until he got to the NFL. John asked his question this way, "Doug, it's obvious you've been a Black quarterback all your life. When did it start to matter?" That's an excellent question to pose, but Williams misheard. He did a double take and repeated what he thought he heard: "What? How long have I been a Black quarterback?" Some reporters in the pack didn't hear Butch John's original question, either, but they did hear Williams, and that's what was published the next day, becoming part of the lexicon of Super Bowl hype.[17]

Washington had won Super Bowl XVII five years earlier with Joe Theismann as their quarterback. Their opponents in Super Bowl XXII would be the Denver Broncos, who were making a return trip to the game, having lost to the New York Giants the previous year. The Broncos looked formidable on the first play from scrimmage when John Elway threw a fifty-six-yard touchdown pass to Ricky Natiel. They followed that with a Rich Karlis twenty-four-yard field goal. Denver's lead was 10–0 when Doug Williams went down hard and didn't get up. Washington's trainer came out to tend to his injured quarterback, but Williams waved him off saying, "Don't touch me. Don't touch me, because if the good Lord lets me get up, I'm going to finish the game." He limped off the field with a hyperextension of his left knee, which had been surgically repaired during his years at Grambling. Outfitted with a brace, he returned to the huddle having missed just two plays. When Williams went down, journalist Michael Wilbon remembered fearing that a potentially shining moment in history for Blacks across America would be lost. "I know what was going on in Black households all across America. 'Oh my God, don't let Doug Williams get pulled out.'"[18]

Years later, Williams said, "Pain? At that time, it was no longer important." He also had spent three hours in a dentist's chair the day before the Super Bowl having root canal work done on an abscessed molar, so his knee wasn't the only thing hurting. Doug Williams responded as he had when facing opposition before. "I knew what was at stake, and I knew I couldn't fail in that situation. I felt the weight of the Black world on my shoulders," he said.[19]

What he did was set the pain aside—the pain of the moment and the pain he had felt dealing with years of racism since his childhood in Zachary, Louisiana, in the 1950s. Williams said he had "milkshakes in my face, eggs thrown at me, rocks thrown at me, you name it. Every Friday, basically, at each end of the intersection of Plank Road there was a cross burning."[20] During the second quarter of Super Bowl XXII, Williams threw nine completions, four of them for touchdowns. Running back Timmie Smith carried the ball five times in that quarter for 122 yards and a fifth touchdown. By halftime, Washington had turned a 10–0 deficit into a 35–10 lead. They extended their string to six unanswered touchdowns when Smith scored again in the fourth quarter, making the final score Washington 42, Denver 10.

Doug Williams was named the Most Valuable Player of Super Bowl XXII on the strength of his four touchdown throws and 340 yards passing. Leaving the field in San Diego, he was reunited in the tunnel with Grambling Coach Eddie Robinson, where the two hugged and cried together.

Later that same night, Coach Robinson was asked about the significance of his former player's performance in the most-watched sporting event of the year. "All those Black kids who saw Doug throw those touchdown passes will be out there throwing the ball now," he said.[21] What Doug Williams did on sport's greatest stage as the first Black quarterback ever to win a Super Bowl was to prove that the fulfillment of dreams is possible and that success opens the door for untold new success stories.

The Man in Charge

In 1988, Tony Dungy was a thirty-two-year-old assistant coach with the Pittsburgh Steelers who marveled at Williams's performance. *Hey, we've got a quarterback*, he thought to himself. "Roger Bannister runs a four-minute mile—no one has done it—and right after he does it, you get three or four guys who do it," said Dungy. "Doug Williams wins a Super Bowl and, all of a sudden, you begin to see Donovan McNabb and Michael Vick and Warren Moon."[22] In the years since Super Bowl XXII, so many African American quarterbacks have led their teams to victories large and small that they aren't referred to as "Black quarterbacks" anymore but simply as quarterbacks. Williams remembered always seeing "Black quarterback" attached to his name whenever it was written. The Super Bowl helped America turn that page in its cultural history for people in all walks of life, not just athletes.

Doug Williams said his victory was "the greatest thing" from the standpoint of a professional athlete. But what he saw as even more significant came nineteen years later when two teams, both with Black head coaches, met in Super Bowl XLI: the Indianapolis Colts with Tony Dungy at the helm and the Chicago Bears with head coach Lovie Smith. "African American players have played in this league for a long time, but very few African American coaches have been given the opportunity to coach in this league," said Williams. "I think what these two men have accomplished lets everybody know it can be done."[23]

In the first forty years of the Super Bowl, a Black man had never entered the stadium as head coach. Then in February 2007, two had been handed the reins of enterprises valued in the hundreds of millions of dollars, entrusted with making decisions that would affect countless people and the bottom line, and responsible for their success and accountable in the event of failure. "It is not perhaps on the level of the White House or the first Black secretary of state or the first Black head of the Joint Chiefs of Staff, [but] it is one more river that we really needed to cross," said sociologist Dr. Harry Edwards, whose sports activism began in the 1960s at San Jose State University with Olympic sprinters Tommie Smith and John Carlos and the Olympic Project for Human Rights.[24]

Dr. Edwards could not have known how prescient his words in early 2007 would be. Nearly 140 million people would watch all or part of Super Bowl XLI as Tony Dungy's Colts defeated Lovie Smith's Bears 29–17 in Miami. Six days later, Senator Barack Obama of Illinois announced his candidacy for president of the United States. He would win election in November 2008 and become the first African American man to take up residency in the White House in January 2009, just in time to see another Black coach win Super Bowl XLIII: Mike Tomlin of the Pittsburgh Steelers. President Obama did not attribute his election to the success of Black coaches in the Super Bowl nor should he. But what those 140 million viewers saw in Super Bowl XLI was two Black men in leadership positions, calling the shots, using their judgment and their experience to make decisions that carried weight and that would change the course of events. Their elevation to those positions and their ability to "faithfully execute" the duties associated with their jobs represented an example in sports of what was possible in society.

"I think we have to understand the history of sports' contribution to the broader culture," said Dr. Edwards. "There is a direct line of ascent from Jackie Robinson to Bill Russell, to Jim Brown to Curt Flood to Doug Williams to Barack Obama."

CHAPTER 5

Politics, Patriotism, and the Power for Change

THE AMERICAN PUBLIC, THE MEDIA, AND THE NFL HAVE WOVEN THE Super Bowl into the fabric of American society by celebrating the same qualities of the game for which we celebrate America itself: the virtues of hard work, perseverance, teamwork, courage, loyalty, reward based on merit, and belief in the American dream that anyone can rise up and succeed if they are determined, dedicated, and refuse to quit. Sports help construct and represent the nation's identity, and around the world no sport is tied more closely to the United States than gridiron football. The military nature of the play itself—its goal of conquering the territory of opponents and the premium placed on strength, leadership, endurance, and the bravery to overcome all obstacles—are emblematic of the nation's history and values.

The Ultimate Expression of America

The NFL's vision statement for Super Bowl 50 in 2016 made the connection between football and patriotism abundantly clear: "Super Bowl is the ultimate expression of America. Nothing unites us or lets us soak up everything we love about our country like the Super Bowl—the human struggle to make it to the top, mixed with the best in music, entertainment and business. Super Bowl 50 is about American optimism on full display for the world to see."[1]

The Super Bowl has been, from its origin, deliberately and shamelessly crafted as a patriotic symbol of America itself. "It was a conscious effort on our part to bring the element of patriotism into the Super Bowl,"[2] said former NFL Commissioner Pete Rozelle. The NFL waves the flag and celebrates the triumph of the American spirit, the successes and contributions of Americans in military and community service, the promise of America's youth, especially the strength and skill of the nation's young men. The league is proud that its product has become woven into the American identity. "It is a great responsibility," said Anna Isaacson, the NFL's senior vice president for social responsibility. "We are more than just our games on Sundays." NFL players have been part of USO delegations to visit American forces stationed overseas since the 1960s and the Vietnam War. Since 1968, the Super Bowl has been broadcast live to American troops around the world via the Armed Forces Network (AFN). The first year it was distributed by AFN, the game broadcast was on a tape delay. It airs live now. "The feedback that we've received from those that get to watch our games is amazing," said Isaacson. "Feeling connected back to family and friends is really important for their welfare and their well-being."[3]

The connection between sport and nationalistic pride in the United States has existed virtually as long as the sports themselves. American flags along with red, white, and blue bunting have decorated outdoor and indoor sports venues since the nineteenth century. American presidents have bestowed their blessing on major league baseball by throwing out the first pitch of the season, a tradition that dates back to 1912 and President William Howard Taft. The playing of "The Star-Spangled Banner" became part of the soundtrack of American sporting events at the first game of the 1918 World Series between the Chicago Cubs and the Boston Red Sox. On September 4, 1918, the day before the game was to be played in Chicago, a bombing at the federal courthouse building there killed four people, including two postal workers. Thirty others were injured. The bombing was believed to be a protest against US involvement in the Great War, which had already claimed the lives of more than one hundred thousand American soldiers fighting in Europe. As a tribute to those who had perished at the courthouse the previous day, a military band played "The Star-Spangled Banner" during the seventh inning stretch of the World Series game at the first Comiskey Park. Standing on the field, Boston third baseman Fred Thomas, who was on furlough from the US Navy, snapped to attention and saluted. "The onlookers exploded into thunderous applause and rent the air with a cheer that marked the highest point of the day's enthusiasm," reported the *New York Times*.[4] The overwhelming response from the 19,274 fans in the park that day led Cubs ownership to play the song at game two the following day, also during the break between the top and bottom of the seventh inning. When the series moved to Boston, the Red Sox organization moved "The Star-Spangled Banner" to the beginning of the game, when it planned to honor veterans who had returned from fighting in Europe. It would not become the official national anthem until 1931, but the song had found its patriotic place at the beginning of countless sporting events since, including every Super Bowl.[5]

The Super Bowl as Symbol

Also wrapped up in the symbolism of the Super Bowl is the success of American business and of the United States as a leader in the parade of nations. It speaks to the ascendancy of the consumer society and of leisure in modern America. The emergence of the Super Bowl, which was played exclusively in warm weather cities for its first fifteen years, coincided with the rise in population and influence of the Sunbelt and the migration of people and businesses to the West and South, away from the Northeast and the "Rust Belt." In 1967, when the Super Bowl was first played, the US population hit two hundred million, and the fastest growing regions were in the western and southern states. The celebration of Super Bowl Sunday has come to be identified with new frontiers and new beginnings, as well as big money and big power. It is a day that represents a "powerful populism that concentrates the nation's passions" on one professional football game.[6]

The first president to make a White House connection with the Super Bowl on behalf of his "fellow Americans" was Richard Nixon, who served from 1969 until his resignation in 1975. Nixon started the tradition of a presidential phone call to the winning team's locker room in 1970, after the Kansas City Chiefs defeated the Minnesota Vikings in Super Bowl IV. In so doing he elevated the status of the game as an event of such importance and popular interest that it warranted a president taking time away from his Oval Office responsibilities to applaud the efforts of a professional football team.

During his six-minute conversation with Chiefs quarterback Len Dawson, President Nixon spoke of NFL players as role models who possessed the ideals that made America great. "The world looks up to pro football players for courage," he said. Dawson replied, "Thank you, Mr. President. We try to exemplify the best in professional football. I appreciate it, Mr. President, but it wasn't me, it was the whole team that did it."[7] Nixon had used the same phone six months earlier to call astronauts Neil Armstrong and Edwin "Buzz" Aldrin while they stood on the surface of the moon. Nixon was a huge fan of professional football and fancied himself a perceptive strategist. During his years in the White House, he even called Washington Redskins head coach George Allen with suggestions for plays he thought the team should run.

The presidential phone calls continued until Super Bowl 50 in February 2016, when President Obama, in his final year in office, called the Denver Broncos in their locker room at Levi's Stadium and talked with Head Coach Gary Kubiak and defensive star DeMarcus Ware after their victory over the Carolina Panthers. The president, a longtime Chicago Bears fan, said, "I want to let you know that that's about as good a defense as I've seen since the '85 Bears,"[8] and he invited the entire team to visit the White House.

Visits to the White House by professional sports teams go all the way back to 1869, when President Ulysses S. Grant played host to the Cincinnati Red Stockings as they traveled across the country in their inaugural year. The first World Series champions feted at the White House were the 1924 Washington Senators, who posed on the lawn with an almost-smiling President Calvin Coolidge. President John F. Kennedy expanded the parade of champions to include the NBA in 1963, when he hosted the champion Boston Celtics, who represented his home state of Massachusetts.

Taking a Knee during the Anthem

An invitation to the White House elevated the status of sports teams and athletes to the level of national heroes and visiting heads of state. The beginning of this practice in the 1960s demonstrated how important sport had become to the American public, due primarily to its wide distribution via the television sets in millions of American homes. It also gave presidents a political opportunity to be photographed with popular stars who were adored by millions. The first Super Bowl–winning team to make a ceremonial White House visit was the Pittsburgh Steelers in 1980, at the invitation of President Jimmy Carter. His successor Ronald Reagan continued the annual photo ops with Super Bowl champions, and they became a tradition until the Philadelphia Eagles won Super Bowl LII in February 2018.

The Eagles were invited to the White House by President Donald Trump, but only a handful of the players said they were interested in attending. As a result, the president withdrew the invitation in his Twitter post on June 4, 2018: "The Philadelphia Eagles Football Team was invited to the White House. Unfortunately, only a small number of players decided to come, and we canceled the event. Staying in the Locker Room for the playing of our National Anthem is as disrespectful to our country as kneeling. Sorry!"

During preseason games beginning in 2016, Colin Kaepernick of the San Francisco 49ers chose to sit or kneel during the national anthem as a protest against several police shootings of Black Americans. Kaepernick, who had been the 49ers quarterback in Super Bowl XLVII in 2013, said, "I am not going to stand up to show pride in a flag for a country that oppresses Black people and people of color. To me, this is bigger than football and it would be selfish on my part to look the other way. There are bodies in the street and people getting paid leave and getting away with murder."[9] As the regular season began, Kaepernick was joined in his protest by several players on various teams who also chose to take a knee when "The Star-Spangled Banner" was played.

President Trump voiced his anger with the protesting players, most of whom were African Americans, at a rally on September 22, 2017, in Huntsville, Alabama. In front of national and local television cameras, he asked the crowd, "You know what's hurting the game? When people like yourselves turn on television, and you see those people taking the knee when they are playing our great national anthem." His advice was, "If you see it, even if it's one player, leave the stadium, I guarantee things will stop. Things will stop. Just pick up and leave. Pick up and leave. Not the same game anymore, anyway. Wouldn't you love to see one of these NFL owners, when somebody disrespects our flag, to say, 'Get that son of a bitch off the field right now. Out. He's fired. He's fired!'"

Trump's angry words alienated many players and drew quick responses from the league, its owners, and the NFL Players Association (NFLPA). In a written statement Commissioner Roger Goodell said, "The NFL and our players are at our best when we help create a sense of unity in our country and our culture. . . . Divisive comments like these demonstrate an unfortunate lack of respect for the NFL, our great game and all of our players, and a failure to understand the overwhelming force for good our clubs and players represent in our communities."[10] New England Patriots owner Robert Kraft, who had been a vocal Trump supporter, said, "I am deeply disappointed by the tone of the comments made by the President on Friday. I am proud to be associated with so many players who make such tremendous contributions in positively impacting our communities." His statement continued, "There is no greater unifier in this country than sports, and unfortunately nothing more divisive than politics. . . . Our players are intelligent, thoughtful and care deeply about our community and I support their right to peacefully affect social change and raise awareness in a manner that they feel is most impactful."[11]

Coming to the defense of the players he represented, NFLPA Executive Director DeMaurice Smith said that their opinions "are protected speech and a freedom that has been paid for by the sacrifice of men and women throughout history. This expression of speech has generated thoughtful discussions in our locker rooms and in board rooms. However, the line that marks the balance between the rights of every citizen in our great country gets crossed when someone is told to just 'shut up and play.'"[12]

The divisive political debate that surrounded NFL football in 2017 was largely to blame for decreased television ratings for regular season games and for Super Bowl LII in February 2018. The regular season audience fell by an average of 9.7 percent across all networks that held the rights to televise NFL games. That meant that an average of 14.9 million viewers per minute were watching games in 2017, down 1.6 million from the average of 16.5 million viewers per minute the previous year. The ratings for Super Bowl LII also fell. On average, slightly more than 103 million Americans per minute watched the Eagles victory over the Patriots on television, a decline of nearly 10 million viewers from Super Bowl LI in 2016. However, the number of people who streamed the game via the internet increased to more than two million, a trend to be discussed in a later chapter.

After the intensity of criticism from the White House died down, regular season NFL television ratings rebounded during the 2018 season, bouncing back to an average of 15.8 million people watching in any one minute. Total viewership for Super Bowl LIII, which followed the 2018 season, also increased. Its total audience was a healthy 112.7 million viewers per minute, which included home television viewers, the streaming audience, and millions of Americans who watched the game away from their homes or in Spanish.

Winter's Fourth of July

During the ten years between Richard Nixon's call to Len Dawson in 1970 and that 1980 Steelers trip to Washington, DC, the Super Bowl transformed from simply a professional sports championship game into part of our American heritage. In the words of former NFL Commissioner Paul Tagliabue, the Super Bowl became "the winter version of the Fourth of July celebration."[13] A number of important milestones during the decade helped secure this lofty status: (1) The debut of *ABC Monday Night Football* in 1970 made NFL football a major prime-time television product. (2) The TV audience for the Super Bowl increased by 72 percent from 1970 to 1980, hitting an average of 76.24 million viewers per minute for Super Bowl XIV in 1980. (3) The largest crowd ever to watch a Super Bowl in person in the history of the game was at the Rose Bowl on January 20, 1980, as 103,985 fans saw the Steelers defeat the Los Angeles Rams 31–19. (4) For host cities, the game was no longer a one-day event, but it had been transformed to include several days of parties, receptions, official events, news conferences, and fan activities. In the words of Stanford University Professor George Foster, the Super Bowl had become "a pop-up theme park."[14] (5) Super Bowl viewing parties hosted by fans across the country became one of the most popular annual social gatherings.

Commissioner Tagliabue first used the term "winter's Fourth of July" during his "State of the NFL" press conference in January 1991 in response to a reporter who asked why he thought so much public attention seemed to focus on the Super Bowl during times of national stress. American soldiers were fighting in the Middle East as part of Operation Desert Storm, launched just the previous week to force Iraq to surrender Kuwait, which it had seized by force in August 1990. For Super Bowl XXV in Tampa, the NFL gave ABC, its broadcaster that year, additional time for breaking news updates after the first and third quarters so that the millions of citizens watching could stay informed about the troops on the ground in Kuwait and the progress of the battle.

Ten years earlier, in January 1981, the nation's focus before Super Bowl XV was on the release of fifty-two American diplomats and citizens who had been held hostage by the government of Iran for 444 days. Their ordeal had ended five days earlier, when on his inauguration as the fortieth president of the United States, Ronald Reagan released more than $10 billion of Iranian assets that had been frozen by his predecessor, Jimmy Carter. During what came to be known as the Iran Hostage Crisis, people across America tied yellow ribbons around trees to show their support for the hostages and express hope for their safe return. The practice was based on the popular song "Tie a Yellow Ribbon," by Tony Orlando and Dawn, which hit number one in 1973. In a show of solidarity with the American public and as a message of support for the hostages, the NFL wrapped the exterior of the Superdome in New Orleans, which would host Super Bowl XV, with a thirty-foot-wide yellow ribbon. The league also distributed eighty thousand yellow ribbon boutonnieres to fans arriving for the Super Bowl between the New York Giants and the Buffalo Bills.

On Super Bowl Sunday, January 25, 1981, the hostages, still sequestered as a group, reunited with their families and close friends at the US Military Academy. They could see the giant ribbon as they watched the Super Bowl from the Thayer Hotel in West Point, New York.

President Ronald Reagan's second inauguration raised questions in the minds of many about what they saw as a dramatic rise in the NFL's power. They pointed to the decision in January 1985 that moved the public inauguration ceremonies for Reagan's second term from Sunday, January 20, the date of Super Bowl XIX, to Monday, January 21. Their concern was that highly organized, widely distributed, and extremely profitable sports organizations might be exerting undue influence over the nation's institutions and social structure. Most people, however, were unaware of an informal tradition dating back to the swearing-in of President James Monroe in 1817: if Inauguration Day were to fall on a Sunday, it automatically would be moved to the next day so as to avoid conflict with religious observances. Reagan was sworn in for his second term on Super Bowl Sunday, January 20, 1985, at a private ceremony in the White House, and he did the coin toss for the game at Stanford Stadium in California live via satellite, a presidential first. The public ceremony and the inaugural parade were scheduled for Monday, January 21, but bitter cold in Washington, DC, forced cancellation of the parade and the ceremony was moved inside to the Capitol Rotunda.

An excerpt from President Reagan's diary entry for that Sunday follows:

> Late in day members of inaugural committee came to me about canceling tomorrows parade & moving the ceremony into the Rotunda of the Capitol. The weather with wind chill factor is predicted to be more than 20 below zero. At that temp. exposed skin surface is subject to frostbite in about 15 mins. There is no way we should inflict this risk on all the people who would have to be out in the cold for hours.
>
> King Hussein called with Congratulations. The Super bowl was won by S.F. & I flipped the coin on live T.V.[15]

The Super Bowl's "Superpowers"

The NFL had not flexed its muscles to move Inauguration Day, but it has chosen to exercise its "superpowers" when social issues are involved that the league considers to be of great national importance. Similar to any large corporation with a diverse workforce that does business nationwide and relies upon millions of diverse customers, the NFL has long realized that it must be seen as supporting the broadest interests of the populace; it cannot have its actions in any way interpreted as giving tacit approval to any policy that would discriminate against and thereby alienate any segment of its customer base.

That was made abundantly clear after voters in Arizona rejected a referendum in 1990 making Martin Luther King Jr. Day a paid state holiday. The Arizona Cardinals had moved from St. Louis in 1988, and in the spring of 1990, NFL owners selected the team to host Super Bowl XXVII in January 1993, making it the first Super Bowl ever for Arizona. Cardinals' owner William Bidwill had hoped for the referendum's approval at the polls, even though less than 3 percent of Arizona's population at the time was African American. In the weeks leading up to the vote, the NFL warned that the 1993 Super Bowl would very likely be moved out of the state if the referendum were rejected. It was important for the league not to be perceived as being on the wrong side of this national issue. On Election Day 1990, however, a majority of voters in the state answered "No" to the question of whether Arizona should institute the MLK Jr. Day holiday. Some supporters of the referendum complained afterward that pressure from the NFL actually had been one of the reasons for the loss at the polls.[16]

Following the referendum's defeat, Dr. King's widow, Coretta Scott King, started a campaign for events and performers to boycott Arizona until the holiday was instated. As promised, the NFL owners revisited the site selection question at their March 1991 meeting, and they voted to take the game away from Arizona. Following that meeting, Commissioner Paul Tagliabue released this statement: "We should remove the game from political controversy and avoid being made a target. So long as it is in Arizona and the alleged controversy is unresolved, people will reach out and use us as a target." The Rose Bowl in Pasadena was chosen as the alternate site for the game in 1993. But the owners gave the Cardinals conditional approval to host the 1996 Super Bowl, if Arizona voters were to change their minds and vote "Yes" when the Dr. King holiday question reappeared on the ballot in 1992.

The Phoenix area missed out on the estimated $200 to $250 million boost to the economy that would have come with hosting its first Super Bowl. With that economic incentive during the second referendum, 62 percent of Arizonans voted to approve institution of the holiday beginning in 1993. The NFL had demonstrated its power in the political arena, using the Super Bowl, with its attendant economic riches and massive media coverage, as a "big stick" to force social change. Arizona was not the last state to approve the official observance of Martin Luther King Jr. Day. Four more states followed: New Hampshire in 1999 and Virginia, Utah, and South Carolina all in 2000.

Arizona was again at the center of a social issue in 2014, which caused the NFL to actively explore options to its selection of the new stadium in Glendale as the site for Super Bowl XLIX, which was to be played less than a year later in February 2015. Both houses of the Arizona State Legislature passed a bill early in 2014 that would have given business owners in the state the right to refuse service to gay men, lesbians, and other people on religious grounds. Governor Jan Brewer was under pressure from business leaders in the state who said that if signed, the new law would be a financial disaster and could further damage Arizona's reputation. Governor Brewer vetoed the measure on February 26, 2014, saying that the legislation was "broadly worded and could result in unintended and negative consequences."[17] One of those "negative consequences" would have been the loss of another Super Bowl, because with such diverse players and fans, the NFL could never allow itself to be perceived as doing business with or in any way endorsing the actions of any public or private entity whose official policy endorsed discrimination.

Post 9/11 and Homeland Security

The Super Bowl belongs to America and helps define America. That has become increasingly evident in the years since the horrific terrorist attacks on September 11, 2001. The NFL games that had been scheduled for the weekend of September 16, 2001, were all postponed until the following week as Americans mourned the loss of nearly three thousand lives. Also gone was the sense of security in daily life that seemed to have been brutally torn from the fabric of America. Commissioner Paul Tagliabue made the decision not to play any games that weekend after discussions with players union head Gene Upshaw and team owners. The majority of owners reportedly wanted to play the games and show the world that Americans would continue doing what they do, undaunted. In his speech to the nation the night of September 11, President George W. Bush gave voice to their position. "Terrorist attacks can shake the foundations of our biggest buildings, but they cannot touch the foundation of America," he said. "These acts shatter steel, but they cannot dent the steel of American resolve."

The majority of players, however, favored postponing the games, especially those on the rosters of the New York and Washington, DC, teams, the cities that had been attacked. There were also genuine concerns among players on every team about the safety of traveling to games so soon after the three-day nationwide ban on air travel—imposed immediately after the attacks—had been lifted.

Commissioner Tagliabue announced the postponement of the games on Thursday, September 13, which pushed the entire regular season schedule back one week, making Super Bowl XXXVI in 2002 the first ever played on a Sunday in February. The NFL arranged with the National Automobile Dealers Association (NADA) to swap the date of its planned national convention at the New Orleans Superdome, which was scheduled for February 3, 2002, in order to accommodate the Super Bowl. The NFL paid NADA $7.5 million for the costs incurred due to rescheduling, and the league offered to match up to $500,000 of NADA contributions to 9/11 recovery efforts. Commissioner Tagliabue remembered the factors that went into his decision in an interview several years later. "It was clear to me that the NFL had come to be a huge symbol of the qualities Americans like to see in themselves—resilience, working through adversity, never giving up," he said. "The NFL had to do something. The dominant atmosphere was one of death, devastation, fear and paralysis. Put it all together and the thing to do was recognize the despicable nature of the attacks and the horrible loss of life. You did that by canceling games and getting your priorities straight. And then you came back the next week to show resilience and that we were all standing tall in the face of adversity and carrying on."[18]

When the games resumed on the weekend of September 23, 2001, they were presented as public gatherings at which thousands of citizens in each stadium and millions watching on television could commemorate the lives of those lost and show the world that the social and cultural traditions that Americans value as part of their heritage, for which so many of their forebears had fought and given their lives to preserve, would endure. Ensuring the safety of those attending the games and protecting stadiums full of people became the overriding top priority of the NFL. So too for the US Secret Service and the newly formed US Department of Homeland Security, which designated Super Bowl XXXVI as a National Special Security Event (NSSE). As the first sporting event to be so designated—joining presidential inaugurations, State of the Union addresses, and the Democratic and Republican National Conventions—the Super Bowl was officially recognized as one of America's "most celebrated and high-profile events." For the Super Bowl and for every NSSE, the Secret Service assumes its mandated role as the lead agency for the design and implementation of the operational security plan. The Secret Service has a core strategy for these security operations, which relies heavily on established partnerships with law enforcement and public safety officials at the local, state, and federal levels.

With this intense security effort underway behind the scenes, the Super Bowl that took place less than five months after the 9/11 attacks provided Americans a national stage upon which they could express their collective grief and reaffirm their resolve to face adversity with united strength. In a uniquely American spectacle, the Super Bowl brought the spirit and emotions of Independence Day and Memorial Day to the Superdome that February 2002. Fittingly, the representatives of the American Football Conference that day were the Patriots, hailing from the state where the Pilgrims landed in 1620 and where the first shots of the American Revolution were fired in 1775. The players refused to be introduced as individuals, symbolically taking the field to play the St. Louis Rams as one, as simply "the Patriots." At halftime, the world-renowned Irish rock band U2 performed an unforgettable tribute to the victims of 9/11. As they played "Where the Streets Have No Name," two vertical backdrops symbolic of the twin towers of the World Trade Center were revealed with the names of every person killed in the attacks scrolling upward as if to heaven.

The Patriots won that day in what may have seemed to many as a preordained result. It was the first Super Bowl victory for the franchise after forty-two seasons, and the first of what would become a record-setting championship total. The score was New England 20, St. Louis 17, but the results of the event itself were far more important than the results of the game. Accepting the Vince Lombardi Trophy, New England team owner Robert Kraft declared, "Today we are all Patriots." A wounded nation had come together with renewed solidarity and a vigorous commitment to move forward as a society, unbowed and unafraid to pursue the happiness that its people choose. "America was not built on fear," said President Harry S. Truman a generation before Super Bowls were ever played. "America was built on courage, on imagination, and an unbeatable determination to do the job at hand,"[19] said Truman, the president who made the decision to end World War II in the Pacific by dropping nuclear bombs on the Japanese cities of Hiroshima and Nagasaki in 1945. His words defined the American spirit that was on display that February day in New Orleans in 2002 and continues to manifest in ways large and small in all facets of life in the United States, including the arena of sport.

For every Super Bowl since 2002, the Department of Homeland Security (DHS) has had an integral role in the protection of this uniquely American event. Well in advance of the scheduled date for each Super Bowl, the DHS secretary appoints federal representatives and establishes points of contact with state and local authorities as well as the NFL. The federal department provides security assessment and training for local law enforcement and hotel personnel in the area. At airports where Super Bowl visitors will be arriving, the Transportation Security Administration (TSA) adds screeners, more checkpoint lanes, and passenger screening canine teams. All mass transit locations, including bus and train stations, are assigned Visible Intermodal Prevention and Response Teams, which are comprised of federal air marshals, surface and aviation transportation security inspectors, behavioral detection officers, transportation security officers, and canine teams that help secure mass transit terminals and connecting points. The US Secret Service assists with magnetometer training for all venues that use metal detectors, including every possible point of entry to the football stadium, the media center, the "Super Bowl Experience," and all other related entertainment or gathering sites. The Secret Service also monitors social media platforms before the Super Bowl to detect potential or implied threats.

The federal effort to protect the Super Bowl includes the US Customs and Border Protection (CBP) agency, which works with local law enforcement and plays a pivotal role in securing operations on the ground and in the sky around the game. The agency's Office of Field Operations uses mobile X-ray portals to screen hundreds of truckloads every day that arrive carrying all the food and supplies that will be consumed at the big event. The Department of Defense and agents from CBP's Air and Marine Operations section secure the airspace surrounding each Super Bowl stadium on game day, using Blackhawk helicopters and other aircraft to enforce the temporary flight restriction that is imposed by the Federal Aviation Administration. From 3:00 p.m. until midnight local time on Super Bowl Sunday, the airspace for thirty nautical miles around the stadium up to eighteen thousand feet is restricted. Only law enforcement, medical, and military aircraft can be cleared into that area by air traffic control.

The CBP effort includes collaboration with federal, state, and local agencies to intercept any contraband weapons, explosives, narcotics, or counterfeit merchandise. In Atlanta for Super Bowl LIII in 2019, a total of 285,000 fake items were seized with a value estimated at $24.2 million, along with more than two thousand counterfeit tickets for the game. The goal is "to protect businesses and consumers from intellectual property thieves that produce counterfeit and often defective and dangerous merchandise," said CBP Commissioner Kevin McAleenan.

The Federal Emergency Management Agency (FEMA) scans incoming cargo and performs mass casualty training for local responders. It also provides Mobile Emergency Response Support assets. The National Protection and Programs Directorate does cybersecurity scanning and training to detect threats or vulnerabilities. This agency also handles bomb prevention training for public and private security agencies and active shooter preparedness training.

In addition to the stadium and its associated venues, all federal facilities in the host city, including post offices, federal courthouses, and offices are secured for Super Bowl weekend. The Office of Health Affairs deploys BioWatch detectors to avoid potential release of hazardous biological agents. And the Domestic Nuclear Detection Office deploys mobile detection units to safeguard against the worst conceivable attack on an American gathering.[20]

Wardrobe Malfunctions and Governmental Oversight

In its early years, the NFL struggled to attract national attention, operating outside the mainstream, where its play and business practices largely escaped the scrutiny of policymakers. However, its ascension to the level of universal awareness and ubiquitous media exposure made everything that happened in every game—even something that lasted only 9/16 of a second—subject to criticism and potential governmental oversight.

That fraction of a second during the halftime show at Super Bowl XXXVIII in 2004 fostered a national discussion of American values, including how young children should be protected from certain content in the media. And it was the stimulus for new legislation passed by Congress the following year and for a legal battle that reached the US Supreme Court. The headliner for the 2004 halftime show in Houston was Janet Jackson, and during a racy duet of the song "Rock Your Body" with Justin Timberlake, her right breast was exposed for 9/16 of a second. The game was airing live on CBS, with an average audience per minute of eighty-nine million people. Timberlake had just sung, "Bet I'll have you naked by the end of this song," when he pulled away part of Jackson's costume. In what Timberlake described as a "wardrobe malfunction," more of Ms. Jackson's anatomy was uncovered than was originally intended. She quickly covered her right breast. The song ended, and CBS went to commercial before the start of the second half between the New England Patriots and the Carolina Panthers.

Justin Timberlake, then twenty-three years old, apologized that evening, saying, "I am sorry if anyone was offended by the wardrobe malfunction during the halftime performance at the Super Bowl. It was not intentional and is regrettable." Janet Jackson did not make a formal statement following the telecast, but under pressure from CBS, she issued a written statement on Monday, February 2, 2004. "The decision to have a costume reveal at the end of my halftime show performance was made after final rehearsals," she wrote. "MTV was completely unaware of it. It was not my intention that it go as far as it did. I apologize to anyone offended—including the audience, MTV, CBS and the NFL." The next day she repeated her statement in a recorded video.[21]

MTV, which along with CBS was owned by Viacom, issued a statement shortly after the game: "The tearing of Janet Jackson's costume was unrehearsed, unplanned, completely unintentional and was inconsistent with assurances we had about the content of the performance. MTV regrets this incident occurred and we apologize to anyone who was offended by it." An apology also came from CBS executives: "CBS deeply regrets the incident that occurred during the Super Bowl halftime show. We attended all rehearsals throughout the week and there was no indication that any such thing would happen. The moment did not conform to CBS broadcast standards, and we would like to apologize to anyone who was offended."[22]

It is apparent that a sizeable number of people—who did not expect a Super Bowl telecast to expose them or their children to partial nudity—were offended. The Federal Communications Commission (FCC), which regulates broadcast television, received a reported 540,000 indecency complaints. The public outcry was directed not simply at CBS, but also at the NFL for staging entertainment that was not suitable for all ages, and at MTV for producing the show. The FCC's judgment, announced on September 22, 2004, was to fine CBS and MTV a combined $550,000 for "violating decency standards." In the FCC's official finding of liability, Chairman Michael Powell's statement read, "As countless families gathered around the television to watch one of our nation's most celebrated events, they were rudely greeted with a half-time show stunt more fitting of a burlesque show." CBS immediately began an appeals process that lasted until 2012, but members of Congress were not willing to wait for the case to work its way through the judicial system.

The "wardrobe malfunction" spurred Congress to pass the Broadcast Decency Enforcement Act of 2005, which imposes substantial fines for broadcasting "obscene, indecent or profane material." The act amended the Communications Act of 1934, which had established the Federal Communications Commission in the first place. It added specificity to the procedures for dealing with violators and fixed the maximum fine per incident at $500,000. It directed the FCC to "take into account factors with respect to the violator's: (1) degree of culpability, including whether the offending material was live or recorded and scripted or unscripted; and (2) ability to pay, including whether the violator is a company or individual and the company's size and the financial impact that a penalty would have on an individual." In addition to fines, the FCC can now also "require the offending licensee or permittee to broadcast public service announcements that serve the educational and informational needs of children and reach an audience of up to five times the audience estimated to have been reached by the obscene, indecent, or profane material."[23] One important exemption set down in law was that local stations could not be held liable for content provided to them by their network. So local CBS stations could not be fined if anything in the programs fed to them live by their affiliated network was objectionable.

The FCC's $550,000 fine was overturned by a federal appeals court in November 2011 as "arbitrary and capricious." The court said that the FCC had not adequately defined the "bounds of decency." The Justice Department responded by filing a 243-page petition on behalf of the FCC, appealing dismissal of the fine by the US Supreme Court. But the high court rejected that appeal in June 2012, upholding the lower court ruling that had allowed the fine to stand. Chief Justice John G. Roberts Jr. warned, however, that because the FCC had updated its rules in the years following the halftime performance of 2004, any similar offense that occurred could now be punished.

"It is now clear that the brevity of an indecent broadcast—be it word or image—cannot immunize it from F.C.C. censure," wrote Justice Roberts in a two-page opinion that put the CBS case to rest. Recalling the performance by Jackson and Timberlake, he noted, "The performers subsequently strained the credulity of the public by terming the episode a 'wardrobe malfunction.'"[24] Nine-sixteenths of a second during one Super Bowl telecast had changed broadcasting regulations in the United States.

The Super Bowl's Impact on American Culture and Society

WHEN THE FIRST SUPER BOWL WAS PLAYED IN 1967, THE ONLY HOLIDAY in the United States during the month of January was New Year's Day. The next federal holiday on the calendar was February 12, which commemorated Abraham Lincoln's birthday. That was followed closely by George Washington's birthday on February 22. These were days of national recognition for the historic contributions made by these two remarkable leaders, but typically they weren't days for celebration and parties. More often than not, Americans in the post–World War II era heard the terms "Lincoln's birthday" and "Washington's birthday" followed by the word "sale." The two holidays were combined into "Presidents' Day" by the Uniform Monday Holiday Act of 1971. The advent of the Super Bowl in the late 1960s gave citizens, particularly those in northern climes, a "time-out" from winter and an excuse to get together with friends and family. A new holiday was born.

The Super Bowl Sunday Holiday

In many ways Super Bowl Sunday has taken on the characteristics of our official national holidays. People gather for a common purpose, and they change their daily routines for holidays. Super Bowl Sunday combines the essential elements of virtually every American holiday. It includes the gathering of family and friends and the feasting that are central to the celebrations of Thanksgiving, Christmas, and other religious holidays, along with the television connection associated with Thanksgiving, Christmas, and New Year's Day. Add to that the commercialism of many national holidays, among which the Christmas season is preeminent, and the celebration of America that is intrinsic to Independence Day, Memorial Day, Veterans Day, and other conspicuous annual displays of patriotism. The Super Bowl has become "winter's Fourth of July," and as such it is one of the annual national traditions that define us as uniquely American.

What Super Bowl Sunday lacks are the historic ties or religious observances connected to most official holidays. Nor does it involve the considerable obligations that are associated with other holidays such as buying presents, hosting or visiting family members, preparing meals and guest rooms, or attending religious services. However, in the eyes of Pope Francis, the Super Bowl is not without spiritual or positive social potential. In a video message he recorded for Super Bowl LI on Sunday, February 5, 2017, the pope said that great sporting events "like today's Super Bowl are highly symbolic, showing that it is possible to build a culture of encounter and a world of peace." The pontiff voiced his hope that the Super Bowl may be "a sign of peace, friendship and solidarity to the world." A lifelong soccer fan, the pope often spoke of sports as "a privileged place to learn virtue and practice fraternity." In his native Spanish he said that "by participating in sports, we are able to go beyond our own self-interest and—in a healthy way—we learn to sacrifice, to grow in fidelity and respect the rules."[1]

When you consider all the ways in which people can be divided in a nation with ever-multiplying options and platforms for entertainment and new sources of information and disinformation each year that widen the political spectrum far beyond liberal and conservative, the Super Bowl offers us a reason to share time in friendship and celebration. When the ties that bind us feel stretched and frayed, this annual event brings Americans of every generation, every color and orientation, national origin, and political ideology together in a way that, as the pope said, goes "beyond our own self-interest." That makes this one football game rare and ever more special.

The Super Bowl has become New Year's Eve, the Fourth of July, and Mardi Gras rolled into one, leading many people to suggest that Super Bowl Sunday, or perhaps the Monday after, be designated an official federal holiday in the United States. The reasoning is that an official designation would recognize the fact that the majority of Americans have already made it a holiday by their collective actions. In fact, more people watch at least a portion of the Super Bowl (give or take two hundred million) than have voted in any US presidential election. (The number of voters in the 2020 presidential race was 159,633,396, according to Federal Elections Commission data.)

This massive audience has become as diverse as America itself. During the regular season, the majority of NFL television viewers are male, but Nielsen reports that the gender split among viewers is regularly 51 percent male and 49 percent female for the Super Bowl. That represents a trend toward gender equality that has occurred during the early years of the twenty-first century. As recently as 2009, Super Bowl viewers were 61 percent male and only 39 percent female. The audience also closely reflects the diverse ethnic composition of the US population.

In January 2017, Heinz Ketchup launched a brand campaign leading up to Super Bowl LI, which included a petition drive to win formal designation of the Monday after the Super Bowl as a holiday the company called "Smunday." The petition read:

> We can all agree that going to work the Monday after the "Big Game" on Sunday is awful. So as far as we're concerned at Heinz, we as a nation should stop settling for it being the worst workday of the year. We don't settle for that awesome football Sunday to be just like every other day of the year. No. We eat. We drink. And we be merry, having the tastiest times of our lives. But then the very next day we settle for that Monday being a terrible workday.
>
> Statistics show over 16 million people call in sick or just don't show up to work. And for those that do, productivity plummets so far that the country loses on average around $1 billion (true story). Enough with the madness. This is where YOU come in.
>
> Sign the petition to make the day after the Big Game a National Holiday. Share it with friends, family and even strangers and get

THEM to sign it. If we get over 100,000 signatures, it will be sent to Congress.

If we can make Big Game Sunday awesome, we can make the Monday after awesome too. Make that Monday more like Sunday. Make it a SMUNDAY and have more Sunday on your Monday than any of us have ever had in our lives. Don't settle. Sign it. For your sanity. For your family. For your country.[2]

The petition drive fell short of the one hundred thousand signatures the company said it needed to deliver the proposal to Capitol Hill. Had it reached the floor of Congress, it is very likely that one of the proposal's strongest opponents may well have been the NFL itself. The American public has made Super Bowl Sunday a significant holiday by virtue of the inertia created when millions of people do the same thing at the same time. No vote in any legislature is needed to officially establish what already exists. And consider the impact of incorporating the words "Super Bowl" into the title of a federal holiday, be it on a Sunday or a Monday. Such a designation would effectively put the title into the public domain, thereby removing it from its status as the sole property of the National Football League. The NFL in no way would want to jeopardize the revenue stream it receives from its exclusive Super Bowl licensing agreements, which exceed $1 billion per year.

The Super Bowl Fosters Social Interaction

When millions of people in any society all direct their attention to one event or celebration that occurs just once each year, traditions develop, expectations are fostered, and the routines of life change. The communal bonding around the Super Bowl, as with other holidays, helps fill the need that most humans have to participate in the culture that surrounds them, to be "in the loop," not "out of touch." On December 26, no one wants to tell friends that "I forgot yesterday was Christmas" or "I didn't get any presents." On the day after the Super Bowl, the best way to ensure inclusion in conversations at work or at school, even for non-football fans, is to have at least a minimal knowledge of what transpired: which team won and what made the game special (or not so special).

Winter's Fourth of July has become a reason for gathering with family and friends that didn't exist on any calendars before 1967. Now an estimated ninety to one hundred million Americans get together at Super Bowl parties here in the United States and hundreds of thousands more gather at locations around the globe. An informal survey of 100 to 150 college students ages eighteen to twenty-four, which I do each year in my classes, shows that 86 percent of them spent their Super Bowl Sunday at a party, either one that they threw themselves or that was at the home of friends or family members. That percentage each year for the past decade ranged between 75 and 85 percent. Most people, regardless of age, prefer not to be alone on holidays, and the same proves true for Super Bowl Sunday.

In America, overindulging has become synonymous with holiday celebrations. Millions of Americans eat and drink far more on Super Bowl Sunday than on ordinary Sundays, even if they aren't celebrating the victory of their favorite team. In fact, Super Bowl Sunday ranks as the second largest food consumption day of the year in the United States behind only Thanksgiving Day. The Calorie Control Council estimates that Super Bowl viewers consume an average of 2,400 calories in four to five hours of watching the game. That compares to the average daily food intake for American men of 2,640 calories and of 1,785 calories for women. The National Chicken Council estimates that 1.38 billion chicken wings are consumed on Super Bowl Sunday. At 81 calories per wing, that's more than 111 billion calories alone, before anyone eats one slice of pizza. Americans order 12.5 million pizzas for their Super Bowl parties, according to the American Pizza Community website. Super Bowl Sunday and Halloween, both unofficial holidays in the United States, are the two busiest days of the year for pizza makers. Guacamole has become such a Super Bowl party favorite that more than 5 percent of the annual California avocado crop is consumed on just that one day. Add in the seventy million pounds of avocados imported from Mexico for the week of the game, and you've got a lot of guacamole.

The increased consumption of alcohol on Super Bowl Sundays is accompanied by a spike in calls to alcohol and addiction rehabilitation centers and an average of 15 percent more arrests for driving under the influence, when compared to other Sundays during the same winter months. And DUI violations by drivers who have had previous drunk-driving arrests rise by an average of more than 20 percent. Police see regional impacts depending upon which teams are playing and the "spirited" response of their fans. Arrests for driving under the influence reportedly doubled in New England on February 1, 2015, after the Patriots defeated the Seattle Seahawks in Super Bowl XLIX. That game ended with Malcolm Butler's interception, which preserved the lead and the victory for New England.

Viewing and posting comments, photos, and videos on social media now appears to be almost as popular an activity on Super Bowl Sunday as partygoing. To be "in the loop" in twenty-first-century America means that you are almost certainly active on social media. Various surveys show that between 70 and 80 percent of Americans use Facebook and that, around the world, the platform has roughly three billion active users. Just as many are regular users of YouTube. Social media interaction on the day of the Super Bowl has increased dramatically in a very short time, signaling a major change in how people experience the event by sharing their thoughts, impressions, and photos with friends and family across town or across the world.

During the week leading up to Super Bowl LVII in February 2022, the NFL recorded a total of 1.8 billion impressions across the league's social platforms, which was an increase of 42 percent over the previous year's game. The NFL saw a record 618 million video views across social media that week, which was 51 percent more than for Super Bowl LV. Each year since, the total video views and social media posts have seen double-digit increases.

In its sixth annual Super Bowl Survey, Burson, Cohn and Wolfe (BCW) found that 82 percent of millennials say that they check social media or online news outlets during the Super Bowl telecast. Seven out of ten said that using social media brought them closer to the game, and 43 percent of social media users said they look for commentary from their close friends as a way to connect during the game. "The Millennial mindset about activities related to a big sports event matches the mood of a generation consistently seeking new types of stimuli," said Scott Elder, senior vice president of PSB research, which collaborated on the survey. "The survey shows there remains plenty of room, and a willing audience, to expand opportunities surrounding the Super Bowl." Facebook is the platform of choice for Super Bowl fans, with 49 percent of fans from all age groups telling BCW researchers that they planned to use Facebook during the game, twice as many as use Instagram (24%) or Twitter (now "X") (22%). In a result from the survey that was both exciting news for the telecast's advertisers and a demonstration of how ads have for many become entertainment to be enjoyed and shared with friends, 82 percent of fans said they use Facebook to share what they think are the best Super Bowl ads.[3]

Consider the online activity that originates from just the fans in the stadium during each Super Bowl. Seventy-two percent of the 67,827 who attended Super Bowl LVII at State Farm Stadium in Arizona used a total of 31.5 terabytes of data on February 12, 2023, alone. That is more than double the total digital storage for every item in the Library of Congress. WiFi usage at the game tripled in just seven years from Super Bowl 50, when the 71,088 fans at Levi's Stadium used a mere 10.15 terabytes on February 7, 2016.[4]

I Win, You Lose

One of the joys of being a sports fan is celebrating the victories of your favorite team with fellow fans and lording those victories over the fans of losing teams. What helps connect sports fans is their "in-group bias," which unites individuals with communities of like-minded souls who follow the same teams, and their "out-group biases," which separate them from those who identify themselves with rival teams. Fans commonly "bask in the reflected glory" of their team's success. The tendency of individuals to associate themselves with the successful, the famous, or the celebrated was first researched scientifically by Dr. Robert Cialdini at Arizona State University. According to his research, published in 1976 in the *Journal of Personality and Social Psychology*, after a winning football game, not only were fans more likely to wear clothing that endorsed the football team, but they were also more likely to use the pronoun "we" to describe the events of the game as compared to fans after a losing football game. How many times on the day after the Super Bowl have you heard someone who is wearing the jersey of the team that won say proudly, "We won the Super Bowl"? Basking in reflected glory, or "BIRGing" isn't limited to sports. Telling a story of a chance encounter with a celebrity, such as sitting next to that person on a plane or dining at the same restaurant, may serve to connect you with that celebrity's fame and success, even though you played absolutely no role in its creation.

The opposite of BIRGing is CORFing. That is when you "cut off reflected failure." Most people prefer to connect themselves with success, so when their team loses, the CORF reflex can kick in. That is when fans seek to distance themselves from the loss and avoid being negatively evaluated along with an unsuccessful franchise. Sports fans with strong allegiances to a team may attribute a loss not to the team's performance, but to other external factors, such as playing conditions or officiating.[5]

Changing Patterns of Behavior

For many years a myth, which still survives in some quarters, circulated that suicide rates climb around the holidays, particularly at Christmastime. However, data from the Centers for Disease Control and Prevention show that the opposite is true. Most studies demonstrate that the social connections that bring us together on special occasions, creating threads of conversation and communication, have actually resulted in declining rates of suicides nationwide. Our social interactions with our fellow human beings are in fact maximized during holidays, including the Super Bowl, and this serves as a "buffer" to help reduce stress and depression.[6]

An Associated Press story in January 1993 promulgated another myth regarding human behavior during the Super Bowl. Reporting on a study done by sociologists at Old Dominion University, the story said that incidents of domestic violence rose by a frightening 40 percent on Super Bowl Sundays, when compared to other Sundays during the year. Shortly after the story was released, a coalition of women's groups held a news conference in Pasadena, California, which was to be the site of the upcoming Super Bowl XXVII, to point a finger at the game as "the biggest day of the year for violence against women." These Super Bowl abuse stories garnered so much attention that NBC aired a public service announcement before the 1993 game to remind men that domestic violence is a crime.

However, one of the authors of the study, Janet Katz, a professor of sociology and criminal justice at Old Dominion, told the *Washington Post* the next day, "That's not what we found at all." One of the most notable findings from the small number of cases studied, she said, was that an increase of emergency room admissions "was not associated with the occurrence of football games in general, nor with watching a team lose." In fact, a much wider study published in 2007 in *Human Organization*, the journal of the Society for Applied Anthropology, concluded that the belief that domestic violence crisis calls increase during holidays in general, including the Super Bowl, is unsubstantiated.[7]

On the day of the Super Bowl, so many of our regular life routines are affected by the inertia of more than one hundred million Americans simultaneously fixing their gazes on video screens for three to four hours or more. Retail stores are measurably quieter as sales drop by 20 percent or more compared to other Sundays during the winter. The same is true at golf courses, theaters, and amusement parks, which all register reduced attendance. Air travel may be busier before and after the Super Bowl, with the increased demand resulting in higher airfares. But on that Sunday, people would rather watch the game than hear a score update from the pilot. Major airlines see a diminished number of travelers and have trimmed the number of flights to match their supply with the reduced demand.

There is less vehicular traffic on American roads and highways during the hours between kickoff and the raising of the Lombardi Trophy, but because of the high rates of alcohol consumption, Super Bowl Sunday is one of the most dangerous days of the year to drive. California Department of Insurance reports that there are more drinking-related crashes on that day in California than on any other Sunday in January or February.

Statistics compiled during a five-year period from 2009 to 2013 showed a 77 percent increased probability for alcohol-related injuries or fatalities throughout California on Super Bowl Sunday. In Los Angeles County, there was a 57 percent increase, and in San Diego

County, it was a startling 117 percent. "Drivers and passengers should be aware of the high crash risk from drinking and driving associated with Super Bowl Sunday," said Robert Bouttier, the chief executive of the Automobile Club of Southern California. "We encourage everyone to make a plan: designate a sober driver ahead of time, contact a ride-sharing service or use a taxi or public transportation."[8]

Gambling with the Future

Gambling is among the oldest of human behaviors. Evidence from ancient civilizations shows that as long as there have been contests, people have gambled on the outcomes. Wagering existed for centuries before the NFL, but the Super Bowl is without equal in stimulating bets. Every year, more money is wagered on the Super Bowl than on any other single-day sporting event. The American Gaming Association estimated that Super Bowl LVIII in 2024 generated $23.1 billion in wagering. The confidence that fans have in their favorite teams—or in what they see as their expert knowledge of the NFL—has led millions to gamble their money in amounts large and small on the outcome of the Super Bowl or on any number of variables surrounding the game.

Super Bowl gambling totals have dramatically increased since the legalization of sports betting in more than thirty-five states following the 2018 US Supreme Court decision to overturn the Professional and Amateur Sports Protection Act. This represents good news for the NFL and the networks that distribute the game live because people who have money on the outcome of games are more excited to tune in and tend to watch for longer periods of time. When more people spend more time viewing, overall audience ratings go up.

If the outcome of the game were the only bet to be made, the total amount wagered on the Super Bowl each year would certainly be lower, but every year there are thousands of propositions, or "prop bets," available that add to the pot. These range from which team will score the first touchdown and the total number of turnovers in the game, to how long the selected performer will take to sing the national anthem, and what color liquid (usually Gatorade) will be spilled over the winning coach. The origins of the prop bet go back to Super Bowl XX in January 1986, when the Chicago Bears faced the New England Patriots in the New Orleans Superdome. During the 1985 regular season, Bears Coach Mike Ditka sent 335-pound defensive lineman William "Refrigerator" Perry into the offensive backfield to carry the ball five times on short yardage situations. He scored two touchdowns and became an instant folk hero. When the Bears made it to the Super Bowl, Las Vegas bookmaker Sonny Reizner thought he could generate some action by making the first proposition bet: "Will Refrigerator Perry score a touchdown in Super Bowl XX?" Reizner did. Perry did. With the Bears leading 37–3 in the third quarter, the "Fridge" took the ball from Chicago quarterback Jim McMahon, rumbling in from one yard out for a touchdown that NBC's Dick Enberg said "registered 3.8" on the Richter scale. Now, the number of prop bets is limited only by the creativity of bookmakers.

Over the years, the NFL and its security personnel diligently worked to protect the integrity of games by keeping gambling interests out. In 1963, Commissioner Pete Rozelle suspended Green Bay Packers running back Paul Hornung, whom *Sports Illustrated* called "the biggest star in pro football," and All-Pro defensive lineman Alex Karras of the Detroit Lions for the entire season as punishment for placing bets on NFL games. Five other Detroit players implicated in the gambling were fined but not suspended. In his announcement of the suspensions, the commissioner reassured the public by stressing that the outcome of no games had been compromised: "There is absolutely no evidence of any criminality. No bribes, no game-fixing or point-shaving," he said. "The only evidence uncovered in this investigation, which included 52 interviews with players on eight teams, was the bets by the players penalized. All of these bets were on their own teams to win or on other NFL games."[9]

When the Supreme Court made its ruling in 2018 that legalized sports gambling state by state, the NFL's immediate response was to request federal protection. Commissioner Roger Goodell said his league was "asking Congress to enact uniform standards for states that choose to legalize sports betting." Declaring that "our fans, our players and our coaches deserve to know that we are doing everything possible to ensure no improper influences affect how the game is played on the field," he recommended four core principles for federal guidelines:

1. There must be substantial consumer protections.

2. Sports leagues can protect our content and intellectual property from those who attempt to steal or misuse it.

3. Fans will have access to official, reliable league data.

4. Law enforcement will have the resources, monitoring and enforcement tools necessary to protect our fans and penalize bad actors here at home and abroad.[10]

The number of possible variations among more than thirty-five different state statutes creates a frightening puzzle for sports organizers as well as a myriad of opportunities for those seeking to exploit any loopholes or oversights. The federal regulation of sports gambling requested by Commissioner Goodell aligns with the September 2018 initiative by Senator Chuck Schumer (D-NY) and Senator Orrin Hatch (R-NV), who has since retired. Included in their recommendations were:

- All sportsbooks should use only official league data to determine outcomes.

- The sports leagues themselves should be involved in determining what bets would be accepted.

- Anyone under twenty-one is prohibited from placing a sports bet in any state.

- Entities taking bets should not target youth in their advertising and should properly disclose dangers of betting.

- Sports wagering operators should report suspicious activity and share information with sportsbooks, the leagues and state regulators that could help uncover anything that compromises the integrity of games.

In recognition of the seismic shifts in the sports betting landscape—and perhaps following the adage "if you can't beat 'em, join 'em"—the same league that in 2012 had made the dire forecast that legalized gambling would "irreparably harm amateur and professional sports," announced in January 2019 that it was forming a new partnership with Caesars Entertainment. The multiyear deal made Caesars the "official casino sponsor of the NFL" but did not include any special arrangements for wagering on NFL games at Caesars casinos. Two years later, the league signed sportsbook partnership agreements with Caesars Entertainment, DraftKings, and FanDuel and designated FOX Bet, BetMGM, PointsBet, and Wynn-BET as "approved sportsbook operators."

Commissioner Roger Goodell's job did not get easier when the US Supreme Court swung open the door for states to offer legalized sports betting. By geometrically increasing the number of dollars up for grabs and the number of gambling outlets in states with varying levels of experience dealing with organized crime, the possibilities for abuse are also bound to increase. Law enforcement authorities may also be faced with potential problems from the illegal bookmaking operations that will see legalized sportsbooks cut into their illegal handle, reducing their share of the business.

Roger Goodell is the custodian of the nation's most valuable sports properties: the NFL and the Super Bowl. He looked back onto the league's one-hundred-year history as he described the mission that lies ahead: "As it was for my predecessors, there is no greater priority for me as the Commissioner of the National Football League than protecting the integrity of our sport." He knows that as more states make legalized sports gambling an option for their citizens and visitors, protecting the value of the league properties grows even more difficult and complex. Former New Jersey Senator Bill Bradley, a member of the Basketball Hall of Fame, saw the dangers ahead when he wrote, "Athletes are not roulette chips, but sports gambling treats them as such. If the dangers of state-sponsored sports betting are not confronted, the character of sports and youngsters' view of them could be seriously threatened."[11]

The Super Bowl Provides Community Upgrades

The holiday most often associated with gift giving is obviously Christmas, but the NFL has embraced the practice as part of every Super Bowl. Fans don't exchange gifts at Super Bowl parties, but the league's corporate social responsibility initiatives have benefited millions of people in the cities that have hosted the event. NFL Charities was established in 1973 "to support education and charitable activities and to supply economic support to persons formerly associated with professional football who were no longer able to support themselves." This nonprofit organization was funded with monies generated by the licensing of NFL trademarks and team names. In the early 1990s NFL Charities began making an annual $1 million legacy grant to Super Bowl host cities to create Youth Education Towns (YETs). Host committees were required to match the NFL donation and commit to operating and raising additional funds for the NFL YET for a minimum of ten years after their Super Bowl took place. NFL YET facilities and programs vary, as do the number of children served, but most include interactive fitness equipment, classrooms, technology and multimedia labs, physical fitness zones, recreation fields, and other resources. In some locations, NFL YETs offer full-day school programs, as well as afterschool services.

There are now NFL YET centers in nine cities that have hosted Super Bowls, plus Honolulu. Hawaii has never hosted a Super Bowl, but it was the site of thirty-one NFL Pro Bowls. The league partnered with the Boys and Girls Clubs of America in 2003 to manage the initiative and work with the local NFL YETs to ensure that each location offered programs and services that would effectively meet the needs of the communities they served through educational enhancement, technical training, life-skills development, and recreational opportunities.

NFL Charities, which in 2012 was expanded and renamed the NFL Foundation, has broadened its annual Super Bowl gift giving to include far more community initiatives beyond Youth Education Towns. The league would make a donation of $1 million in seed money, and each year's Super Bowl host committee would raise matching funds to underwrite the programs for which they see a need in underserved areas of their regions. A major initiative for Super Bowl XLV, hosted by the Dallas Cowboys in Dallas–Fort Worth, was SLANT 45, which stood for Service Learning Adventures in North Texas. Elementary school students in thirty-three different school districts identified problems in their community or school and worked as teams to design and then implement solutions. Former Cowboys running back Daryl Johnston chaired the SLANT 45 project, which registered more than forty-four thousand children. They collectively delivered 445,814 service hours that helped change their communities and provided each youngster with an awareness of what it means to volunteer and work together for the common good.

Perhaps the most significant gift-giving impact on a community that hosted a Super Bowl was in Indianapolis for Super Bowl XLVI in 2012. Civic leaders there called the event "a transformational moment in the city's history" with a "lasting impact." The NFL's customary $1 million contribution was used to start an effort that raised $154 million from public and private partners to be invested in long-term community improvement.

The Chase Near Eastside Legacy Center was built as part of the Super Bowl Legacy Project and stands today as an $11.3 million testament to that impact. A fitness and learning center with a menu of services for youth, families, seniors, and neighborhood residents, it was part of a plan to improve the quality of life for an entire neighborhood. The thirty thousand residents on the near east side of Indianapolis call it the "crown jewel" of their neighborhood. "I think what the NFL did, and the Super Bowl Legacy project did was to give the stage and the spotlight and the bullhorn for these aspirations of what they wanted to happen in this community, and in fact, that is happening," said James Taylor, the 2012 Super Bowl Legacy Project director.[12]

In the years since 2012, that area of Indianapolis also witnessed a housing renovation and development boom. When the Legacy Project began, there was a 40 percent vacancy rate in near east side neighborhoods. Five years later, one hundred new homes had been developed—homes for families who may not have been able to afford one before the project began. "Most of the homes are affordable homes developed for low to moderate income families. We are really proud of the work that has happened because of the Super Bowl Legacy project," said John Franklin Hay, Near East Area Renewal Director.

The generosity and community pride generated in each host city begins with the NFL's selection of a city and its annual gift, which beginning in 2024 has been increased to $1.5 million. If anyone in Indianapolis whose life changed for the better through the legacy of Super Bowl XLVI were asked if Super Bowl Sunday is a holiday, they'd likely answer with a resounding, "Yes!" Each year community leaders in the cities selected to host upcoming games prioritize what they see as their pressing needs. When the San Francisco Bay area hosted Super Bowl 50 (the only Super Bowl not using a Roman numeral as its official designation), the host committee awarded one grant each week for fifty weeks leading up to the Super Bowl with the goal of making a positive change in one of three areas: youth development, community investment, and sustainable environments.

Chair of Houston's host committee in 2017, Ric Campo described the impact of the Super Bowl as a platform providing the ability to promote your city "as a great place to live, work and play, and also create a community dialogue to improve people's lives one experience at a time." The "Touchdown Houston" legacy for Super Bowl LI awarded seventy-eight grants to community organizations that were working to fight poverty, prevent homelessness, improve literacy, education, and teacher development, and promote the health and wellness of citizens in eleven Texas counties.

The Birth of an American Tradition
One enduring gift that the Super Bowl has bequeathed to American culture is the tradition of dousing the winners of major contests with Gatorade or whatever liquid is nearby. From high school championships and rivalry games to the sidelines of college and professional games, the "Gatorade bath" has taken its place as an integral part of season-defining celebrations.

When Head Coach Bill Parcells was doused with Gatorade after the New York Giants victory over the Denver Broncos in Super Bowl XXI, more than eighty-seven million people were watching that Sunday in January 1987. That postgame celebration in the Rose Bowl gave birth to a tradition that has endured and thrived now for more than three decades. This, however, was not the first Gatorade bath, but it was the most widely witnessed and therefore created the greatest impact.

The first victim of the sticky shower was Bears Head Coach Mike Ditka on November 25, 1984, following a regular season game. The Bears were on the verge of clinching the Central Division of the National Football Conference. Their 39–3 thrashing of the Minnesota Vikings that day capped an impressive three-year turnaround for the Bears, who had finished ten of the previous fifteen seasons with losing records. Defensive tackle Steve McMichael conspired with defensive tackle Mike Hampton and linebacker Mike Singletary to dump the Gatorade cooler over Ditka's head as the game ended. Ditka, who prided himself on his natty sideline attire and hair always in place, did not like getting soaked and he let his players know it. He stayed dry the rest of the season, which ended with a loss in the conference championship game to the San Francisco 49ers.

The following season, the New York Giants resurrected the Gatorade bath. The Giants started the season with a record of three wins and three losses, which did not meet Coach Parcells's expectations. In the week leading up to their game against divisional rival Washington on October 20, 1985, Parcells gave his starting noseguard Jim Burt grief, telling him that Washington's offensive lineman Jeff Bostic was going to "eat him up." After the Giants won the game 17–3, Burt decided to celebrate and take his anger out on his coach by pouring the Gatorade cooler over Parcells's head. The following week the Giants won again, and this time, the Giants Pro Bowl linebacker Harry Carson did the honors. As long as the Giants kept winning, Bill Parcells did not mind getting wet. "It's fun," he said. "If you have fun, fine. It's not all life and death."[13]

When Parcells took the Giants to their first Super Bowl, where they made franchise history by defeating the Broncos 39–20, the coach had the time of his life and loved getting wet. His sticky legacy has stuck, soaking thousands of triumphant coaches across America ever since.

CHAPTER 7

Count the Dollars— Billions and Billions of Them

In 2009, noted journalist Allen St. John wrote an in-depth behind-the-scenes look at all the variables that go into the making of the Super Bowl by placing his magnifying glass on Super Bowl XLII, the first played at the Cardinals' home stadium in Glendale, Arizona. Its title was "The Billion Dollar Game." Fifteen years later, taking into account the economic impact of the Super Bowl on its host city and the nation as a whole, the number has soared to roughly $40 billion per year. This American "holiday" created by commercial interests has paid off far beyond what Pete Rozelle, Lamar Hunt, or anyone at its inception could have ever imagined.

Let's Do the Math

A large portion of the huge economic impact of the Super Bowl is the money spent by Americans who aren't attending the game. Research done annually for the National Retail Federation (NRF) by Prosper Insights & Analytics estimates that fans throwing or attending Super Bowl parties or just watching the game at home collectively spend more than $15 billion each year. The NRF estimate for Super Bowl LVIII in 2024 was $17.3 billion. "You don't have to be a football fan to celebrate the Super Bowl," said NRF President and CEO Matthew Shay. "Whether it's to see who wins, watch the halftime show and commercials or just get together with friends, this is the biggest party since New Year's

Eve." And those billions of dollars aren't just for beer and pizza. "Retailers are ready whether you need food, team jerseys, decorations or a new TV," said Shay.[1]

Surveys by the NRF show that at least 200 million American adults plan to watch the Super Bowl each year. Of those, 80 percent plan to buy food and beverages, 13 percent will purchase team apparel and accessories, 9 percent say they will buy a new television to watch the Super Bowl (and no doubt try to impress their friends and family), 8 percent will get some new decorations, and 6 percent will buy furniture such as chairs or sofas.

Supermarkets see a spike in their usual Sunday sales figures early on the day of a Super Bowl, as party hosts fill their shopping carts with last minute items and guests grab bags of snacks, beverages, and other foods to present to their hosts. Takeout restaurants and fast-food delivery establishments naturally see business spike in the late afternoon and evening of Super Bowl Sunday.

Online and mobile retail sales figures reflect a different buying pattern on the day of the "big game." Based on data from a survey done by Criteo of 625 US online retailers not including Amazon, game day online and mobile sales for Super Bowl LIII in 2019 were significantly lower before the game started than on an average winter Sunday. However, the number of purchases surged during the second quarter and peaked at the end of the game, when orders for sporting goods and apparel skyrocketed by a multiple of twenty times greater than average. The post–Super Bowl increase in sales of NFL gear and accessories was 1,823 percent above average. The Criteo study showed that categories other than sports-related items like clothing and jewelry also noticeably increased after the Super Bowl.[2]

When you add up all the money spent on grocery items, beer, and soft drinks, plus millions of takeout pizzas and big-ticket items, the average Super Bowl investment for each adult viewer comes to more than $80 per person. The NRF says the biggest spenders are between the ages of thirty-five and forty-four (more than $120 spent per viewer), and Americans who are sixty-five or older spend the least (approximately

$40 per person). Geographically, fans in the Northeast spend the most on average and those in the Midwest tend to spend the least.

In the month of January each year, demand for new televisions is at its peak because the bigger the screen and the more advanced the technology, the closer viewers will feel to the action on the field. Retailers are willing to offer deep discounts to entice football fans to buy. They are also motivated to sell their existing stock of television sets because every January at the annual Consumer Electronics Show, the newest technology and the latest upgraded televisions are introduced. These new models typically hit the consumer market in the early summer months, so clearing soon-to-be dated inventory from their shelves is a priority for stores and online retailers during the first few months of the year.

A fraction of the more than $15 billion in gross retail sales related to the Super Bowl is diminished by returns: reports show that up to 25 percent of the TVs sold in the weeks before the Super Bowl are returned to retailers shortly after the game.[3] The return of nondefective, used merchandise for a refund is called "wardrobing." That big new television on your friend's wall that showed every detail of every play in vibrant color may not be there a few days later. But if you were impressed, it served its purpose.

The Economic Impact on Host Cities

The most intense impact of the Super Bowl, economically and in virtually all other categories, is felt by the cities and regions that host the event. The impact is realized in short-, medium-, and long-term benefits. In the short term—the period leading up to and immediately following the game—cities can expect to reap an additional $300 to $600 million in economic activity, and they get the opportunity to showcase their region to a national and international audience. In the one to three years following the event, host cities hope they can achieve future benefits. If they promoted their assets and attractions well enough in the weeks before and during the game, visitors who couldn't see or do everything during their Super Bowl visit will return as tourists to do more. This impact also includes television viewers who were attracted to the area by what they saw in the media so that they too make plans to visit. When Super Bowl

LI was being planned in Houston, Mayor Sylvester Turner described the importance of being the host city: "This is our opportunity to tell Houston's story on an international stage." Pointing out that 142 languages are spoken in Houston and the city is home to ninety-two foreign consulates, Mayor Turner said, "Many people outside the city don't see Houston as the most diverse city in the country—many people are still surprised by that. We are more than cowboy hats and cowboy boots."[4]

Over the long term, the facilities and infrastructure upgrades that are made to accommodate the Super Bowl remain for years to come as valuable community resources. And the increased activities and events that are staged in host cities can be catalysts for change in the areas of youth, volunteer, and cultural development. These all have value, if not a readily quantifiable figure that would show up in an economic impact study. Perhaps the most valuable extended benefit is the city and region's enhanced reputation as a place to successfully stage major events such as national trade shows and conventions and additional sports championships like future Super Bowls or the NCAA Final Four. Virtually every city that hosts a Super Bowl, regardless of its total population, improves its status and moves into the top tier of major cities in the eyes of the American public. For example, the population of New Orleans is quite a bit smaller than that of Columbus, Ohio, but its reputation as an elite center for events and tourism is considerably greater having hosted so many Super Bowls.

The prestige of hosting a national "holiday" and the spotlight it shines on the people of the region and the progress and successes of their institutions and industries have been intoxicating attractions for NFL owners and their local community leaders since the Super Bowl established itself as a valuable institution. That wasn't the case until after Super Bowl III in Miami in 1969. As discussed in chapter 4, it was unclear whether the Super Bowl would be a true championship worthy of national attention or simply a season-ending exhibition game between a major professional football league and a minor league circuit. That was until the New York Jets of the AFL upset the Baltimore Colts in Miami, thus ending the NFL's domination of the game. Miami hosted the second and third Super Bowls at the Orange Bowl because after two consecutive convincing victories by the NFL's Green Bay Packers, there were no serious contenders bidding to bring the third game to their cities. New Orleans had expressed an interest in hosting, but that didn't get serious until after the Jets victory elevated the status of the AFL and of the championship game. There was no Superdome yet in Louisiana, but New Orleans did win the rights to host Super Bowl IV in 1970 at Tulane Stadium, and since then the number of bidders has blossomed. The number of different regions of the United States that have served as official host cities has grown to sixteen with the addition of Las Vegas for Super Bowl LVIII.

The number of host cities probably would have remained at only ten or eleven if the NFL had not relaxed the criteria that was initially used to select successful bidders. Commissioner Pete Rozelle's vision for the Super Bowl was that it would be played at a neutral site in an area that could attract visitors in the winter, so an average daily temperature in January of at least 50 degrees Fahrenheit (10°C) or a climate-controlled indoor stadium was stipulated as a criterion for hosting. A prospective

Super Bowl Venue	Games	Years
Miami	11	1968, 1969, 1971, 1976, 1979, 1989, 1995, 1999, 2007, 2010, 2020
New Orleans	11	1970, 1972, 1975, 1978, 1981, 1986, 1990, 1997, 2002, 2013, 2025
Los Angeles/Pasadena	8	1967, 1973, 1977, 1980, 1983, 1987, 1993, 2022
Tampa	5	1984, 1991, 2001, 2009, 2021
Arizona	4	1996, 2008, 2015, 2023
San Diego	3	1988, 1998, 2003
Atlanta	3	1994, 2000, 2019
Detroit/Pontiac	2	1982, 2006
Houston	2	1974, 2004
Stanford/ Santa Clara, CA	2	1985, 2016
Minneapolis	2	1992, 2018
Jacksonville	1	2005
Dallas/Arlington	1	2011
Indianapolis	1	2012
NY/NJ	1	2014
Las Vegas	1	2024

city also was required to have a stadium that could seat a minimum of seventy thousand fans, hotels that could provide at least nineteen thousand hotel rooms, plus a range of nearby facilities to accommodate practice sites for two teams, a media and accreditation center, and space for parties, concerts, and other affiliated promotions and attractions.

As a result, twenty-four of the first twenty-five Super Bowls were in warm weather climates, except for Super Bowl XVI, at what was then a seven-year-old Silverdome in Pontiac, Michigan. It was a climate-controlled indoor venue with football seating for 80,311 that served as home for the Detroit Lions. Four of the first ten Super Bowls were at the Orange Bowl in Miami, the home of the Dolphins. Three of the first ten were in New Orleans at Tulane's stadium where the Saints played, and two were played in Southern California, Super Bowls I and VII, at the Los Angeles Memorial Coliseum, which was the home field of the Los Angeles Rams.

More NFL team owners and cities sought entry into this tight, exclusive circle of Super Bowl hosts, fueling the competition. The owners themselves were the only ones who had a vote when decisions were made regarding where the next Super Bowls would be played. Many owners tried to win the support of their fellow owners by offering them gifts, such as the use of a yacht free of charge for a week in Miami, 150 free tickets for family, friends, and associates to Busch Gardens as the reward for a vote favoring Tampa, and Jacksonville sweetened the pot with Arnold Palmer signature putters from the PGA Tour. However, the most compelling factor in host city selection year after year has been that the game should be awarded to a city that built a new, state-of-the-art stadium or to an owner for years of unflagging service to the NFL.

The open bidding process continued until October 2017, when the league announced that it would no longer take bids from individual cities. Instead, the NFL set up a Super Bowl and Major Events advisory committee comprised of seven owners and two team presidents and gave it the responsibility to identify potential host cities. Then the NFL's events staff begins negotiations with the team owner and representatives from each selected city. Describing the new procedure, the NFL's senior vice president of events, Peter O'Reilly, said, "The process is focused on identifying the really optimal destination for the Super Bowl, as opposed to a process where you may have multiple cities spending significant time and energy around a bid process."[5] The key word there is "destination," which harks back to Commissioner Pete Rozelle's initial vision for the Super Bowl as an attraction for thousands of fans in the wintertime. The first Super Bowls awarded under this new process, announced at the NFL owners meeting in May 2018, were both warm weather destinations: Arizona in 2023 and New Orleans for LVIII in 2024. In the fall of 2020, the NFL moved the New Orleans date to 2025 because the expanded seventeen-game regular season that was approved for the 2021 season pushed the Super Bowl one week later in February, concurrent with Mardi Gras. Mardi Gras already fills the hotels in the Big Easy, so the Super Bowl would have crowded out visitors already destined for New Orleans.

The days of competing host committee offers and the enticement of lavish gifts accompanied by arm-twisting from owners may now be history, but it may be more difficult for the NFL to win the concessions it demands from host cities that haven't had to assemble attractive bids in order to be considered for selection. Those concessions represent a major commitment by a community with a significant investment of dollars that seriously cuts into the overall economic benefit of hosting a Super Bowl.

The Host City Balance Sheet

The infusion of cash that comes from staging a major event of national import that will attract thousands of visitors is what cities crave. The hard truth is that it costs a lot of money to make a lot of money. On the positive side of the ledger are:

1. Direct spending by participants, including the NFL, its subcontractors for operations and hospitality, and at least five thousand credentialed members of the media. That number reached six thousand for Super Bowl LVIII in Las Vegas.

2. The average room rate for each hotel room occupied by one of these "participants" or by the thousands of spectators and visitors who arrive, multiplied by the number of nights they stay in town. The minimum stay most hotels will book is four nights, and the "participants" usually stay at least a full week.

3. The amount of money each participant spends each day on food, transportation, and entertainment multiplied by the total number of days they spend in the market.

4. The average spectator and visitor spending (above and beyond their hotel bills) per person, multiplied by the number of days they stay in town.

5. Direct spending by partners and sponsors who do business with the NFL.

6. Any additional spending.

The money spent by participants or visitors does not stop circulating after one transaction. For example, hotels use the revenue they receive for each room (usually double or triple the room rate for a regular weekend in February) and buy more food and supplies, pay overtime, hire additional part-time personnel, pay higher utility bills and taxes, and do much more of what is called "indirect spending." Travel and event experts say the formula for determining the true economic impact is the total amount of direct spending—items 1 through 6 above—multiplied by 2.25. Therefore, $100 million in direct spending yields an economic impact of $225 million.

But that's just the "incoming" side of the balance sheet. On the outgoing side are items such as:

1. Capital construction for new venues or upgrades to old ones, plus road building or repair and additional infrastructure expenses, such as the expansion of the Louis Armstrong New Orleans airport terminal before Super Bowl XLVII in 2013, which carried a price tag of $305 million.

2. The direct cost of hosting an event, which includes all dedicated personnel, extra police, and security. These include all the changes and services that the NFL requires.

3. The post-event costs of restoring venues to their previous condition, clean up, storage, and processing of all required reports and tax forms.

The *Atlanta Constitution* obtained the list of specifications required by the NFL from the Atlanta Super Bowl Host Committee for the game played at Mercedes-Benz Stadium in February 2019. The cost of each item had to be paid for with funds raised from local Atlanta businesses, contributors, and taxpayers in Atlanta, Fulton County, and the state of Georgia. Included were:

- Free hotel rooms for eight nights for each participating team, including 150 standard rooms, two "presidential" suites, and five other suites.

- Rent-free use of Mercedes-Benz Stadium for the game and other venues, such as the Georgia World Congress Center for ancillary events that included the Super Bowl Experience and the NFL media center.

- The State of Georgia owns the stadium through the Georgia World Congress Center, so it contributed to the event by not charging any regular fees that would be paid by any other visiting event or convention.

- Assignment of ten security officers to each team hotel during the day and five during the night for every night of the teams' stays.

- Police escorts for the team owners to and from the game.

- Approximately ten thousand parking spaces for game-day use, with the parking revenue retained by the NFL.

- Installation of up to two thousand banners on street poles and setting up a "social media monitoring and response center."

- And despite all the work and investment of time and resources made by the host committee, the NFL provided no free tickets. The committee could buy up to 750 tickets at face value.[6]

The list of confidential NFL requests for Super Bowl LII in Minnesota was a 153-page document obtained in 2014 by the *Minneapolis Star Tribune*. In addition to the types of expenses listed above for Atlanta, the Minnesota Super Bowl Host Committee had to pay for:

- The waiver of local government licensing fees on 450 courtesy cars.
- Anticounterfeit enforcement by local police.
- The creation of "clean zones" within a one-mile radius of the stadium and a six-block radius of the NFL headquarters hotels, which included the cost of sanitation and the relocation of any homeless people in those areas.
- Twenty free billboards across the Twin Cities.
- Installation of NFL-preferred ATMs at the stadium.
- Up to two "top-quality bowling venues" reserved at no cost to the league for the Super Bowl Celebrity Bowling Classic.
- The hotels where the teams were to stay would be obligated to televise the NFL Network for a year before the Super Bowl—at no cost to the league.
- Free access to three "top-quality" golf courses during the summer or fall before the Super Bowl.
- If cell phone signal strength at the team hotels was not strong enough, the host committee—at no cost to the league—would be responsible for erecting "a sufficient number of portable cellular towers."
- The league also asked the local media to "provide significant advertising and promotional time" for the NFL Experience in the month leading up to the game, specifically at least twenty color pages of free space, in aggregate, in leading daily newspapers

to promote the game and four weeks of free promotions on at least six local radio stations, including at least 250 live or prerecorded ads.[7]

Beyond simply the plus and minus side of the balance sheet, there are three other factors that need to be calculated before the net local economic impact of a Super Bowl can be determined. These are the "displacement effect," the "crowding-out effect," and "leakage." Hotels and restaurants would have had other patrons, and other events may have been held at local venues if not for the Super Bowl. Plus, local residents and any visitors would have spent money on entertainment, gifts, apparel, and other regularly available services, so the revenue that all of these would have generated was "displaced" by the Super Bowl. An excellent example of the displacement effect was in Las Vegas for 2024. The city's hotels and casinos would be full every Super Bowl weekend whether the game is being played there or not.

The crowding-out effect takes into account the reality that a Super Bowl or other major event keeps away locals who don't want to deal with the traffic and crowds. These two effects combine to further reduce the net impact of Super Bowl spending in the host region. "Leakage" refers to dollars spent on goods and services provided by companies not based in the region, so this money does not go into the local economy. A prime example of leakage was at the one Super Bowl hosted by Jacksonville, Florida, in 2005. The city did not have enough hotel rooms to accommodate all the visitors, so six cruise ships were brought in to handle the overflow. All the money paid to the cruise ship operators for rooms, food, and onboard services literally floated away when the boats left port.

After all the pluses and minuses, what is the economic impact of hosting a Super Bowl? The market research firm Rockport Analytics, based in West Chester, Pennsylvania, has been preparing annual economic impact reports for host committees for the better part of the past decade. For Super Bowl LII in Minnesota in 2018, the Rockport Analytics report titled "Super Bowl LII: The Bold North Delivers" said that the gross amount of incremental local spending was $450 million. This derived from 125,000 visitors to Minneapolis–St. Paul and from the event "participants" who spent $179 million on staging the game, broadcast and media coverage, and event hosting.

But from that number the analysts subtracted $80 million for the value of regular tourism that ordinarily would have occurred in the Twin Cities during that time period but was displaced by the Super Bowl. That brought the net local spending total down to $370 million. Then the analysts subtracted another $78 million in leakage, the value of goods and services that were provided by vendors from outside the Twin Cities area. That dropped the total benefit for Super Bowl LII to the local community down to $292 million. On the positive side of the ledger, Rockport Analytics reported that the event generated an incremental $32 million in local and state tax receipts. And they added another $108 million to account for what is referred to as the "ripple effect," which is the amount of wages earned by local workers during the weeks of Super Bowl activities that they would spend in the area during the rest of the year. The bottom line reported to the Minnesota Super Bowl Host Committee was a total economic impact on the gross domestic product for Minneapolis–St. Paul of $400 million. Considering that the state of Minnesota spent $348 million and local taxpayers paid another $150 million to build the new stadium that attracted the Super Bowl, news of this $400 million return was just what they wanted to hear.[8]

However, several economists dispute the accuracy of these economic impact studies. After Super Bowl XLIX in 2015, the second one played at the new stadium in Glendale, Arizona, a study done by Arizona State University reported that the benefit to the region totaled $719 million, making it the all-time leader in economic impact. The president of the North American Association of Sports Economists, Victor Matheson of the College of the Holy Cross, said the consensus among sports economists is that estimates this high are greatly exaggerated. "If they can come up with a large, plausible number, that's what they want," Matheson said. "The NFL uses this for two reasons: They use it to get all sorts of government payments to host the Super Bowl, and they use the Super Bowl as a carrot to dangle in front of otherwise reluctant taxpayers. They say, 'build a stadium and we'll make sure you get a Super Bowl.'" Matheson has been studying the economic impact of Super Bowls for more than twenty years, and he says that the net increase in revenue for host cities is more like $30 to 130 million.[9]

The City That Always Wins

Las Vegas did not host a Super Bowl in the event's first five decades, but with the arrival of the former Oakland Raiders to begin play at Allegiant Stadium there in 2020, the NFL awarded Nevada its first for 2024. However, Las Vegas never needed to host the game to reap a huge benefit. In 2019, the Las Vegas Convention and Visitors Authority reported that 306,000 people came to the city for Super Bowl week and spent $426 million dollars on accommodations, entertainment, transportation, and other expenses. After the pandemic year of 2020, the number of visitors climbed to 311,000 in 2021, bringing with them more revenue for Vegas businesses and more tax money collected by local and state governments. Sportsbooks in Nevada casinos reported that a record $179.8 million was wagered there on the game in 2022. Of that total, 9 to 10 percent is profit for the casinos. The total amount gambled in Las Vegas during a Super Bowl week when the city isn't hosting the game fell off slightly in 2023 as more states legalized sports gambling but came back strong to $185.6 million when the city hosted the game in 2024.

Despite the increased competition for sports betting from other states, the reported impact of more than $400 million for Las Vegas in 2019 is even higher than the Rockport Analytics estimate for most cities that actually did host the game. In addition, the gross revenue total for Las Vegas, when it doesn't host the Super Bowl, is not offset by any taxpayer or host committee expenditures for facilities, services, or NFL-required upgrades. The Las Vegas Convention and Visitors Authority put its estimate for the total economic impact at $500 million in 2024.

Even if the host city net revenue for each Super Bowl is a more conservative $150 to 200 million and the net for Las Vegas when the city doesn't host the game is only $400 million, the gains for both cities combined would annually exceed half a billion dollars. Add that to the estimated $23 billion in wagering nationwide plus the $17 billion in retail sales, and our running total is up to $40.5 billion.

Television Advertising

The price of television commercials in the Super Bowl broadcast always gets a lot of attention in the weeks leading up to the game, primarily because they are the most expensive commercials of the year on American television. I dig deeper into Super Bowl advertising in a later chapter, but when the average price for a thirty-second Super Bowl spot hit $1 million in 1995, there was no turning back. In the years since, that price tag has grown geometrically. The top price for a thirty-second commercial in the telecasts of Super Bowl LVII in 2023 and LVIII in 2024 cost advertisers $7 million. It is estimated that FOX in 2023 and CBS in 2024 sold $600 million worth of advertising for their respective Super Bowl Sunday programs.

This does not include the commercials that each local FOX, CBS, ABC, or NBC station sells when its network televises the Super Bowl. Your local station usually gets four thirty-second slots per hour during a Super Bowl telecast, which it sells to local businesses like nearby car dealers or pizza delivery restaurants. With a huge, guaranteed audience, the rates charged for these commercials in each of the 210 American television markets are multiplied several times over the cost of an average local spot that would air any other Sunday evening. The larger the local television market (New York City is number 1 with 7.1 million TV homes), the higher the price charged for local commercials. This incremental local TV advertising revenue could add another $50 to 100 million to the overall economic impact figure.

Then add the revenue from the commercials that are sold in the Super Bowl–related programming that is produced by ESPN, the NFL Network, and others that serve sports fans but do not televise the game. These networks and platforms see tremendous value in associating their brands with the big game during the week leading up to the game and on game day. Together, the ESPN networks and the NFL Network annually air approximately 100 to 150 hours of this "surround programming." In every one of those hours, there are twelve to fourteen minutes of commercials with prices set based on the anticipated audience of viewers who can't get enough information, opinions, or predictions leading up to the Super Bowl or interviews and analysis after the game. The ratings for these programs are a fraction of the game telecast itself, but they generate millions of dollars in revenue. So does sponsorship of Super Bowl content on websites that cover the NFL, from Pro Football Talk, to Bleacher Report, Barstool Sports, Yahoo! Sports, ESPN.com, ESPN Deportes, and several other Spanish-language sports websites.

A conservative estimate for all the advertising connected to the Super Bowl each year—the network that televises the game and its affiliated sports network and local TV stations, plus the other sports networks, websites, and mobile services that don't air the game—is $800 million. Adding this to our running total of $40.5 billion brings the annual economic impact to $41.3 billion.

The Price of Watching in Person

What we haven't yet counted are the total dollars spent on tickets for the game and cost of transportation to the host city by fans who do not live in the local area. The average price for a ticket to Super Bowl LVIII was estimated at $8,600. Multiplied by the 61,629 seats at Allegiant Stadium in Las Vegas, that represents another $530 million in spending.

To attend the game, a large percentage of fans have to fly to the host city. The NFL team hosting the game is allocated 5 percent of the available tickets to sell to its season ticket holders, so only about 3,500 are lucky enough to attend the game in their home city. Subtract them from the stadium seating capacity for football, and that leaves more than fifty thousand fans who have to fly or drive in from far-flung destinations. Round-trip airfares vary widely from city to city across the United States, but using an average of $500 per ticket for an estimated fifty thousand visitors traveling by air to the Super Bowl totals $25 million. If this accounted for all the people at the game, that's where the air transportation total would end. But each year, more than five thousand credentialed media cover the game, in addition to the personnel from the teams, the NFL, and its operations and nonlocal credentialed support staff. That's another thirty-five thousand people who need transportation. Most cities report at least another fifty thousand or more out-of-town visitors who won't be attending the game but come for the excitement of the week, and attractions like the NFL's Super Bowl Experience. Depending upon how many of them drove in from nearby states, the airlines could have handled another twenty-five to thirty-five thousand travelers. Add the thousands of people who work the game or represent the NFL and its other thirty-one cities, and that could mean another $30 million in round-trip airfares, for a grand total of approximately $55 million spent on air transportation. The cost of hotel rooms occupied by all these people is covered in the host city economic impact figure that we calculated earlier.

The Running Total

Our previous running total of $41.3 billion included roughly $17 billion in retail sales across the country, $23 billion in wagering, the economic impact on the host city of $150 to 200 million, and $800 million for the purchase of television/media advertising. Add the money spent on tickets to the game—around $530 million, give or take—and $55 million for the cost of air transportation, and the running total jumps to roughly $41.9 billion in an annual economic impact for a Super Bowl.

The Cost of Calling in Sick

American businesses in all fifty states wind up contributing to the Super Bowl's total economic impact in the form of lost productivity. The firm of Challenger, Grey and Christmas produces an annual report with the Workforce Institute at Kronos on lost productivity that can be attributed to the Super Bowl. On the Monday after Super Bowl LVIII in 2024, their survey estimated that 16 million people planned to call in sick, a few of them unable to deal with the grim reality of their favorite team suffering a loss, but most unable to deal with the mass quantities of beer, pizza, chicken wings, and guacamole consumed the previous day. Millions of other employees were projected to either arrive an hour late for work on the Monday after the game or leave work an hour early. And during the five-day workweek preceding the Super Bowl, six out of ten workers who are interested in the game spend an estimated ten minutes per day talking about it instead of working on their assigned tasks. Calculating the average hourly wages for all these people missing time at work, the grand total for lost productivity attributed to the Super Bowl is a staggering $6 billion.[10]

"Over the years, calls have been made to make Super Bowl Monday a national holiday, which would give fans time to decompress after the big game. For companies that cannot be that generous, it's best to use the game as a morale-building experience," said Andrew Challenger, vice president of Challenger, Grey and Christmas. "Employers should accept that people are going to spend some of that time Monday discussing big plays or best commercials. Consider allowing employees to come in a bit later and encourage fans to bring in leftovers from their Super Bowl parties and throw a potluck during lunch. Use this opportunity to increase morale and workplace satisfaction," he added.[11]

With the introduction of the NFL's seventeen-week season in 2021, the Super Bowl may occasionally fall on the Sunday before the official Monday observance of Presidents' Day in February. During those years, the lost productivity figure should be reduced because many employers would already be granting their employees that day off.

The Bottom Line

By adding the $6 billion estimate for productivity losses by American businesses on the Monday after the Super Bowl to our running total of $41.9 billion, the total economic impact of a Super Bowl comes to approximately $48 billion. That figure is larger than the yearly gross domestic product for many nations including Bahrain, Bolivia, Paraguay, and Iceland. The Super Bowl is truly a "Billions and Billions of Dollars Game."

CHAPTER 8

Brands Worth Defending

THE SUPER BOWL IS THE BIGGEST EVENT IN THE MOST POPULAR AMERican sport with a national and international reach and appeal. More Americans watch television on Super Bowl Sunday than on any other day of the year. The game and the halftime show make it the highest-rated entertainment show each year. Advertising campaigns for a variety of products and services launch via commercials designed to amuse us and stick in our memory. And we are introduced to trailers for new movies that will premiere later in the year.

The NFL described the Super Bowl as "American optimism on full display for the world to see," in its vision statement for Super Bowl 50. The event's unparalleled success makes it the most valuable sports event brand in the world. Every year, *Forbes* magazine compiles a brand value report that factors in the amount of revenue per day from media, sponsorships, tickets, and licensed merchandise, and every year the Super Bowl tops that list. Its value as a brand is now more than double that of the second-place event, the Summer Olympic Games.

Nothing Compares to the Super Bowl Brand
What makes brands valuable is how they communicate by triggering associations and emotions in ways that words alone cannot. They establish familiarity, reliability, and permanence. They connect us with our passions, our memories, and with our fellow fans. Those connections come with the inherent social benefit of membership in and identification with a large, vocal affinity group. When you hear the words "Super Bowl"

spoken, see a story about the game, or randomly think about when your team or favorite player was in the Super Bowl, what comes to mind? The fun you had watching the game with friends or at a party. The joy of a victory shared or a defeat lamented. Perhaps you were fortunate enough to attend the game with a parent, family member, or friend, and you remember every detail of the travel, where you stayed, what you ate and drank, the laughs you enjoyed together. Brands command a premium in their collective history, memories, and reputation, with every player, every team, and every story, past and present, adding to the accrued value. A great brand is a story well told.

Marketing professionals measure "brand equity," which is defined as the "set of assets and liabilities linked to a brand, its name and symbol, that add to or subtract from the value provided" to, in the case of sports, a league, team, event, organization, athlete, or their fans and customers. That value is determined by how people perceive and experience the brand. Its assets can include fan loyalty, awareness, and the perceptions of quality that enhance consumer confidence and produce competitive advantages, which include the ability to charge more for media distribution rights and advertising associated with the brand and for the tickets sold to fans who choose to attend.

What, then, are the Super Bowl's brand assets? You can start with the game's history of more than a half-century of excitement and suspense. Of great teams from the Green Bay Packers and the Pittsburgh Steelers to the San Francisco 49ers and the New England Patriots. And of special performances by charismatic stars, starting with Bart Starr and Joe Namath and continuing with Terry Bradshaw, Joe Montana, Tom Brady, Patrick Mahomes, and so many more whose achievements and personalities have become part of Super Bowl lore. The combined value associated with just these few teams and players is formidable, but they represent only a fraction of the Super Bowl's total brand assets.

Another of the Super Bowl's brand assets is its strong American fan base and the loyalty that millions of fans feel for their favorite teams. "Sports like football are deeply embedded in the culture," said Michael Oriard, author of *Brand NFL: Making and Selling America's Favorite Sport*, who spent four years after graduating from Notre Dame as a lineman for the Kansas City Chiefs. "They're organic in some way to the communities in which they're played. You grow up with football. You pick your favorite NFL team as a seven-year-old kid, and these attachments are deeply rooted in American life and the game is deeply rooted in American culture."[1] More than half the US population identifies themselves as NFL fans, and of those 180 million people, 72.6 million say they are avid fans of the league. When fans are asked which sport they are most interested in month by month, the NFL is the most popular in eleven out of the twelve months, with June being the exception, when more fans are interested in Major League Baseball. This massive, devoted following has made the NFL the premier sports and entertainment brand, bringing people together socially and emotionally like no other and translating into a major asset when the football season culminates in its single, winner-take-all championship game.

Fans show their devotion and loyalty by spending billions of dollars each year on NFL licensed apparel and merchandise. Every item emblazoned with the NFL shield, the words "Super Bowl" and "Pro Bowl," the Super Bowl and Pro Bowl logos, and the team names, nicknames, colors, symbols, emblems, helmet designs, and uniform designs is a valuable brand extension. When the Super Bowl was first played in 1967, it was rare for fans of any sport to wear hats or jerseys with team logos or colors when they attended games. In wide shots taken of stadium crowds from that era, people wore their normal street clothes and looked far different from the fans we now see clad in the official jerseys and jackets of their favorite players and teams. And they aren't all men. In 2010, the NFL launched its "Fit for You" campaign to market licensed apparel that would be fashionable and practical for women. Twenty wives of famous players and coaches helped model the clothing, which was a departure from the NFL's previous "shrink it and pink it" philosophy for its women's wear offerings. "We've taken the approach that we have the right products for women and now have products that fit them," said Tracey Bleczinski, who was the NFL's vice president of consumer products. "We're tapping into fast fashion."[2]

The commitment by men and women to purchase NFL merchandise and make these branded items part of their wardrobe is evidence of a deeper connection that they have with those teams than if they were just interested spectators watching from a stadium seat or from their sofa at home. Nike knows the value of that connection. In October 2010, the company agreed to pay an estimated $1.1 billion for a five-year licensing deal that would outfit all NFL teams in Nike-designed uniforms beginning with the 2012 season. That agreement has now been renewed twice, extending it until the year 2028 at terms that were not disclosed. Since Super Bowl XLVII in 2013 between the Baltimore Ravens and San Francisco 49ers, every player in every Super Bowl has worn multiple Nike swooshes, which are seen live on television by more than one hundred million viewers, as well as in online and social media coverage and in countless publications every year. The value of that massive exposure and how it translates into the sale of Nike-branded merchandise in North America and around the world obviously provides the apparel maker with a strong return on the licensing fees paid to the NFL. And every time these millions of buyers are seen wearing their team colors in public, the NFL's brand awareness and reach are broadened and deepened.

A Story Well Told and Controlled

The NFL earns approximately $2.5 billion per year from its licensing and sponsorship partners, which include brands ranging from Gatorade—the NFL's official sports nutrition partner since 1983, making it the longest tenured partner—to Quaker Oats, the "official hot cereal and granola bars," Intuit, the "official financial and accounting software provider," and Nike. With the opening in 2019 of legalized sports gambling in several states, the NFL signed its first official casino, Caesars. The list of official partners has grown to thirty-nine, with fourteen of them joining the fold since 2020. This list will continue to grow as long as companies trust the value that comes with identifying their brands with the NFL brand.

In his introduction to the guidebook that governs how the brand can be used, Commissioner Roger Goodell said, "The NFL has the unique responsibility to uphold the highest standards. Our fans—comprising the largest and most diverse audience in sports entertainment—expect no less. That is the reason every communication by the NFL and its business partners has the potential to significantly impact respect for the NFL."

When the league succeeds and thrives, its official partners also realize an increase in the value of that connection. Surveys by Turnkey Intelligence show that NFL fans who correctly identify a sponsor with the league are more likely to buy that product or service. Marriott, the NFL's official hotel since 2011, appears to have benefited the most, with 67 percent of fans who made the connection saying that they would be more inclined to stay at a Marriott property than at another hotel. The NFL sees the protection of its brands as a responsibility it shares along with partners like Marriott. "The business decisions we make and the communication we produce should be supportive of and consistent with our brand positioning and values," said Goodell. The values laid out by the NFL include its tradition and heritage, teamwork, excellence, its embrace of community and diversity, integrity, and innovation.[3]

The league created a checklist for how its partners should communicate the NFL brand:

- Conduct business in ways that support the NFL brand positioning and values.

- Produce products and communications that support the NFL brand image.

- Conduct ourselves in ways that are consistent with what people expect from us and with the standards that we have set for ourselves.

- Set the bar high and expect anyone involved with the NFL— whether employee or partner—to meet those standards.

- Take the lead in bringing new ideas to the sport of football and our unique sports/entertainment product.

The "Communicating the NFL Brand" guidebook contains more than forty pages of specific examples of backgrounds for ads that may or may not be used, the size of the NFL logo in relation to sponsor logos that appear together in any messaging, permissible typefaces and color palettes, and even how the fifty yard line graphic should appear. The identity guidelines go into granular detail to ensure that whenever an NFL logo, mark, or image is seen, it will always appear in the most positive light. The NFL's style guide for a Super Bowl is even more comprehensive, running to 130 pages. Every design application is demonstrated, from how the NFL shield and the game logo may be used to the color palette, gradient backgrounds, approved font styles and elements. "The NFL mission is to stay true to the great game of football and the positive values that our game represents," said Commissioner Goodell. "It is in our mutual interest for the NFL to continue to be widely respected and a positive influence on millions of fans of all ages and walks of life. These guidelines will help us achieve that goal."

Number One and Still Growing

The more people who care about a product, who sample, consume, and respect it, the greater the value that accrues to the product. The Super Bowl has been the most-watched television program each year since 1984, first exceeding the level of one hundred million viewers per minute in 2010 with all live viewing platforms combined. Super Bowl LVIII, Kansas City Chiefs versus the San Francisco 49ers on February 11, 2024, achieved the ultimate high-water mark for American television. More people watched that game than any other program in the history of the medium. An average of 123.7 million viewers were tuned in per minute, watching either on CBS television, Univision in Spanish, via digital streaming on Paramount+, or on Nickelodeon. More than 200 million people in the U.S. watched at least a portion of the live event.

One of the factors that contributes to the huge viewing audience each year is the timing of the Super Bowl: in the midst of what is the coldest part of winter for much of the country. "A lot has to do with people staying put—the weather," said the late Hall of Fame coach and legendary broadcaster John Madden. "It's not like, 'Well, should I go boating? Should I go to a picnic? Should I lay out in the sun?' You can't do anything; you gotta stay in your house. So, I think it's the bigness of the game. The fact that you have two weeks to get ready to play it. The fact that we're going to be done that day. The finality of it. Then the weather."[4] The Super Bowl's unrivaled live audience, augmented by the reduced number of outdoor recreation options, makes the event perhaps the only true mass media outlet left standing in our splintered communications landscape. And that is decidedly a brand asset.

Complementing the live viewing audience is the multiplatform, multinetwork media coverage that the Super Bowl receives each year, reaching a near-saturation point in the week preceding the game. The NFL itself has two in-house media assets that add their own brand of promotional value: the NFL Network and NFL Films. The NFL Network's eighty-plus hours of coverage begin each year with Super Bowl Opening Night on the Monday before the game and then uses the combined efforts of hundreds of broadcast professionals, ex-coaches, and players to analyze how the two teams match up, tell the stories of the teams, the individual players, and coaches, to produce as much pregame hype as is humanly possible.

NFL Films was founded by Ed Sabol in the 1960s. Ever since its inception, the NFL has generated a mythology that makes it seem larger than life. Every NFL Films production delivers the powerful promotional message that NFL football is filled with dramatic storylines and hard-working heroes who fight together against all odds. NFL Films focuses on the intensity, the beauty, and the fun of professional football using slow-motion video, close-ups of expressive faces and dirty hands, low-angle shots that make the players appear larger than life, and documentary-style narration with an underscore of stirring music. Their programs are meant to be entertaining for women as well as men, driving interest and audience for the ultimate game each year, the Super Bowl.

The NFL doesn't have to pay a dime for some of the most valuable promotion that its players and teams receive every year. Fantasy football now has an estimated 62.5 million players in the United States, and research shows that they are more likely to attend games, read sports news, watch sports highlights, and spend money on sports than fans who aren't fantasy players.[5] The burgeoning of the internet during the mid-1990s gave rise to online fantasy games led by CBS SportsLine and Yahoo! When these and other fantasy platforms were offered free of charge at the beginning of the twenty-first century, the ranks of players began to take off. Those fans are the ones who engage with content, programs, and live games more than any other fan base. And that represents value to the platforms, networks, and the NFL.

The emergence of the smartphone opened the floodgates in 2008, when the Fantasy Sports and Gaming Association reports that the total number of fantasy players jumped from nineteen million to thirty million in just that one year. The NFL saw the demand for specialized coverage of only the scoring plays that pile up the fantasy points, and in 2009 the league launched the NFL Red Zone pay channel. The NFL doesn't release data on the total number of Red Zone subscribers, but it does say that the channel now accounts for about 10 percent of all weekly NFL viewing. The debut of NFL Red Zone was followed in 2010 by the premiere of the NFL's own fantasy platform on NFL.com.

The rapid growth in the popularity of fantasy football must be considered one of the factors that helped push viewership of the Super Bowl dramatically upward at that same point in time. The TV audience totals from 1995 through 2007 hovered in the range of eighty-five million to ninety-three million viewers per minute. But in 2008, that jumped to 97.45 million, and in 2010, the audience surpassed the one-hundred-million-per-minute plateau for the first time, with an average of 106.48 million viewers. Most fantasy leagues conclude competition before the Super Bowl happens, but the increased player and team awareness and the stronger connection that fantasy players have with the NFL product has proven to be an important asset and enhancement for the NFL brand.

The NFL brand also benefits from the remarkable success of the EA Sports Madden NFL Football video game. The game debuted in June 1988 and was named for John Madden, the primary NFL analyst on CBS TV at that time, who had retired after ten winning seasons as coach of the Oakland Raiders, including victory in Super Bowl XI. The game has sold more than 130 million copies worldwide since, for total sales of more than $4 billion.

Announcing a new partnership extension in May 2020 among EA Sports, the NFL, and the NFL Players Association (NFLPA), Commissioner Roger Goodell said, "The expansion of this partnership is not only about the continued success of the Madden NFL franchise but also the creation of new avenues for our fans to connect with the sport they love." The new contract commits the three parties to develop games in new genres, expand esports programs, and create additional experiences for fans across more platforms. DeMaurice Smith, then the executive director of the NFLPA, described Madden NFL as a pivotal point of connection for NFL players, the sport, and its fans. "We have a shared vision to expand the fanbase of football through interactivity, and we're thrilled to continue our strong partnership with EA Sports to bring this to life in more ways than ever," he said.

"It's incredible how many people have enjoyed Madden NFL over the years, and the impact it's had on not only teaching the sport of football, but growing the love of it as well," said Cam Weber, executive vice president and group general manager for EA Sports. "Every year Madden NFL is the game that kicks off our season of EA Sports games, and it continues to be one of the titans of the game industry." Video game players who learn more about how pro football is played and grow to love the sport are destined to become longtime NFL fans and consumers. EA Sports reports that worldwide the average video game player is thirty-five years old, with 16 percent in the thirteen- to twenty-one-year-old age range in which brand preferences and allegiances are being formed.[6] Millions of young people playing a game for fun, which also connects them with the players, teams, and exciting action of professional football, provides the NFL with yet another powerful asset.

The Power of Cross-Promotion

The NFL's advertising partners belong on the list of brand assets themselves. With their promotional campaigns linking popular products with the game and its fans, the early release of their new commercials online and during the telecast, and even their supermarket displays, they are the companies responsible for focusing consumer attention on Super Bowl Sunday. Consider the marketing value of the "Pepsi Halftime Show" to the Super Bowl and the NFL for the decade from 2013 through 2022. As soon as the halftime act was announced, Pepsi began populating social media and the internet with videos and interviews of the performers, heightening the anticipation of the game months before anyone knew which two teams would play. The company also put messages promoting the halftime show on half a billion PepsiCo product packages. "We turned a 12-minute performance into a 12-month marketing opportunity," said Adam Harter, who was PepsiCo's senior vice president for marketing, media, sports, and entertainment. Pepsi maximized its value as the halftime sponsor by blending advertising, content, music, and pop culture. It was transformed into "a moment of celebration and unity," said Harter.[7]

The cross-promotional synergy between the NFL and Pepsi helped make the Super Bowl halftime the highest-rated segment of the telecast, with an average of more viewers per minute than any game action. Their decade of success increased the value of the halftime sponsorship so dramatically that when it came time to renew the contract in 2022, the NFL's asking price had skyrocketed. PepsiCo decided to continue its official NFL partnership but not renew the halftime sponsorship so that the company could focus on other promotional opportunities, many on digital streaming platforms that attract more younger demographics than linear television. With its new Apple Music sponsorship, halftime has set new records for viewership, hitting 129.3 million viewers per minute in 2024. That made Usher's performance at halftime of Super Bowl LVIII the most-watched entertainment show in American television history.

The tradition of throwing Super Bowl parties also can be seen as an asset in the same way that the tradition of family gatherings for Thanksgiving is an important asset for the farms and stores that sell turkeys. The National Retail Federation reports that roughly one fifth of all Americans who plan to watch the Super Bowl each year also intend to host a party on that Sunday. When a sporting event moves from the realm of appointment viewing to become the center of social activity by millions of Americans, it has significantly added to its value. The timing of the game in early February and during prime-time hours also serves to enhance its value. If the Super Bowl were played in the summer or fall, it would compete for leisure time with outdoor activity and vacations that take people away from their homes and out of regular television-viewing routines. The winter schedule helps support the large number of television viewers and partygoers.

One final listing for the positive side of the ledger is the labor peace that the NFL and the NFL Players Association have assured themselves until the year 2030. A ten-year collective bargaining agreement was approved by owners and then ratified by the players in March 2020. This long-term agreement between the league and its players means that there should be no interruption in the schedule and therefore no threat to revenue generation from the NFL's various media rights and licensing deals. For any organization to guarantee its ability to provide a supply of product and to make money unabated for a decade must be counted as a most valuable asset.

Defending Assets Doesn't Win Popularity Contests

The NFL's detailed identity guidelines discussed earlier make it very clear as to how serious the league is about protecting the value of its brand assets. Companies that want to market their products to the millions of Americans who will watch the Super Bowl but who, unlike Gatorade or Frito-Lay, haven't paid to be sponsorship partners with the NFL are forbidden from using the words "Super Bowl" or "Super Sunday" in any advertising or promotion. That is why, leading up to the game, we see and hear plenty of messages telling us to get ready for the "big game" by purchasing snack food X, beverage Y, or flatscreen television Z.

The NFL has long held the opinion that using the "big game" in advertising constitutes "ambush marketing," so in 2006 the league applied to trademark "big game." "There's been a decades-long practice of companies that do not have the official rights trying to create the mistaken impression that they do," said Gary Gertzog, the league's general counsel at the time. "They try to come up with clever ways to garner the association." The NFL's application to the US Patent and Trademark Office was opposed by Stanford University and the University of California, whose football teams have competed in the "big game" since 1892. Objections were also filed by several companies, including Anheuser-Busch, KFC, Papa John's, Time Warner Cable, Domino's Pizza, Yum Brands, and Dell. Craig Mende, a lawyer at the Manhattan law firm Fross, Zelnick, Lehrman & Zissu, represented nine companies that opposed the league's attempt to secure a trademark. "They had gone along with the NFL's desire that if they didn't have licenses, they should not be able to use 'Super Bowl,'" said Mende. "But to force people not to use 'Big Game' made it impossible for companies to fairly communicate what they might do around the Super Bowl. It seemed that the league was overreaching."[8] One year later, the NFL withdrew its trademark application.

The NFL has never been timid in the defense of its brand. In 1999, the league sued Coors Brewing to block a planned campaign that pitched Coors Light as the "Official Beer of NFL Players." Coors had made the licensing agreement with Players Inc., which was then the marketing arm of the NFL Players Association. The NFL suit stated that identifying Coors Light as the official beer of its players was "both literally false and a violation of the NFL's exclusive trademark rights." It alleged that the Coors promotion "irreparably and irretrievably damages" the economic value of the league's trademark by implying that "Coors Light has a sponsorship with the NFL when it clearly does not." A federal district court judge in New York sided with the NFL and issued an injunction against the campaign, which intended to put the "official beer" slogan on signs, posters, and inflatable footballs to be distributed at the end of NFL games during the 1999 season.[9]

The NFL did receive some criticism when its concerted efforts to protect the Super Bowl brand took the form of threatened legal action against churches. Prior to Super Bowl XLI in February 2007, Falls Creek Baptist Church in Indianapolis invited members of the community to attend its "Super Bowl Bash" to watch the CBS telecast of the game from Miami on a projector in the church hall. There was huge local interest in Super Bowl XLI because the hometown Colts led by Peyton Manning were playing the Chicago Bears. The church planned to charge a $3 admission fee as a fundraiser. Someone from the NFL spotted a promotion for the gathering on the church website, and Pastor John D. Newland said that he received an overnight letter from the league demanding that the party be canceled. The NFL objected to the church's plan to charge a fee to attend and its use of the words "Super Bowl" in its promotions. Pastor Newland said he offered to drop the admission fee and stop using "Super Bowl" in any further promotion, but he was told that the league's longstanding ban of "mass out-of-home viewing" prevented the church from using a projector or any screen larger than a fifty-five-inch diagonal.[10]

The NFL's position was then and remains today that the rights they sell to television networks to broadcast the Super Bowl provide entertainment content to viewers free of charge and that any "mass out-of-home" gathering could affect the size of the audience and therefore diminish the value of those broadcast rights. "This is not about churches," said Brian McCarthy on behalf of the NFL. "We've never investigated a church or gone into a church with a ruler to see how big the TVs are. We've been telling churches and other groups for years what they can and cannot do when it comes to such parties. You shouldn't have to pay for something that's free."

Falls Creek Baptist Church canceled the event. "It just frustrates me that most of the places where crowds are going to gather to watch this game are going to be places that are filled with alcohol and other things that are inappropriate for children," said Newland. "We tried to provide an alternative to that and were shut down." The following year, the church organized a few in-home parties for Super Bowl XLII, which they combined with Sunday school classes, but the hometown Colts weren't in that game.

The Other Side of the Ledger

The Super Bowl's brand assets and the NFL's vigilant defense of them make for an impressive positive side of the event's brand equity equation. But what are its liabilities, and are those liabilities the same as the NFL's liabilities as a whole? The Super Bowl brand and the NFL brand are intrinsically interwoven, but there are significant distinctions that can be drawn.

The Super Bowl's audience is four to five times larger than for NFL regular season games, which means there are millions of people who experience the Super Bowl and receive its messages who do not see what happens in those other games. If the Super Bowl is the only professional football game you see each year, you might be surprised that the games played each week do not feature splashy musical performances at halftime. The television coverage of regular season games rarely includes any content from the site during halftime, with networks choosing to fill the time instead with their studio hosts and analysts, who review highlights and add their commentary. These are still professional football game broadcasts, but the show is decidedly different from a Super Bowl.

Fans who watch or attend games every week are far more likely to see players injured or taken to the sidelines for observation or into the medical tents for concussion protocols. To these fans who consume so much more NFL content on a regular basis, the sport can take on a different character than the Super Bowl, which has had relatively few players suffer serious concussions during the game. During the NFL preseason and regular season of 2023, there were 219 player concussions diagnosed, but not one in Super Bowl LVIII, which concluded the season. That was up from 213 in 2022, but compared to the 2015 season, when there were 275 concussions recorded, that is a 20 percent reduction in eight years. The sight of Miami Dolphins quarterback Tua Tagovailoa stumbling on the field after taking a hit in October 2022—and the millions of times the video was replayed—prompted the NFL and the NFL Players Association to take additional precautions. Symptoms of ataxia were added to the list of mandatory "no-go" conditions that prohibit the return of an injured player to the field. Ataxia is defined as abnormality in a person's balance, stability, or motor coordination or dysfunctional speech.

The relatively few concussions suffered during Super Bowls does not remove the risk of debilitating head injuries from the Super Bowl's list of brand liabilities. The movie *Concussion* was released on Christmas Day 2015, just six weeks before Super Bowl 50 was to be played in Santa Clara, California. In the film, Will Smith portrayed Dr. Bennet Omalu, whose autopsy on four-time Super Bowl champion and Pro Football Hall of Famer Mike Webster in 2002 revealed the condition known as chronic traumatic encephalopathy (CTE). Many of the NFL players who attended a screening of *Concussion* before its release said it was difficult to watch. "This touched my soul," said Keith McCants, who was a linebacker in the NFL from 1990 to 1995. "I watch this movie and I know we were paid to hurt people. We were paid to give concussions. If we knew that we were killing people, I would have never put on the jersey."[11]

Bob Costas, who was NBC's host of *Sunday Night Football*, attended a prerelease screening in late November 2015, and he connected the story of Mike Webster's tragic death at age fifty to NBC's game telecast on December 6, 2015, from Pittsburgh, where Webster had played most of his seventeen-year career. "I thought that the movie would make an impact, and I thought this was a way not only for NBC to acknowledge it, but to get out in front of it," said Costas in an interview four years later. He wrote an essay to deliver at halftime of that game between the Steelers and the Indianapolis Colts, which attributed the suffering of players like Webster to what he described as the "brutality" of the sport. Costas reported that his bosses at NBC Sports told him that they wouldn't change a word of the essay but that he could not present it on air because NBC was in sensitive negotiations with the NFL for the rights to Thursday night games at the time.[12]

NBC did not get "out in front" of the story in the way Costas had hoped, but Americans in large numbers did see the NFL portrayed as insensitive to the health risks faced by its players and dismissive of Dr. Omalu's findings. The movie had box office receipts of $10.5 million in its opening weekend and $34.5 million for its total domestic theatrical run. The danger of head injuries was underscored in Super Bowl 50 a month and a half after the film's release, when an audience of just under 112 million viewers per minute saw two players suffer concussions in the third quarter. Carolina Panthers wide receiver Corey "Philly" Brown, who was twenty-four, and the Denver Broncos twenty-three-year-old linebacker Shaquil Barrett both were taken from the field and did not return to play. Then in July 2017, the *Journal of the American Medical Association* published the results of research done by the University of Boston School of Medicine on the donated brains of 111 former NFL players. Evidence of CTE was found in 110 of the samples.[13]

The cumulative effect on public opinion was predictable. A poll of one thousand football fans during the summer of 2017 by the University of Massachusetts at Lowell and the *Washington Post* found that 77 percent of those questioned thought head injuries leading to long-term health issues in the sport were "a major problem." Only 15 percent said it was a "minor" problem, and 6 percent said it was not a problem at all.[14]

"If you have the belief among the fans that somehow players end up worse from playing this game," said DeMaurice Smith, who was executive director of the NFLPA, "to me that is a very distinct and significant threat down the road."

After initially discounting Dr. Omalu's findings in 2002 and downplaying the long-term health risks from head injuries in professional football for many years to follow, the NFL began its Game Day Concussion Diagnosis and Management Protocol in 2011, reviewing and updating the policy annually. In 2016, the NFL and NFL Players Association established the Field Surface Safety & Performance Committee to perform research and advise on injury prevention, improve testing methods, and adopt tools and techniques to evaluate field surface performance and playability. The league has made several rule changes to make the game safer by changing kickoff returns, mandating the use of helmets with advanced safety features, banning the lowering of the helmet to initiate contact, and eliminating blind-side blocks.

The NFL's safety efforts and the more than $100 million invested by the league in research have not eliminated concussions suffered in practice or on the field, but they have helped to blunt some of the criticism. In his letter announcing the launch of "Play Smart, Play Safe" program in September 2016, Commissioner Roger Goodell said, "Our game, of course, is a contact sport. Fans love to see the action on the field, including the big hits. While we can never completely eliminate the risk of injury, we are always striving to make the game safer—for our professional athletes down to young athletes first learning how to play."[15] The parents of young athletes, however, do not appear to have been convinced, and that could represent a long-term threat to the popularity of professional football. An NBC News/*Wall Street Journal* poll released on the Friday before Super Bowl LII in February 2018 showed that 46 percent of parents with a child in the home would encourage their children to play sports other than football, primarily due to their concerns about concussions.[16] That represents an increase of 9 percent of parents who had the same concerns just four years earlier.

In the fall of 2009, the National Federation of High School Associations reported that a total of 1,109,278 boys were playing eleven-man football for their high school teams. Ten seasons later, that number had declined by 9.3 percent, down to 1,006,013 players. The problem that this decline represents to the NFL is not one of filling their rosters in the years to come. There will always be individuals willing to risk their bodies (and brains) in exchange for the reward of multimillion dollar contracts. The threat is to the fan base, which may begin to shrink because one of the primary drivers of sports fandom is the experience of playing the sport as a child. The fewer players participating in a sport now, the fewer fans it is likely to have in the future. That would absolutely fall on the "liability" side of the ledger.

Points off for Bad Behavior

Whenever an NFL player is arrested, especially if the charge is domestic violence, the NFL is subjected to criticism for promoting a sport that rewards powerfully built young men for pursuing and colliding with other human beings. These arrests can tarnish the NFL shield by association because they naturally generate far more public attention than when similar charges are leveled against suspects without the celebrity status of NFL players. *USA Today* began a database of NFL player arrests in January 2000. For the twenty years from 2000 through 2019 inclusive, the database lists 953 arrests for a variety of charges ranging from disorderly conduct and reckless driving to five players arrested for manslaughter and three for murder. That sounds like a lot of crime, but the rate of arrests for NFL players is about half the national average for men in the twenty-one- to thirty-nine-year-old age group. Each year there are approximately sixteen hundred active players on NFL opening day rosters. The number of arrests each year is approximately 1.5 percent of the total NFL player cohort. For the US population, the arrest rate for men in their age bracket is slightly more than 3 percent. To its credit, the NFL has never sought to diminish the relevance of its player arrests by using figures showing that crime among its players is far less prevalent than in the general population.

One of those three arrests for murder by players has cast a shadow for twenty years. On January 30, 2000, the St. Louis Rams defeated the Tennessee Titans 23–16 in Super Bowl XXXIV at the Georgia Dome.

Baltimore Ravens All-Pro middle linebacker Ray Lewis was in Atlanta for the game, and in the early morning hours following the Super Bowl, he was arrested outside a nightclub in the city's Buckhead district and charged with murder in the stabbing deaths of two men. Lewis, who was then twenty-four years old, spent two weeks in jail. Five months later, he pleaded guilty to a reduced charge of obstruction of justice for statements he had made to his two fellow defendants at the scene to keep their mouths shut and for incomplete statements made to police. Lewis was sentenced to one year of probation, and the murder remains unsolved.

After Ray Lewis entered his plea in an Atlanta courtroom on June 5, 2000, NFL spokesman Joe Browne said: "The serious charges were dropped, and he was entirely cleared of those charges." Browne concluded by saying, "We are going to continue to work as hard as we can to see that National Football League players will not be involved in these tough and tragic situations."[17] The NFL fined Lewis $250,000, but he was not suspended by then-Commissioner Paul Tagliabue.

Ray Lewis played thirteen more seasons for the Ravens, retiring after the 2012 campaign. He was inducted into the Pro Football Hall of Fame in the summer of 2018, but the unanswered questions about what happened that night after the Super Bowl in Atlanta have, for some people, tainted his legacy. Even though the incident is in the receding past, the NFL can never be happy to see the words "Super Bowl" and "murder" in the same sentence. That is not a positive association.

The crime that proved to be the NFL's greatest liability in the past two decades was not a murder, but the assault by Baltimore Ravens running back Ray Rice on his fiancée Janay Palmer in an Atlantic City, New Jersey, casino elevator in February 2014. Rice played six seasons for the Baltimore Ravens and won a Super Bowl ring in 2013 when the Ravens defeated the San Francisco 49ers in Super Bowl XLVII. Rice was indicted on charges of aggravated assault at the end of March 2014, on the day before he and Palmer were married. Commissioner Roger Goodell announced four months later that Rice would be punished with a two-game suspension. But that was before a video surfaced from inside the casino elevator showing the ferocious punch that sent Janay Palmer to the floor and Ray Rice subsequently dragging her unconscious body into the corridor. During its investigation, the NFL said that its request to see any video in the possession of law enforcement agencies had been denied. On the day that the video was shown nationwide on *TMZ*—September 8, 2014—the Ravens terminated Rice's contract and the NFL announced that it would suspend him indefinitely. But in the media maelstrom that followed, the NFL was made to appear as if it had initially been satisfied with giving Rice a two-game "slap on the hand" and that it was willing to tolerate domestic abuse by its stars. Cries went up from many quarters demanding Goodell's resignation.

The commissioner's response was not to resign, but to admit that the league had made mistakes and to resolve that "now I will get it right and do whatever is necessary to accomplish that." At a news conference on September 19, 2014, he told reporters, "At our best the NFL sets an example that makes a positive difference. Unfortunately, over the past several weeks we've seen all too much of the NFL doing wrong. That starts with me." The commissioner announced that former FBI director Robert Mueller had been hired to lead an investigation of league policies and procedures and would have "full cooperation and access." Goodell pledged that any shortcomings uncovered by Mueller would "lead to swift action. The same mistakes can never be repeated."

He said that the NFL would provide funding for the National Domestic Violence Hotline and the National Sexual Violence Resource Center. The commissioner said that there would be swifter and stricter discipline for players who behave unacceptably, citing domestic abuse and violations including child abuse, illegal use of firearms, drugs, and alcohol. And he promised more comprehensive training for players and league personnel on the issues involved.

Robert Mueller's report in January 2015 recommended more training and better supervision for members of the league office charged with investigating such issues, as well as more thorough "investigative guidelines and standards." Mueller said the NFL needed policies that required information sharing between the league and its thirty-two clubs during investigations and that the NFL's security department should be expanded to include a specialized team for domestic violence issues and sexual assault cases.

Ray Rice last carried the ball in an NFL game in 2013. As that memory fades, the NFL would much prefer Americans to remember instead its strong response to problems and its willingness to admit mistakes and make changes that will have a positive impact and align the league with partners committed to fighting society's ills. If more people come to see the NFL shield as protection for victims and not as a defensive barrier behind which predators can hide, the brand will be able to weather whatever storms may be over the horizon.

In his book *Blink: The Power of Thinking without Thinking*, Malcolm Gladwell presents research showing how people rapidly draw conclusions based upon relatively little information. "All our senses, memories, expertise and imagination combine to form the subjective image we have of any brand," he wrote.[18] The impressions that the NFL wants its fans to associate with the brand and the Super Bowl are wrapped up in the "American optimism on full display" that the league envisioned for its second fifty years. It is optimistic that its many efforts will make a "positive difference," among them: (1) the NFL's continuing commitment to improving the communities that are home to its teams and to Super Bowls; (2) the millions of dollars spent building a better, safer game; (3) its advocacy for social justice and human rights and against the oppression of minorities; (4) the fight against domestic abuse; (5) the league's health and nutrition initiatives to benefit America's youth; and (6) providing the best entertainment to every fan who attends a game, whether it be at a spectacular, innovative new stadium, a proud, historic building steeped in tradition, or any other location on any media platform.

Depending upon its effectiveness in the fulfillment of these goals and its ability to keep the public focused on the positive side of the ledger and the progress being made, the NFL will have years in which its brand's assets outshine the liabilities. However, it is sure to experience times ahead when the liabilities threaten to undermine the league's optimism. The decisive factor for the security and enhancement of both the NFL and the Super Bowl brands will be the continued interest and support of millions of people who care about their teams (regional and fantasy), who get excited about new draft picks and new games (at the stadium or on their mobile devices), and who look forward to watching or attending the next "big game."

CHAPTER 9

The King of the Advertising Jungle

IN THE JUNGLE THAT IS ADVERTISING IN THE UNITED STATES, THE Super Bowl is king. It provides the largest audience, charges the highest prices for commercials, and generates more revenue than any other event or single entertainment vehicle on the calendar, year after year. And the Super Bowl is unique in that it is the only program that millions of people say they watch just to see the commercials. This surely adds luster to the Super Bowl's crown.

More Viewers Mean More Money
The numbers are astounding and on the rise. For Super Bowl LVIII, CBS sold an estimated $600 million worth of in-game advertising. When you add $90 million more for the ads that ran during pregame and postgame programming, February 11, 2024, was a day worth more than half a billion dollars for CBS. That $690 million haul was equal to 30 percent of the network's total annual rights fee of $2.1 billion. The rights paid for by CBS to the NFL cover the network's eighteen-week Sunday afternoon package and include a Super Bowl every fourth year in rotation with FOX, NBC, and ESPN/ABC.

During the ten years from 2013 to 2023, the price for a single thirty-second commercial in the Super Bowl increased from $3.8 million to $7 million, a jump of 84 percent. Inflation in the United States during the same ten years was 28 percent, according to the federal consumer price index. The price of a Super Bowl commercial nearly doubled in that decade, but the total number of television viewers reached by that advertising message in 2023 showed an increase of only 3.2 percent over 2013, from 111.5 million viewers per minute to 115.1 million people ten years later. The conclusion that can be drawn is that the commercial "real estate" in the Super Bowl is now more valuable to advertisers than it has ever been.

The Super Bowl was not the king of the advertising jungle in its early years. It was an extra playoff game added to the end of the NFL year. Advertisers treated it almost as if it were just that: one more game that gave them the opportunity to reach football fans. Commercials in the first several Super Bowls were the same ads from the same sponsors that had run during regular season games and other entertainment programming the previous fall. Granted, the number of people who tuned in to watch the Super Bowl was greater than for games during the season, but the event had not separated nor distinguished itself as a vehicle with far greater potential and opportunity for advertising. For example, the famous commercial in which a young fan offers his Coke to an exhausted Pittsburgh Steelers defensive tackle "Mean Joe" Greene is widely considered to be one of the best Super Bowl spots of all time, because that is where it gained its greatest exposure. But the ad actually launched in October 1979, and it aired several times before appearing in the Super Bowl XIV telecast of January 20, 1980. To Coke's added advantage, Greene played in that game, which the Steelers won 31–19 over the Los Angeles Rams. "Mean Joe" was named All-Pro in ten of his thirteen seasons and was inducted into the Pro Football Hall of Fame in 1987. Companies like Coke were not creating new campaigns for the Super Bowl. Instead, it ran the same ads that it had been using during the fall but paid a higher price per commercial based on the larger audience numbers.

The Birth of "the Super Bowl Commercial"
That all began to change after Super Bowl XVIII in 1984. During the third quarter of that game in which the Los Angeles Raiders were thumping the Washington Redskins, Apple ran a one-minute commercial that had never been seen before. It used themes from George Orwell's dystopian novel *1984*, first published in 1949, to introduce Apple's new line of Macintosh computers. The book had envisioned a future in which

an omnipotent "Big Brother" sought to control the minds and behavior of the masses. Conceived by the creative team at the Chiat/Day agency and directed by Ridley Scott, whose breakthrough success was the film *Alien* in 1979, the sixty-second short film offered the Macintosh as new technology that could be used to expand freedom, not surrender to control. It closes with the tagline, "On January 24, Apple Computer will introduce Macintosh. And you'll see why 1984 won't be like '1984.'" The first Macintosh computers went on sale Tuesday, January 24, 1984, two days after the Super Bowl telecast.

Apple's ad account manager at the time, Fred Goldberg, said, "It was the first time that anybody did something so outrageous on the Super Bowl." In an interview with *Business Insider*, Goldberg said, "I didn't immediately know it was going to be what it was, but it sure was a really great way to introduce the product and get attention." That it was. Apple sold $155 million worth of Macintosh computers within three months after the Super Bowl in 1984. The only time that Apple paid to air the one-minute "1984" spot was during the game, but it generated so much popular interest that it was shown repeatedly on news and talk shows. Apple estimated they reaped an additional $150 million worth of free advertising from this additional exposure.[1]

It didn't have to air more than once to show other advertisers the power of the Super Bowl as a launchpad for new products and campaigns. The value of putting an advertising message in front of a huge audience, many of whom were now going to pay closer attention to the commercials, was not lost on the NFL's television partners. The Super Bowl telecast in January 1984 reached an average of 77,620,000 people per minute on CBS, a 50 percent larger audience than the game had ten years earlier in 1974. That audience had broadened demographically, making it more attractive to advertisers who wanted to sell their products and services to everyone regardless of their age, gender, ethnic background, level of education, or income. When Super Bowl XIX rolled around the following year, the memory of the "1984" Apple ad created anticipation for viewers about what might come next, not necessarily on the field, but during commercial breaks.

Apple paid CBS $525,000 for the sixty seconds of advertising time in Super Bowl XLVIII. The asking price for a standard thirty-second primetime commercial that year was $368,000. The following year, 1985, Super Bowl XIX was the first to be aired by ABC as part of the network's new rights contract for *NFL Monday Night Football*. The size of the audience in 1985 increased by 10 percent, jumping from 77,620,000 in 1984 to an average of 85,530,000 viewers per minute. But ABC raised the price for a thirty-second spot by 42.5 percent to $525,000. That was a steep price hike, but with the perspective of history it appears miniscule.[2]

Prices Climb Skyward

To approach the rates now being charged for thirty-second Super Bowl commercials, you would have to multiply the 1985 rate of $525,000 by thirteen, an increase of 1,300 percent. The standard by which television advertising is sold is "cost per thousand," which is abbreviated CPM, the "*M*" standing for the Latin "*mille*," the Roman numeral for one thousand. A company such as McDonald's or Ford, which bought a thirty-second spot in Super Bowl XIX, reached one thousand viewers for $6.14. That was slightly cheaper than the average CPM of $6.52 for all other television programming in primetime Monday through Sunday in 1985.

Ten years later, the asking price for a Super Bowl spot in January 1995 broke the $1 million mark. ABC charged $1,150,000 for a thirty-second spot during Super Bowl XXIX, which was seen by 83,420,000 viewers. The cost per thousand had more than doubled in a decade to $13.78, whereas the average CPM for primetime television stayed below $10. In only five years, the million-dollar commercial became the $2 million commercial. Since 2000, the going price for thirty-second television spots during the Super Bowl has steadily climbed from $2.1 million to $7 million in 2024. The prices for Super Bowl commercial slots each year are never "flat rates."[3] Advertisers who buy more than one ad during the game get a volume discount, and ad placement—when the ads run during the telecast—also affects the price. A commercial during the first quarter is always more expensive than one scheduled for the fourth quarter, because the score is almost always close in the early stages of the game, but if it's a blowout by the fourth quarter, the number of viewers declines.

The first and last ads in each commercial break cost a bit more than the commercials that are sandwiched in between during each "pod."

Advertisers that buy several months in advance also get a price break, whereas a company that waits until two weeks before the game, when the two teams have been determined, pay "full retail." One additional wrinkle: the network televising the Super Bowl during any particular year may choose to "bundle" the commercials it sells with ads in other programming. NBC, for example, has stipulated in the past that its Super Bowl advertisers also buy time in their Olympic telecasts if they occur in the same calendar year. With so many variations in the pricing scale, it is virtually impossible to determine an exact figure that a specific advertiser paid for its spots, and most purchase agreements include a nondisclosure clause.

During the twenty years from 2000 to 2020, the price for a Super Bowl ad more than doubled, but the total audience grew by only 15 percent over that same twenty-year span. The increased prices have not affected demand. Virtually every year, the network airing the game reports that its inventory of Super Bowl ads is sold out several weeks before the day of the event. The buying decisions made by national advertisers obviously take more factors into consideration than the simple math of dividing cost per commercial by the number of viewers.

The Most Valuable Advertising Real Estate

The "real estate" in the Super Bowl and the viewers watching it are clearly more valuable than for any other sports property. As a point of reference, advertisers can reach a thousand viewers in a regular season NFL game for about half the price of reaching the same number in the Super Bowl. "Buying a Super Bowl ad doesn't simply reach the largest audience in media," said Digital Content Next CEO Jason Kint in an interview with *Bleacher Report*. "It sends an economic signal to the audience/public that your company has worth, value and products so strong that you can buy a Super Bowl ad for them. The latter is key to brand advertising."[4]

The total of all national advertising "real estate" in a Super Bowl is approximately fifty-one minutes, plus another seven minutes, which is allotted to the network's local stations who then get to charge their highest ad rates of the year to the car dealers, pizza restaurants, and other businesses that want to reach the largest possible number of people in their regions. In a game telecast that runs an average of three and a half hours, commercial breaks make up at least 25 percent of the total content. The total advertising content will vary depending upon how much time the broadcasting network and the NFL decide to set aside for promotion of their own shows and products.

When every thirty seconds can bring in $6 to $7 million, *not* selling every second and collecting the maximum advertising revenue is a brave decision by a network. But the networks and the NFL realize how valuable it is to reach such a huge audience with promotions. In 2018, for example, NBC sold only thirty-nine minutes and forty seconds to national advertisers so that it could use nine minutes and forty seconds to promote NBC programming, most of it the Winter Olympic Games, which began in South Korea the following week. CBS used more than nine minutes to promote its upcoming shows in Super Bowl LIII in 2019. With thirty-second spots selling for upward of $5 million then, those nine-plus minutes could have commanded an extra $90 million for NBC or CBS for their respective Super Bowl telecasts. FOX, however, did increase its gross revenue from Super Bowl LIV in 2020 by using only six minutes and twenty-five seconds for promotion and selling the remaining time. The amount of time in Super Bowl commercial breaks that the NFL reserves for its own league messages has held steady at about two minutes for several years.

The primary objective for advertisers across all media is to increase awareness of their product or service among the largest possible percentage of a strategically selected target audience. For example, the target audience for soft drinks is a different group of people than for champagne; the set of potential buyers for lower-priced economy cars does not often overlap with people older than fifty who tend to be interested in buying luxury cars. The maker of each product needs data on who is buying that item at what time of the year. They then position their commercial messages in the shows that their target demographics watch and via the media they use during the months in which the intent to purchase is highest.

Companies also want to instill a favorable disposition toward their product that distinguishes it from other options in the market. A person who is familiar with a product and sees it in a favorable light is predisposed to consider that product and then develop an intent to purchase. Advertisers can cultivate greater awareness, favorability, and purchase intent by increasing the reach of their commercial message and the frequency with which it is delivered. The chances are very low that someone who sees or hears a message only once or infrequently will become a buyer.

Advertising in live sports programming, on television or online, offers advantages that can make it more effective and more valuable than advertising in other forms of entertainment or content. More than 90 percent of sports is watched live. It is not often recorded for playback after the fact because as soon as the result of the competition is known there's no suspense and therefore far less interest in watching what happened. That means that the commercials and sponsored elements in sports programming are far more likely to be seen by viewers, not fast-forwarded through or skipped over during playback. Another advantage of advertising in sports content is that each sport, team, or event has a predictable core audience. A certain percentage of fans who follow the Boston Red Sox, Chicago Bears, or any sports team will watch their games whenever they are broadcast, regardless of where the team is in the standings or playoff race. When demographic data for these people are collected, advertisers can match them up with the products they routinely buy.

Another important factor in the sports advertising equation is "positive image transfer." By advertising in NFL games, the makers of pickup trucks want viewers to connect the power, stamina, toughness, and durability they see on the football field with the same qualities of the advertised trucks. Advertisers who sponsor golf or tennis events want to connect their products with the precision and the luxury lifestyle associated with those sports. Sponsors who team up with celebrity athletes hope that the positive image projected by successful and personable stars will also shine on the product they are endorsing, increasing its favorability.

Its unique advertising advantages put the Super Bowl in a class by itself. A company that buys an ad in the Super Bowl connects its brand with the number-one television and entertainment property in America. Its presence in the Super Bowl helps elevate that company and its product to the top tier in the public's collective cognition. A company does not have to be number one in its field to be considered elite if it successfully projects that image as a brand leader. "It's a premier event, and McDonald's should be there," said R. G. Starmann, a former senior vice president at McDonald's. In an interview with the *New York Times* during his tenure at the fast-food giant, he said, "The millions of people who watch are all McDonald's customers. As long as the Super Bowl fits with what we're trying to do, it will be part of our plan."[5]

Who's Watching?

Who are those millions of people watching the Super Bowl that advertisers are eager to reach? Research by the Nielsen Company shows that the average age of Super Bowl viewers is forty-seven, which is younger by three years than during the regular season. The "big game" is the highest rated television show of the year in *every* age bracket, including teens. In an era in which viewership has been splintered across multiple platforms with so many entertainment choices that appeal to narrow segments of society, the Super Bowl stands alone as the last bastion of what was once "traditional" television. Those were the days when most homes had only three or four channels to choose from, before cable boxes and the proliferation of subscription video services. On average, 40 to 45 percent of all households in America are watching on Super Bowl Sunday, which represents two-thirds or more of all television viewing during the game hours, despite the hundreds of other options available.

This massive audience has become as diverse as America itself. During the regular season, the majority of NFL television-viewing audiences are male, but Nielsen reports for the Super Bowl the gender split among viewers is regularly 51 to 53 percent male and 47 to 49 percent female. That represents a trend toward gender equality that has occurred in the early years of the twenty-first century. In 2009, Super Bowl viewers were 61 percent male and only 39 percent female. The audience also closely reflects the diverse ethnic composition of the US population. The US Census Bureau reports that America is 76.9 percent white/non-Hispanic, and the most recent Nielsen surveys show that this group accounts for 74 percent of the Super Bowl viewing audience. The portion of viewers that is African American is 11.2 percent, roughly equivalent to the percentage of Blacks in the general population, which stands at 13.3 percent. The same holds true for Asian Americans, who represent 5.7 percent of the population and 4.4 percent of the viewing audience. Persons of Hispanic/LatinX origin make up 17.8 percent of the population, but significantly fewer are Super Bowl viewers. Only 9.2 percent of the annual TV audience is Hispanic.[6]

The median income of adult viewers watching a Super Bowl is $77,000 per year, which is about $4,000 more than the income average for regular season NFL fans. Interestingly, the larger the household income, the larger the percentage of viewers in those homes. The Nielsen Company reports that more than 73 percent of Americans living in households in which the annual income is more than $500,000 are watching the Super Bowl. That percentage gradually declines as annual income declines: from a 61.7 percent rating in homes making $250,000 to $500,000, to a 54.4 percent rating in homes in which incomes range between $75,000 and $100,000, down to only 30.5 percent of homes that report incomes of less than $10,000 per year. The skew toward a higher income audience for the Super Bowl helps explain why luxury brands buy commercial time there and not in other sports programming.

The Perfect Stage for Premieres

The Super Bowl is the perfect platform upon which to introduce a new product to a mass audience or to debut a new campaign for an existing product. If it has never been seen nationwide before, the new look will attract the attention of millions of potential buyers. The key here however is the "mass audience." For products such as automobiles, which appeal to a broad spectrum of people, nothing compares to the Super Bowl. The auto industry is regularly the largest market category for Super Bowl advertising, ranging from three to four automakers to as many as nine different makes advertised in one telecast. Technology companies, telecommunications providers, and video streaming services are constantly introducing new products for mass consumption, so the mass audience of the Super Bowl is perfect for them. However, a product or service that appeals to only a narrow sector of the American public likely would be better served and save money by advertising in specific programming that reaches a far smaller number of viewers but a greater proportion in its target market.

The most important factor that separates the Super Bowl from all other advertising vehicles is the dramatic increase in reach that it delivers via the internet and social media. Companies can attract millions of people to watch "sneak previews" of their new commercials by posting them to multiple sites in the weeks leading up to the big game. And in the two to three days after the game, millions more want to see replays of their favorites and find out which ads were judged to be the best by various polls, chief among them the *USA Today* Ad Meter, introduced in 1989.

In the days before and after Super Bowl LVII in 2023, the Booking.com commercial featuring Melissa McCarthy garnered 128 million online views, for which the company paid zero dollars. That's more views than the spot received during FOX's telecast of the game. An average of 115 million viewers per minute watched the game. The online views more than doubled Booking.com's reach to 233 million people. As a result, the $58.09 the company paid to reach one thousand viewers was slashed by more than half to $25.75. Adding the online reach to the massive television audience makes buying a Super Bowl ad a bargain, even if the price tag is $6 to $7 million dollars per unit.

Audience surveys report that a sizable percentage of viewers prefer Super Bowl commercials that feature recognizable celebrities like Melissa McCarthy. Bryan Buckley, who has directed more than seventy Super Bowl ads, says, "Casting is the most important thing in a Super Bowl commercial. It's number one." Buckley directed the memorable Snickers commercial in 2010 that featured then-eighty-seven-year-old actress Betty White getting muddied in a pickup football game. Marketable celebrities, entertainment value, and humor all factor into how well people like an ad. And if they like the commercial, there is a greater likelihood that they will remember it, which increases brand awareness and makes potential buyers feel good about the brand. Buckley says it is "essential" for advertisers to know their audience and its diversity and for the creative team to "nail the story" and connect with the entire audience.[7]

USA Today recognized that Super Bowl commercials had become a cultural phenomenon back in 1989, when the newspaper started its annual Ad Meter survey. Thousands of viewers are asked to rate each of the commercials they see during the telecast. In 1989, the ad that got the most points featured Dana Carvey and Jon Lovitz from *Saturday Night Live* in a spot for American Express. The Super Bowl commercial that fans voted their favorite over the first thirty years of the Ad Meter poll was Budweiser's "Puppy Love" from 2014. Created by the Anomaly advertising agency, the spot tells the story of a golden Labrador puppy's friendship with a Clydesdale on an idyllic American ranch. With the lyrics and music of Passenger's "Let Her Go" in the background, the puppy and the massive horse end up bringing their owners together. "The genesis of the spot was observing a genuinely friendly [exchange] between a Clydesdale and a puppy on one of our Clydesdale breeding ranches," Budweiser Vice President Brian Perkins told *USA Today* in 2014.[8]

Nothing Beats Exclusivity

The ultimate goal of any advertiser, especially those spending millions of dollars on Super Bowl ads, is to prompt people to take action: visit the company on social media, go to its website, and then buy the product. If sales don't increase along with brand awareness and favorability, the campaign is a failure. A study by the Stanford Graduate School of Business of six Super Bowls and the advertising impact in fifty-five cities found that there was one major difference maker in generating sales: exclusivity. If a brand were the only advertiser in its category, the Super Bowl would help it generate increased sales volume per household and total revenue. But when competitors' ads were also seen in the telecast, those gains diminished. For thirty-three years beginning in 1988, Budweiser (now AB InBev) paid extra to be the only brewer running ads in the Super Bowl. The Stanford study found that in the short run after a Super Bowl, Budweiser increased its sales by an average 15.75 percent per household over its competition. "Budweiser's long-standing association with the

Super Bowl is paying off during this peak sales period," said the researchers. They calculated that Budweiser received a 172 percent return on its advertising investment.[9] In Super Bowl LIV, AB InBev ran ads for four of its brands: Budweiser, Bud Light, Michelob Ultra, and Michelob Ultra Pure Gold. With the bill for four commercials in the $20 million range, plus the undisclosed premium paid for exclusivity that kept its competitors out of the Super Bowl, a 172 percent return on investment amounts to an ocean of beer.

After Super Bowl LVI in 2022, AB InBev decided not to renew its exclusivity agreement and instead to use those extra dollars to spread its marketing across different platforms. AB Vice President for Consumer Connections Spencer Gordon said, "with today's plethora of screens and platforms, the notion of Super Bowl advertising exclusivity isn't as defined as it was in '89."[10]

The exclusivity agreement began in 1989, when Anheuser-Busch pioneered a new form of customized Super Bowl advertising. To maximize its effectiveness, Anheuser-Busch negotiated with the NFL and that year's broadcaster, NBC, to become the first-ever exclusive beer sponsor for the Super Bowl. Its "Bud Bowl" campaign was a series of sequential thirty-second commercials that featured an animated stop-action gridiron matchup between "Bud" and "Bud Light" bottles wearing helmets and running plays in a stadium filled with cheering beer cans and bottles. The action in each of the five individual episodes was tailored to coincide with its placement in the game, beginning with NBC's team of Bob Costas and analyst Paul Maguire doing the play-by-play for the opening kickoff of "Bud Bowl I." Exclusivity prevented any other beers from being advertised between the Bud Bowl episodes, so fans could focus on the storyline of the beer-versus-beer contest, right along with the stories playing out during the live contest between the San Francisco 49ers and the Cincinnati Bengals at Joe Robbie Stadium in Miami.

Perhaps the most innovative part of the campaign was a commercial that aired in the days leading up to Super Bowl XXIII that invited viewers to watch the game in order to see the Budweiser commercials. When the spot began, "Football fans get ready for the battle of the century," it wasn't directing attention to the matchup between the NFC and AFC champions, but instead to the clash between "unbeaten Budweiser" and "undefeated Bud Light." To guarantee a large audience, this promotional spot also offered viewers who watched Bud Bowl I a chance to win $100,000. It told fans to "pick up your official scorecard" at any store selling Anheuser-Busch products and "use it to follow the action. You could win big." The call to action at the end of the spot was to "Get ready, get set. On January 22nd Bud Bowl I. This time it's for real."[11]

This was several years before Super Bowl commercials were available for "sneak peaks" on the internet, but Anheuser-Busch and its ad agency team at St. Louis–based D'Arcy Masius Benton & Bowles had designed a campaign that created "buzz" about what new entertainment viewers would see during the game's commercial breaks. Their vision laid the groundwork for what we now take for granted: promotional hype surrounding the online premieres of new Super Bowl ads from several advertisers each year.

The concept of beer bottles playing the role of football players was developed by Bill Oakley, creative director at the DMB&B ad agency. In an interview with *Sports Illustrated*, he explained how he had "camped out in his garage and constructed a miniature football stadium constructed out of plywood and Astroturf remnants."[12] Oakley said he remembered putting a quarter into gumball machines as a kid to buy tiny plastic football helmets, so he bought dozens of little helmets in red and silver and jimmied them onto bottles of Bud and Bud Light.

Oakley and the DMB&B creative team brought their pitch— and the plywood stadium from his garage—to a meeting with the Anheuser-Busch executives, which included Chairman August Busch III, a man with a reputation as one of the toughest bosses to please in America. As Oakley and his three colleagues played out their make-believe gridiron scenario in front of Busch, he remembered seeing a smile slowly creep across Busch's face. The agency got the green light and a $3 million budget to turn their rinky-dink idea into a series of Bud Bowl spots that would unspool as a game-within-a-game throughout the entire Super Bowl XXIII telecast.

The first Bud Bowl episode takes place just before the opening kickoff as we hear a Bud "player" say, "Let's turn out their light," to which his

Bud Light opponent says, "Let's kick some Bud." Costas tells the viewers, "We've got a real 'brew-ha-ha' going on here." The next commercial in the sequence ends with the score "Bud Light 7, Budweiser 3," and the third one takes the action to halftime. Two more episodes aired during the second half of Super Bowl XXIII, the first as action closed out the third quarter of Bud Bowl, with Bud Light now leading 21–17. The last of the five commercials has placekicker "Budski" advancing onto the artificial turf with two seconds left to hit the field goal that gives the Budweiser team a triumphant 27–24 victory. In the last scene, a helmeted Bud Light bottle leans into the camera and says, "Wait 'til next year!"

The Bud Bowl returned in 1990, and it continued for eight Super Bowl telecasts, more than enough time for Anheuser-Busch to accomplish the goal of dethroning Miller Lite as the number-one seller in the light beer category. Miller had a stranglehold on the market, having stood virtually alone since its introduction in 1973. Bud Light was launched in 1982, but it still trailed Miller Lite in sales seven years later when Bud Bowl debuted. Bud Light soared past Miller Lite in 1994 shortly after Bud Bowl VI, and it has never looked back, surpassing its old gridiron rival Budweiser as well. Bud Bowl showed what was possible in a mass media sports event if you monopolized the advertising "playing field" in your product category and then tailored a campaign to marry the commercial content with the live game action itself.

Not All Buyers Are Welcome

What started with Bud Bowl I has morphed over the decades into several new iterations of advertising hybrids that strive to blur the lines between the sport and its commercials, overlapping and integrating the content to increase the effectiveness of its delivery to the intended audience. Viewers of sports content regularly see sponsor logos and messages on graphics that are superimposed over game venues and action, lineups or replays that are sponsored, commercials as short as six seconds each that are shown in a video box alongside another box that continues to show live pictures from the site of the contest, and sponsor logos that have been stitched onto players' uniforms and emblazoned on equipment. These hybrid forms of advertising have become common in telecasts of Major

League Baseball, the NBA and WNBA, the NHL, auto racing, and several other sports, but not in the Super Bowl. The NFL commands the highest rights payments from its media partners because of the size of the audience it delivers, so it has been able to resist the trend in other sports toward increased commercialization. The league maintains its prohibition against any commercial messaging superimposed over live game action, keeping the televised product less cluttered and "cleaner" than what is now seen in the coverage of many sports. If its viewing audience were smaller, the NFL might have to make compromises to support increases in rights fees and sponsor revenue.

The NFL also prohibits any advertising in the Super Bowl from a long list of product categories that do not align well with the league's stated goals of upholding the highest standards and projecting positive values that will be widely respected. These include:

- Contraceptives, condoms
- Dietary/nutritional supplements
- Establishments featuring nude/seminude performers
- Firearms, ammunition, weapons
- Gay dating services
- Illegal products/services
- Movies or video games containing objectionable material
- Restorative or "male enhancement" products
- Tobacco products
- Certain restricted pharmaceuticals

Distilled spirits had been a prohibited advertising category until the 2017 regular season and Super Bowl LII in February 2018. The NFL announced prior to that season that it would begin allowing advertisements for distilled spirits, but it placed a limit of only four thirty-second commercials from that category in any single game. And any ad for hard liquor in NFL content had to carry a "prominent social responsibility message" and could not be football themed. Medical cannabis grower

Acreage Holdings had hoped for a similar relaxed policy for Super Bowl LIII with a commercial that used first-person testimonials to extoll the pain-killing power of their product over opioids. "Cannabis has given me my life back," said a patient from Buffalo, New York, who had been taking opioids for fifteen years. The ad ended with a request for viewers to contact their US representatives or senators to "advocate for change now." The ad was rejected despite the fact that marijuana had been legalized for medical use in thirty-three states and the District of Columbia. It was however, still an "illegal product" in seventeen states.

The NFL is wary of "ambush marketing" that seeks to use the massive popularity of the Super Bowl to draw attention to any product that cannot or will not buy time in the program. In January 2010, a gay dating website called ManCrunch pitched a commercial to CBS in which two male fans in football jerseys are seen kissing. When the ad was rejected, the company distributed a news release nationwide, generating almost as many impressions, if not more, than it would have received had the commercial been accepted. "There's a separate cottage industry based on getting your Super Bowl spot banned," said Barbara Lippert, an ad critic for *Adweek*. "You get all the free publicity, and you never have to actually pay the media cost."[13]

One of the non-broadcast ambush marketing cases the NFL dealt with was at Super Bowl XXXVI in New Orleans in 2002. Proctor & Gamble had bought a billboard across from the Superdome that showed a box of its Tide detergent and read, "Because there are more than XXXVI ways to ruin your clothes. Enjoy the Big Game." Proctor & Gamble wasn't an NFL official partner at the time. The league had no power to remove the billboard, so thousands of people attending the game at the Louisiana Superdome made the connection between Tide and the Super Bowl because of the Roman numeral in the ad. Seven years later, P&G did join the ranks of official sponsors for its Gillette, Head & Shoulders, Vicks, Old Spice, Duracell, CoverGirl, Always, and Tide brands, with the detergent designated as the "official fabric care of the NFL."

When the Super Bowl returned to Atlanta in 2019, its official soft drink was faced with a territorial challenge. Pepsi had been an NFL partner since 2002 and had resumed its sponsorship of the Super Bowl halftime show in 2013, but Atlanta had a significant Coca-Cola presence because the beverage maker has been headquartered there since the late nineteenth century. To make sure that both Atlanta residents and visitors would connect Pepsi with the Super Bowl and not Coke, PepsiCo proceeded to blanket the city with more than 350 ads on billboards, the sides of buildings, recycling bins, and even the walls of MARTA train stations. Their messages included: "Pepsi in Atlanta, How Refreshing"; "Hey Atlanta, thanks for hosting. We'll bring the drinks"; and "Look who's in town for Super Bowl LIII."

The marketing director for PepsiCo North America, Greg Lyons, said the promotion was "a big spend for us. We are absolutely leaning in to make sure that we are painting Atlanta blue for the Super Bowl." A Coca-Cola spokesperson responded by telling CNN, which also calls Atlanta home, "As Atlanta's hometown beverage company for over 130 years, we're thrilled to help our city welcome everyone to town for the Big Game, including our friends from Pepsi." Coke delivered its advertising messages to the national television audience by buying an ad from CBS that ran directly before the national anthem of Super Bowl LIII. Coca-Cola has regularly advertised in Super Bowls because the sale of commercials in the telecast is not limited to just NFL official sponsors. And its hometown message was making a $1 million donation to Atlanta's National Center for Civil and Human Rights, which allowed the museum to provide free admission to its exhibits from January 28 through the end of February. Coke versus Pepsi, another standoff.[14]

"Holy Grail" or "King of the Jungle"?

Over the years, many ad executives and writers have referred to the Super Bowl as the "Holy Grail" of advertising to denote its singular nature in the quest to deliver commercial messages that will have the greatest impact on the largest number of people. Comparing the Super Bowl to the most-valued but long-sought Christian relic may no longer be the best analogy. The advertising business has changed dramatically in the years since the "Holy Grail" description was first attached to the Super Bowl. Digital advertising now grosses more dollars per year than television advertising, and audiences have been splintered across so many new video on-demand services, direct-to-consumer platforms, and varied technologies that the business appears to be very much like a jungle. Advertisers are confronted by a growing forest of options that can be confusing as they seek the best routes to reach new and old customers alike. In that "jungle," however, there is one landmark that stands alone, visible to all: the Super Bowl. It is the last living survivor of the species that once was mass media in the United States. In advertising, the Super Bowl is the unquestioned "king of the jungle."

CHAPTER 10

The Media and the Super Bowl

WHEN THE NFL DEBUTED ON TELEVISION IN THE FALL OF 1939, IT WAS simply one of several sports that the early broadcast networks tried out to see how well they might translate to electronic transmission and how many people would buy televisions as a result. The primary business then for each of the networks was the manufacture of radios and televisions. Broadcasting sports and entertainment was meant to stimulate sales of their hardware. During the 1940s and 1950s, the broadcast champion was Major League Baseball. Its two leagues had long been established in the nation's largest cities, its biggest stars were national celebrities, and most Americans identified themselves as baseball fans. But through the ensuing decades, as virtually everyone in the country fell into the habit of watching TV every day, baseball had difficulty competing with professional football as a television sport. "If God was looking to create the perfect programming for TV, it would be the NFL for a variety of reasons," said former NBC Sports President Dick Ebersol. "The obvious: It's spectacular. It's violent in some ways. It has a ballet section to it. It has a brass section to it, with the loud personalities who always seem to come along with almost any game. Then from a practical standpoint, unlike almost all the other major sports in America, it fits into a finite period of time," he said. "It has quarters. It has halves. People can wander out and get a sandwich. It gives every play about a half a minute or more to be treated like a jewel, to be analyzed, to be touched, to be petted. It gives you enough time to breath the atmosphere of the crowd."[1]

A Sport Made for Television

The fact that professional football is so perfectly suited for television has contributed greatly to the growth of the NFL and to its broad popularity. The sport was born in Midwestern cities during the pretelevision era that was dominated by baseball, boxing, and college football, but it came of age after millions of Americans acquired their first TV sets. The decade of the 1950s witnessed the explosion of the medium, taking it from a novelty in 1950, when the US Census Bureau reported that less than 9 percent of homes had TVs, to the live video connection that instantly delivered entertainment, news, and sports to 95 percent of the nation's homes in 1960. In 1953, when television was not yet in half of American homes, the first network to air NFL regular season football games was the DuMont Network on Saturday nights. DuMont owned stations in New York City, Pittsburgh, and Washington, DC, so every game during the season originated from one of those three cities. Ray Scott, who provided play-by-play for CBS at Super Bowl I, II, VI, and VIII, worked for an agency in Pittsburgh that was part of the DuMont package. Scott said that DuMont was delivering the NFL product to so many viewers that then-Commissioner Bert Bell told him, "You know, Scotty, don't ever tell any other owner I said this, but we should probably pay you people."[2] The NFL never did pay a network to televise its games, and the DuMont Network folded in 1956, bringing its football experiment to a close at the end of the 1955 season. Just a few years later, the penetration of television, reaching 95 percent of American homes, was a hugely important factor for Lamar Hunt and his fellow "Foolish Club" owners, when they agreed, months before a single AFL game had been played, to sign a contract with the ABC television network to air games every Sunday beginning in the fall of 1960.

The cover of *Time* magazine on December 21, 1962, which featured Vince Lombardi and the Green Bay Packers, proclaimed pro football "the sport of the '60s." The article described "football, as the pros go at it," as a "game of special brilliance, played by brilliant specialists. . . . So precise is the teamwork that a single mistake by one man can destroy the handiwork of ten. . . . Action piles upon action, thrill upon guaranteed thrill, and all with such a bewildering speed that at the end the fans are literally limp. . . . No other sport offers so much to so many. Boxing's heroes are papier mâché champions, hockey is gang warfare, basketball is for gamblers, and Australia is too far to travel to see a decent tennis match. Even baseball, the sportswriters' 'national pastime,' can be a slow-motion bore." *Time* magazine saw sports history changing, but its writers and editors could not have foreseen how "the sport of the '60s" would conquer the decade.[3]

At the close of the 1950s, professional football was played in only twelve American cities, and not one of them in the Southeast. There were no teams in Florida or Texas, nor a single team based in the Mountain Time Zone. Only one game each season—the NFL championship game—aired nationwide on network television. The NFL's regular season games every autumn weekend were broadcast only on regional television networks. By the end of the 1960s, the number of cities with teams would more than double, with twenty-six teams playing in twenty-five cities (New York had the Giants and the Jets), and regular season games would be nationally televised each week on two networks: CBS and NBC.

The AFL debut in 1960 brought professional football to six cities without NFL franchises: Boston, Buffalo, Dallas, Houston, Denver, and Oakland. When the AFL's Los Angeles Chargers moved to San Diego for the 1961 season, another new city gained a pro football team. Then the AFL expanded to Miami in 1966 and to Cincinnati in 1968.

Prompted by the competition from the new AFL, the NFL began to ride the expansion wave by adding its own Dallas franchise in 1960, primarily to compete with Hunt's Dallas Texans. When Hunt moved his team to Kansas City in 1963 and renamed it the Chiefs, another major market joined the pro football family. The NFL added three more expansion teams in the 1960s: the Minnesota Vikings in 1961, the Atlanta Falcons in 1966, and the New Orleans Saints, who began play in 1967.

National television coverage was a major factor in creating demand for the sport to spread to more cities where games could be watched but that did not yet have franchises. These cities had growing populations, plenty of rich investors, and pride in their communities that fueled a desire to establish teams they could call their own. This expansion from twelve to twenty-six fan bases across the United States, with at least one in every time zone, created a much larger appetite for media coverage and information about those teams and about the two leagues that would merge by the end of the decade. The Super Bowl in its first year, 1967, dethroned the World Series from its perennial top spot in sports television viewership. The first World Series was televised in 1947, but no game in baseball history up to 1967 could boast the fifty-one million viewers who watched Super Bowl I on CBS and NBC combined.

A TV Product Worth Millions

The national television rights fees for professional football grew along with the leagues in the 1960s. After Congress approved the Sports Broadcasting Act of 1961, which exempted national sports broadcasting agreements from federal antitrust laws, the NFL's annual rights payments from CBS increased from approximately $5 million in 1962 to more than $15 million for the 1965 season. The NFL had fourteen franchises in 1965, so the television money was split evenly fourteen ways, with each team's share just more than $1 million per year. The AFL contract with NBC paid the league $7.2 million in 1965, so each of its eight teams collected slightly more than $900,000 per year from that agreement. The arrival of the Super Bowl and the huge earnings potential that it presented would send these numbers skyward.

Rights fees are paid by networks and media distributors to the leagues, which are the owners of the content that will be broadcast. The fees entitle the network/distributor to exclusive rights for broadcasting a set number of games in a specified geographical area, over a defined period of time, at a fixed price. (For example, eighteen games per year for eight years broadcast to the United States and its territories at a price of $2 billion per year.) The rights agreements also provide the networks with promotional and marketing rights so that they can use league marks, titles, stars, and video to promote their broadcasts. This arrangement establishes the network and the league as partners who will both benefit from the success of the NFL and the success of its national (and international) broadcasts. With its rights contract, the network also receives event access and a set number of media credentials per game so that its professional production crews and commentators can do what they need to do to televise each game. Unless negotiated, media rights agreements do not include unlimited usage of highlights from games previously televised, even if the game aired on that network. And despite the high prices, these contracts never include the copyright or ownership of the event or its broadcast. These are always retained by the NFL.

The Super Bowl changed the NFL's media rights picture forever, and the huge fees that it helped generate increased the league's power geometrically. But there were some growing pains. The NFL had less than three months to organize and prepare for its first "AFL versus NFL World Championship Game" on January 15, 1967, so the game at the cavernous Los Angeles Memorial Coliseum was not a sellout. The NFL issued credentials to 338 media representatives, of which approximately thirty to forty each were assigned to CBS and NBC so that their two television production teams could access the stadium and its facilities.

The Recipe for Success: Make the Media Happy

Having served as the public relations director then general manager of the Los Angeles Rams in his years before becoming commissioner of the NFL, Pete Rozelle knew how good media relations could help assure the success of an event or franchise. His strategy was to allocate a $250,000 budget to entertain the members of the press who came to Los Angeles to cover the first AFL–NFL World Championship Game. The league offered press outings to Disneyland and to Santa Anita Racetrack on the Saturday before the game and provided the reporters with free food and an open bar. This conscientious display of hospitality was meant to leave a lasting positive impression on the media, and it worked. Mickey Hershkowitz, the staffer assigned to oversee the media entertainment budget, told Michael MacCambridge in *America's Game* that "Pete said, when the press left the first world championship game, he just wanted to hear them saying, 'Man, this is a lot better than the World Series.'" The strategy worked. Western Union reported that the press covering the first Super Bowl sent reports to their newspapers and wire services "that exceeded the amount filed for the 1966 World Series." Major annual sporting events like the World Series and the Kentucky Derby had the advantage of history and tradition attained over decades, but

Pete Rozelle's goal was for his new championship game to immediately assume its place among that royal company.[4]

Jerry Izenberg covered Super Bowl I in 1967 for the *Newark Star-Ledger*, and he remembered the press contingent in Los Angeles during the week prior to the game as being a fairly small corps of NFL writers. "On the Friday before the game Pete Rozelle held what would become the first of his 'State of the NFL' news conferences," Izenberg told me. "There were only about thirteen guys in the room."[5] Izenberg was surprised that the *New York Times* did not send its lead NFL writer, Dave Anderson, opting instead to assign a West Coast reporter, probably to save money on travel. Without a horde of media to rein in, the NFL had very few restrictions for coverage of the first Super Bowl. "I interviewed players and coaches in their hotel rooms," said Izenberg, who was one of only two reporters to cover the first fifty-three consecutive Super Bowls from 1967 through 2019.

One of Jerry Izenberg's most memorable stories from the first Super Bowl was that of Max McGee, a thirty-four-year-old backup receiver for the Packers who hadn't started a game during the entire 1966 season and had caught only four passes all year long. In their last team meeting the Saturday before the game, Coach Vince Lombardi stressed how important winning Sunday's game would be, so he told the players they had a midnight curfew. Any player violating it would be subject to a $15,000 fine. McGee told Izenberg that when an assistant coach came to his room that night, Max asked him, "Are you gonna do another bed check tonight?" When the coach said "no," McGee knew he could slip out of the hotel and spend the night drinking with two flight attendants he had met. He wasn't worried about playing in the Super Bowl. "I'm a super benchwarmer," he told Izenberg. Max McGee got back to the hotel at 6:30 a.m. that Sunday morning, seriously hung over. During the game, Packers starting receiver Boyd Dowler injured his shoulder in the first quarter. Lombardi replaced him with McGee, who proceeded to score the first touchdown in Super Bowl history on a thirty-seven-yard pass from quarterback Bart Starr. McGee finished the game with seven receptions, two of them for touchdowns, and 138 yards receiving. Packers quarterback Bart Starr was named the game's most valuable player as the Packers beat the Kansas City Chiefs 35–10.[6]

Jerry Izenberg missed his first Super Bowl in February 2020, when he decided not to go to Miami for Super Bowl LIV. Jerry Green of the *Detroit News* was the only journalist who covered fifty-six in a row. He died in 2023 at age 94.

The Audience Loves Change

Several factors helped attract a record number of viewers to watch the Packers play the Chiefs for the championship in 1967: the fact that each league had been nationally televised for several years, curiosity about this first Super Bowl and the merger of what had been two competing leagues and how they would match up, plus the huge promotion done by CBS and NBC to encourage fans to watch on "Super Sunday." When Green Bay returned to the game as the NFL champion in 1968, having soundly defeated the AFL representative the first time out, much of the curiosity was gone, and with it went a sizeable chunk of the TV audience. It fell from fifty-one million to thirty-nine million viewers. The Packers with the same coach, Vince Lombardi, and the same MVP quarterback, Bart Starr, were favored to win, and they did, beating the Oakland Raiders in another lopsided score, 33–14. That made the third edition of the Super Bowl, scheduled for January 1969, highly problematic. The NFL team— this time the Baltimore Colts—was again favored to win by double digits. The AFL champion New York Jets did have a new star at quarterback, Joe Namath, but the same old result was expected: an NFL victory. That kept the television audience well below the standard set by Super Bowl I, coming in at 41.6 million viewers. Had the Colts continued the NFL victory streak rather than losing 16–7, no amount of media promotion could have gotten people interested in tuning in to see what they expected would be the same result.

That's why the AFL victories in Super Bowl III and Super Bowl IV made such a difference for the future prosperity of the league and its new championship structure. On the heels of the Jets upset of the Baltimore Colts in 1969, the Kansas City Chiefs upset the Minnesota Vikings, a team that had just soundly defeated the Cleveland Browns 27–7 in the

NFL championship game and had won twelve of their fourteen regular season games. The Jets and Chiefs represented change, and the one thing over all else that builds audience for the media is change. In sports, that means new stars, new teams, new challenges, new records, upset victories. If the same players on the same team always defeated the same opponents with the same roster, interest would fall to minimal levels. After four Super Bowls had been played, each league could claim two victories, which was a sharp turnaround from the first two games. Change gets people interested, it gets them talking, and that is precisely what the media feeds on. The more people who tune in, the more each network or station can charge for advertising; the subsequent increased profits are the kind of change that media companies love. With more fans taking notice and more money to be made, the NFL and the media saw the makings of a juggernaut.

How to Turn Two Leagues into One

The owners of all twenty-six teams gathered in New Orleans the week following Super Bowl IV. There were two major items on their agenda, the first of which was how to realign the sixteen NFL and ten AFL teams into one league that would play a single league schedule beginning with the 1970 season, according to the timeline laid out in the original merger agreement of June 1966. The first idea had been to assign all sixteen NFL teams to a new "National Football Conference" and the ten AFL teams into an "American Football Conference," but that was soon abandoned due to the obvious imbalance in total teams. The joint committee that had been working out the details of the merger considered several factors, including each team's market size, their stadium seating capacity and ticket prices, team history and rivalries, geography, and the travel time between teams that would play each other regularly within their divisions. The committee came to New Orleans with nine plans, discarding four after preliminary discussions. That left five realignment proposals, none of which won a consensus of support. Commissioner Pete Rozelle decided that the best decision was to draw lots: the committee put the remaining five realignment plans into a cut flower vase in the meeting room and his longtime assistant, Thelma Elkjer, reached in and pulled one out. The plan in Ms. Elkjer's hand that morning of January 17, 1970, decreed the alignment of the new combined league.[7]

The Pittsburgh Steelers, Cleveland Browns, and Baltimore Colts—with considerable urging from Rozelle—had already agreed to move to the AFC. Each of the three teams received $3 million compensation from the league for their "sacrifice." The Steelers and Browns would take their place that fall in the AFC Central division, along with the Cincinnati Bengals and the Houston Oilers (which are now the Tennessee Titans). The Colts would join the Patriots, Bills, Jets, and Dolphins in the AFC East. The table below is the 1970 Conference and Divisional alignment with teams in the order they finished that season.

AFC EAST	AFC CENTRAL	AFC WEST
Baltimore Colts	Cincinnati Bengals	Oakland Raiders
Miami Dolphins	Cleveland Browns	Kansas City Chiefs
New York Jets	Pittsburgh Steelers	San Diego Chargers
Buffalo Bills	Houston Oilers	Denver Broncos
New England Patriots		

NFC EAST	NFC CENTRAL	NFC WEST
Dallas Cowboys	Minnesota Vikings	San Francisco 49ers
New York Giants	Detroit Lions	Los Angeles Rams
St. Louis Cardinals	Green Pay Packers	Atlanta Falcons
Washington Redskins	Chicago Bears	New Orleans Saints

The other major item facing the owners in 1970 was the approval of new media rights deals with CBS and NBC, which would dramatically increase league revenue. These two contracts, along with the agreement reached with ABC the previous year for NFL *Monday Night Football* games to begin in September 1970, represented a milestone never before achieved by any sports league in the United States: NFL games would now be televised on all three major broadcast networks every single season.

The four-year contracts on the table for CBS and NBC called for each of the two networks to televise two Super Bowls, alternating every other year. The estimated figure attached to the Super Bowl was $2.5 million per game, which was the price that CBS had paid for each of its exclusive broadcasts of Super Bowls II and IV and that NBC had paid for its exclusive presentation of Super Bowl III. CBS agreed to pay an additional $18 million per year for rights to televise the NFC regular season and playoff games, and NBC's price for the AFC regular season plus playoffs was $15 million. The price disparity was attributed to the fact that NFC teams were in ten of the top fifteen television markets, the AFC in only seven of the top fifteen. With its telecasts available to a larger audience, CBS could in turn charge more for its advertising. Plus, NFL television ratings during the 1960s had remained higher than the AFL. When the new TV contracts were announced, they made headlines. Combined, CBS and NBC would pay the NFL $35.5 million per year. Add in $8.6 million from ABC for the first season of the new Monday night series, and the NFL's annual television rights revenue hit $44.1 million for the 1970 season, an increase of almost 50 percent over the just-concluded 1969 season.[8]

More Games on TV Means More Viewers for the Super Bowl

Games being shown nationwide on all three major broadcast networks coupled with the runaway success of *Monday Night Football* drove television ratings for the Super Bowl to new heights beginning with Super Bowl VI between the Dallas Cowboys and the Miami Dolphins, which followed the 1971 season. For the first time, Nielsen reported that the total viewing audience on just one network, CBS that year, surpassed the combined two-network audience of Super Bowl I. The average number of viewers per minute for Super Bowl VI was 56.6 million, five million more than the 51.2 million combined who watched Super Bowl I on CBS and NBC. The TV audience every year since has always exceeded that benchmark.

Former NBC Sports President Dick Ebersol, who was an assistant to Roone Arledge at ABC Sports in 1970, said that NFL *Monday Night Football* deserved a lot of credit for this upsurge in popularity: "I believe the single biggest moment in American sports TV was the coming of *Monday Night Football*. It was the coming out party for American sport, because sport had always been something that you just saw on Saturday or Sunday afternoons."[9] *Monday Night Football* became an instant phenomenon, with its entertaining byplay between down-home former Cowboys quarterback Don Meredith and the edgy, opinionated New Yorker Howard Cosell. Arledge said his philosophy was "to make it so damned interesting and exciting that people would stay tuned to it," even if the football game was a blowout or its result had little or no meaning. He had compelling talent in the three-man booth, welcoming celebrity guests from John Lennon to John Wayne, and ABC used new cameras "for all sorts of close shots and reverse angles, and overhead shots, and things that, by and large, people had not done. The result was that *Monday Night* became such an institution that, literally, restaurants couldn't get people to go out to dinner on Monday night. They used to have special nights for women. They would have card games or whatever to attract people," said Arledge. "Everything would stop because people were watching *Monday Night Football*."[10]

Storylines and Dynasties in Primetime

The changes that continued and the stories that developed during the 1970s made NFL football more interesting and more popular, which helped build the Super Bowl into the colossus that it would become in the twenty-first century. The Dallas Cowboys won their first championship after the 1971 season, led by immensely popular quarterback Roger Staubach, who had served in the US Navy after his playing days at Annapolis. There were still 156,800 American servicemen and women stationed in Vietnam that year. The team the Cowboys defeated 24–3 was the Miami Dolphins, which had just completed only their sixth season. The Dolphins returned the following year and did not lose a game in 1972, which focused national attention on a feat never before accomplished in the NFL: an undefeated championship season. For many, it served as a diversion from the bad news that was regularly reported from Vietnam.

The Pittsburgh Steelers franchise, founded in 1933 as the Pirates, had never won a league title. But after being uprooted from the NFL and transferred to the AFC, they became the team of the 1970s, winning four Super Bowls after their 1974, 1975, 1978, and 1979 seasons. From their position as a perennial doormat, the Steelers had reached the top and sustained their success, making them an appealing American story and a major promotional force that helped to continue building the Super Bowl audience.

Four of the ten Super Bowls played during the 1970s were hosted by New Orleans: in 1970, 1972, and 1975 at Tulane Stadium and then in 1978 at the fabulous new Louisiana Superdome. That game, Super Bowl XII between the Dallas Cowboys and the Denver Broncos, would change the course of Super Bowl history: it was the first one played indoors and, more importantly, the first ever in television primetime. Kickoff was at 6:17 p.m. Eastern time. Historically more people watched television on Sunday nights than any other night of the week, and because of the wintry weather over most of the country, more people watch television in January than during any other month. Nighttime pro football had made a sensation beginning in 1970 on ABC, but the Super Bowl had continued as a Sunday afternoon fixture. Sunday afternoons were the customary time slots in which CBS and NBC had televised the Super Bowl in its early years because that's where they had shown all the live regular and postseason games. They knew they could deliver a large, reliable audience without displacing their highly rated Sunday night entertainment programs. But the huge success of *Monday Night Football* turned heads. "There's something about football players at night. The way the stadium lights bounce off their helmets that makes it totally different from the daytime. There's a magical quality to it. There's a dimension that daytime football just doesn't have," said Roone Arledge. "The sense of spectacle with the stadium lights and everything made it just different from other football."[11]

CBS was excited to get a piece of prime-time NFL football in 1978. "There are probably 500,000 people who watch this game who do not watch any other television program all year," said Bob Wussler, then president of CBS Sports, in a piece for the *New York Times* written by Tony

Kornheiser.[12] Almost thirteen million more people tuned in to watch that Cowboys 27–10 victory on Sunday evening January 15, 1978, than had watched the previous year on a Sunday afternoon on NBC. In one year, the Super Bowl television audience had grown by more than 27 percent. There would be no going back. The Super Bowl's future was in primetime.

As the NFL closed the book on the 1970s on January 20, 1980, with the Steelers 31–19 victory over the Los Angeles Rams in Super Bowl XIV, the growth of the Super Bowl into television's most valuable property had proved to be nothing short of stunning. In the decade since Super Bowl V in Miami, the average TV audience for the game had grown by thirty million viewers, and the price of a thirty-second commercial had more than doubled to $222,000. The trajectory was stratospheric, and in the following ten years, the sports media world would change forever.

ESPN Becomes a Promotional Tool for the NFL

There was a familiar face making the rounds in Southern California in the days leading up to that 1980 Super Bowl at the Rose Bowl. Chet Simmons, who had been NBC's programming executive at the first Super Bowl, coordinating the two-network coverage with his counter-parts at CBS, had returned with a new job and a new mission. Hired as the first president of ESPN before the network launched in September 1979, he was looking for programming opportunities that would link the name of his new network with the NFL. In its infancy, ESPN had nowhere near the resources to compete for the television rights to NFL games. The network was paying cable systems a monthly fee to carry its channel. Simmons was hoping he could find some inexpensive ways to connect ESPN and the NFL in the minds of viewers, advertisers, and cable system operators. "When we first started, we knew the opportunity to have professional football was nonexistent," said Simmons. "They're going to take football away from NBC, ABC, CBS, and give it to ESPN? We had a couple of million viewers. But we decided that we would report on it in every way possible that we can."[13] For ESPN's first telecasts on September 7, 1979, estimates suggest that less than three million homes could receive the service. Cable networks were a new option that started to gain attention with the launch of HBO in 1975. By 1979, only about

20 percent of American homes were connected to cable, so promotable content that fans could not find on any of the over-the-air broadcast networks was needed to drive interest and increase distribution.

Bill Fitts, the CBS executive producer of Super Bowl I, had also moved to ESPN, where he worked for Simmons as the head of studio and remote event production. Fitts remembered his conversation with Simmons after he had returned to Bristol, Connecticut, from Pasadena that January. "He told me he had met with Val Pinchbeck [the NFL's senior vice president for broadcasting] and asked if there was anything ESPN could do for the NFL." Pinchbeck said the league was concerned that after the Super Bowl each year, public interest in the NFL fell off until the opening of the new season in late summer. That meant there was no NFL content on television for at least six months each year. When Simmons asked what league events occurred during the offseason, Pinchbeck mentioned the annual NFL player draft in April. That's when Simmons began to hatch a plan that would bring NFL content to the fledgling ESPN network.[14]

He set up a meeting with Commissioner Rozelle back in New York after the Super Bowl. "Pete, I got a crazy idea, but we'd like to televise your draft," Simmons recalled telling the commissioner. "Pete, hardly ever at a loss of words, asked me to repeat my question. I told him that I would like to, we would like to, televise his draft. He said, 'live?' I said, 'live.' The minute you say or whoever says, 'Welcome to the 24th annual players' selection meeting,' or whatever they originally called it, I said, 'we want to go on the air, and we'll stay on for a couple of hours. We'll cover round 1, round 2.' And he said, 'go ahead.'"

With Chet Simmons that day representing ESPN's programming department was Steve Bornstein, who would later serve as the network's fourth president and then as the first president of the NFL Network. Bornstein said the NFL was originally shocked that ESPN wanted to televise the event but that Pete Rozelle "saw I think the opportunity to promote what had previously been a print story and make it into an electronic story." However, he was very particular about what the show would be titled. "Pete would never let us call it 'the Draft.' It was always, 'The NFL's Annual Selection Meeting,' I believe is the proper term," said

Bornstein. He compared it to the way Rozelle stuck with the title "AFL versus NFL World Championship Game" for two years before granting his approval to use "Super Bowl." Bornstein said, "It was only after a few years that he relaxed that, and we didn't have to call it 'the Annual Selection Meeting,' and we could actually call it the NFL Draft."[15]

When the deal was done, Bill Fitts remembers a triumphant Chet Simmons telling him, "Bill, we're gonna do the NFL Draft live!" Fitts's first question was to ask Simmons if he was crazy. "Have you been to a draft, Chet? It's just a bunch of guys on phones in a room." Simmons replied, "Yeah, Bill, but it's the NFL. The NFL. We need to get it on ESPN." Bill Fitts quickly put together a small production team and brought in his longtime NFL researcher, Frank Ross, who identified the best college players who were likely to be selected in the first two rounds of the April 1980 draft. Production assistants started calling college sports information directors to ask for any videotaped highlights they might have of the stars Ross had selected. Fitts's plan was to roll the tape after each player was selected so that ESPN commentators could analyze the player's potential and discuss the difference he might make for his new team. It's hard to believe, considering the hundreds of college football games that ESPN has televised year after year, but the network had done no college football games in its first autumn, so its access to player video was limited.

The NFL Draft made its debut as a television show on Tuesday morning, April 29, 1980, live from the New York Sheraton Hotel. The annual "player selection meeting" had traditionally been held on a Tuesday morning, and no concessions were being made for television. Billy Sims, an explosive running back from the University of Oklahoma, was the number-one pick, selected by the Detroit Lions. Bill Fitts reported proudly that his group had pulled together and edited video of Sims and "all but one or two picks" from the first two rounds. Chet Simmons followed up by negotiating with NFL Films for the rights to every Super Bowl film they had in their library. "We ran days of Super Bowl shows just to have the NFL logo on our air," he said. The following year, as NBC was preparing for its telecast of Super Bowl XV from New Orleans on January 25, 1981, ESPN ran its first "Super Bowl Sunday NFL Films

Marathon,"[16] with highlight films of the first fourteen Super Bowls scheduled back-to-back in the hours preceding the game. The NFL Draft of 1980 and the new cable distribution of NFL Films broke new ground for the NFL. Never before had one sports league managed to distribute and thereby promote its product across four different national networks in the same calendar year. And it showed how astute the NFL was to have so quickly taken advantage of this new media platform.

Everything but the Game

ESPN had become the nation's largest cable network by October 1983, reaching a total of 28.5 million homes. As it turned the corner on profitability and budgets began to grow, so did the aspirations of its young corps of programmers and producers. Producer Bob Rauscher, only a few years after graduating from Syracuse University, was tasked with putting together a plan in the fall of 1985 to take a small team anchored by Chris Berman to cover Super Bowl XX from New Orleans in January 1986. "ESPN wanted to have a live presence at the site of the Super Bowl, where the action was happening," said Rauscher. "To be at the game itself would help legitimize the network." He said he set about the task knowing that the network had three constituencies to serve: the NFL, ESPN's affiliated cable systems that distributed the network nationwide, and the fans watching on *SportsCenter*. That was a tall order to fill with limited resources: Rauscher recalled that his office at the hotel in New Orleans consisted of three director's chairs, a desk, and a typewriter. ESPN did not have a contract to televise any NFL games at that point, but the philosophy that Rauscher promoted was: "We have everything but the game," and "We're the first to arrive on site, and the last to leave."[17]

There were great storylines to follow that year: the Chicago Bears lost only one regular season game under coach Mike Ditka and featured stars Walter Payton, quarterback Jim McMahon, and William "Refrigerator" Perry. Generating even more publicity was a widely distributed music video the Bears recorded called "The Super Bowl Shuffle" to raise money for Chicago area charities. The New England Patriots represented the AFC in their first Super Bowl appearance that year, but they were seriously outshined by the Bears, losing in a 46–10 rout.

The on-site presence of ESPN's *SportsCenter* crew forever changed the coverage of the Super Bowl game, turning it into "Super Bowl week" by creating what came to be known as "surround programming." ESPN never televised the actual game, but it covered everything before it and everything that followed, making the network the destination for fans who couldn't get enough Super Bowl content. Former ESPN president Steve Bornstein said the goal was to produce hundreds of hours "on multiple networks surrounding the Super Bowl, and . . . our legacy is being part of the big show and the big event that occurs in sports and to take it to the next level."

The goal was "to show people what they never saw before, whether it's the commissioner's press conference, or it's the commissioner's party, or it's some of the postgame programming we do."[18] It made ESPN "an integral part of the viewer's experience of the event," said Bornstein. For Super Bowl XLIX in 2015, ESPN's Super Bowl "surround programming" reached its zenith with more than one hundred hours of live coverage and specials spread over nine full days beginning on the Sunday before the game and extending until the Monday after. In the years since, the total days and hours of ESPN television coverage from the site of the game have been scaled back, replaced by less expensive studio programming and plenty of ESPN.com digital content.

The promotional value of more networks devoting more airtime during the season and presenting live reports day after day leading up to the Super Bowl in January 1986 was obvious to the NFL. The compelling storylines and the publicity they received in advance helped Super Bowl XX set a new record for total viewing audience with more than ninety-two million viewers per minute for the entire telecast. It broke the record of 85.5 million that had been set in January 1985, which was the first Super Bowl ever on ABC. The network's new contract with the NFL for *Monday Night Football* had expanded the two-network rotation, a fixture since 1968, to an alternating three-network schedule. ABC brought its *Monday Night* philosophy to the game at Stanford Stadium, using more cameras, more replays, and its signature three-man booth. Frank Gifford was the play-by-play host, with Don Meredith at his side, but the third man was Washington quarterback Joe Theismann, not Howard

Cosell. After fourteen years in the *Monday Night Football* booth, Cosell had decided to step away just before the 1984 regular season began.

The NFL Conquers Cable TV and Sports Radio

The success of ESPN's Super Bowl "surround" coverage proved to be a factor in the negotiations that culminated on March 15, 1987, when the NFL announced that it had reached its first agreement with a cable television network, putting eight Sunday night games during the second half of the season plus the Pro Bowl on ESPN for three years, beginning with the 1987 season. Included in that first contract was the creation of a Sunday evening *NFL Primetime* show that would air video recaps of every game played that afternoon. "I don't think they understood precisely what they were, in fact, allowing us to do," said Steve Bornstein, "which was to televise unlimited excerpt rights of highlights of the afternoon's games that night. Once they saw the product, I think they recognized how potent and how important it would be, I think, to the overall marketability of the sport."[19]

The addition of new NFL programming and live games on cable television was a boon for the entire cable industry, dramatically increasing the sale of subscriptions. In July 1987, ESPN achieved a milestone, becoming the first cable network to reach more than 50 percent of American homes, with 43.7 million subscribers. That had swollen to 100.1 million by the time ESPN reached its peak distribution in 2011.

As more fans saw more games, highlights, and hours and hours of analysis and interviews, the more they wanted to talk about it and share their comments and ideas. ESPN, which then called itself "The Total Sports Network," helped give birth to the sports talk radio business, which in turn helped generate more publicity for the NFL and the Super Bowl. On July 1, 1987, just a few weeks before the first NFL season that would feature live games on four national networks, the first twenty-four-hour all-sports radio station signed on in New York City. WFAN, owned by Emmis Broadcasting, took over the 1050-kHz frequency on the AM dial, which had been occupied by a music station, WHN. A little more than a year later, WFAN would swap frequencies with WNBC-AM (on 660 kHz), one of the country's original fifty-thousand-watt clear-channel stations, increasing the power of its signal and its coverage area to several states. The sports radio trend would steadily build in cities across the country that were home to professional and major college teams, which also had multiple stations and advertisers whose target audience was sports fans. Within five years, ESPN would launch its own ESPN Radio network, linking hundreds of these sports-talk stations together.

Come January each year, all that WFAN listeners wanted to talk about was the Super Bowl, so for Super Bowl XXVI following the NFL's 1991 season, WFAN set up in the lobby of the downtown Minneapolis Marriott the week before the game between Washington and Buffalo would take place at the Hubert H. Humphrey Metrodome. In the same lobby of this designated media hotel, ESPN's Bob Rauscher was ensconced at his studio desk with Chris Berman, Tom Jackson, and Chris Mortenson, broadcasting their menu of "surround programming" shows. Surround TV was giving birth to surround radio.

The trail blazed by WFAN was soon followed by more radio stations selling their own brand of Super Bowl coverage to fans in their home markets. For Super Bowl XXVII at the Rose Bowl in January 1993, the NFL accommodated approximately twenty radio stations at their media center in the Century Plaza Hotel. By Super Bowl XXX in Arizona in 1996, what WFAN had begun became "Radio Row," so many stations wanted to beef up their schedules the week before the game with live interviews and reports from the site that the NFL moved the media into convention center spaces. For Super Bowl LVIII in February 2024, the Super Bowl Media Center at the Mandalay Bay Convention Center in Las Vegas accommodated more than 150 media outlets from across every time zone of the United States. If you were to calculate the collective reach of all these media outlets and multiply that by the number of hours each was broadcasting during the week leading up to the game, it would provide a sense of the incomparable power of the Super Bowl to deliver its stories, promote its stars, and continue to create such an immense impact on the public.

John Madden's New Toy

A technical innovation introduced by CBS during the NFC playoffs and championship game at the end of the 1981 season and then at Super Bowl XVI in January 1982 undoubtedly played a role in attracting new viewers to the sport during the 1980s and in every decade since. The Telestrator allowed John Madden to draw circles and arrows on the screen to show fans at home which players to watch during a replay and what actions to watch for in upcoming plays. Using a visual aid to explain strategy, player assignments, and how plays worked or didn't work helped demystify NFL football for people new to the game who were confused by seeing twenty-two players on the screen, all moving at once on every play. "The thing about the Telestrator," said Madden, "it put everyone on the same level." Madden knew that the Telestrator would make NFL football more accessible to a wider audience. "It doesn't make any difference if you ever played or not," he said. "You can say, 'that guy is going to go there and block that guy.' And that's what the Telestrator did. Then that put every viewer on the same level: man, woman, child, someone just comes over to this country. Once you got that thing and you just point it out. They may not know a lot of other things, but they know what to watch when you put it on."[20]

The Telestrator was invented by Dr. Leonard Reiffel (pronounced "rifle") to help him explain concepts to the viewers of his weekly Sunday morning children's science show, *Backyard Safari*, which began in 1968 on WTTW-TV in Chicago. Dr. Reiffel was doing research at the Illinois Institute of Technology and served as a deputy program director at NASA. He patented and made improvements to his Telestrator then suggested to the weather forecaster at WBBM-TV in Chicago that it might help him bring his forecast maps to life. The sports anchor at the station, Johnny Morris, immediately saw its potential for sports analysis. WBBM was and still is owned and operated by CBS, so it bought four Telestrators from Instructional Dynamics, the company that Dr. Reiffel had set up, and then put the stylus in John Madden's hand.[21]

John Madden enthusiastically embraced the Telestrator as an educational device, and he had fun with it, adding entertainment value to the games. Madden would circle the Gatorade jugs along the sidelines or diagram how he stuffed a duck with a small chicken then stuffed both into a large turkey to serve "turducken" to the TV crew members working on Thanksgiving Day games. Super Bowl XVI on January 24, 1982, the first won by the San Francisco 49ers, still stands as one of the highest-rated Super Bowl telecasts of all time. The show on CBS was watched in 49.1 percent of all American homes with televisions, an average of 85,240,000 people watching every minute of the game in which the 49ers defeated the Cincinnati Bengals 26–21. As the US population has grown, there have been many Super Bowls that were watched by more people, but that percentage of homes has never been surpassed.

The team that everyone wanted to talk about during the 1980s was the San Francisco 49ers. They won the championship four times, after the 1981, 1984, 1988, and 1989 seasons, all with Joe Montana at quarterback and the first three with cerebral head coach Bill Walsh, renowned as the creator of the "West Coast offense." The 49ers got even better when they drafted wide receiver Jerry Rice out of Mississippi Valley State in the first round of the 1985 NFL draft. The 49ers became for the new decade what the Pittsburgh Steelers had been in the 1970s. Talk of dynasties, new offenses, different approaches to the game, and talented young players fueled the fans' appetite for more media coverage.

FOX Rocks the Boat

When the FOX Network launched in October 1986, it wasn't looking to attract sports fans. It started as a collection of just seven random, independent television stations from across the country that had no network affiliation with ABC, CBS, or NBC. The plan was to offer alternative entertainment to attract a younger adult audience than those watching the shows that filled the evening hours on network affiliates. The first regularly scheduled show on FOX was a late-night talk show hosted by Joan Rivers, described by one reviewer as "a comic stiletto quick to skewer." In 1987, *Married . . . with Children* debuted to reviews that called it "unapologetically crude." It was followed by *The Tracy Ullman Show*, which included animated shorts each week that became *The Simpsons*. FOX was clearly a renegade network that was trying to chip away at the edges of the big three networks' audience, but it wasn't taken seriously until its chairman, Rupert Murdoch, outbid CBS for NFL television rights in 1993.

In the *New York Times* of December 18, 1993, Richard Sandomir wrote, "The tradition of watching Sunday afternoon pro football took a startling turn yesterday when the National Football League announced that Rupert Murdoch's FOX Network—the network of Al Bundy and Bart Simpson—had outbid CBS for the right to televise National Football Conference games, beginning next season."[22] It was "startling" in that the new contract ended a relationship between the NFL and CBS that went back to 1961 and in that the amount FOX bid was $100 million per year higher than the offer CBS made attempting to retain its incumbency. Murdoch's bold move rocked what had been three decades of stability for CBS and NBC and predictability for football fans tuning in. It replaced an era of steadiness and tradition with one of volatility and constantly shifting sands blown by ever-increasing gusts of cash that would swell to the billions.

FOX jumped headfirst into the sports business for the beginning of the 1994 season, bumping CBS from the three-network Super Bowl rotation. Murdoch, an Australian by birth, brought fellow Aussie David Hill to the United States from London, where he had helped Murdoch launch Sky Sports. Murdoch gave Hill the charge to build a sports division and an open checkbook. "I arrived here with a blank sheet of paper, and I had eight months to create FOX Sports," said Hill. "There wasn't even a logo; there was no music. There wasn't a studio; there wasn't a control room. There was nothing."[23]

Hill's first hire was former Oakland Raiders coach John Madden as his number-one analyst. Madden and Pat Summerall had been the top announcing team at CBS for several years, so they were now available. They made the move to FOX together, along with their producer, Bob Stenner, director Sandy Grossman, and CBS production executive Ed Goren, who would serve as executive producer at FOX. "What we had was a period of nine months, Ed Goren and myself, and a few other people," said Hill. "We were able to sit down and look at the way everyone covered football and say, 'Well, we like this, and we like that.' Ninety-eight percent of the package we loved. All we wanted to do was duplicate. Then what we tried to do was say, 'Well, how can we try and improve things? How can we make it better?' That's how FOX Sports evolved."

One change the FOX team decided on early was to make its pregame show one hour every Sunday before the 1:00 p.m. EST kickoffs. CBS and NBC traditionally aired half-hour pregame shows. Hill's reasoning was that "the best lead-in for football was football." To create the FOX NFL pregame show, he applied a proven formula: "I needed someone to talk offense, someone to talk defense and someone to be a coach—it's very simple. So you go out and find the best offensive guy that you can find, the best defensive guy you can find, and the best coach."

On offense, he hired Terry Bradshaw, who had won four Super Bowl rings with the Steelers. For defense, he brought in Howie Long, a former All-Pro lineman for the Oakland Raiders in eight of his thirteen seasons, who six years later would be elected to the Pro Football Hall of Fame. For the "coach" position, he found a man who had won a national championship as a college player, a national championship as a college coach, and also owned a Super Bowl ring: Jimmy Johnson. Host James Brown also was hired away from CBS and told that the objective at FOX was to educate the audience, but never to bore them. "'Let them enjoy it' was exactly what we were told," said Brown. "Have an edge about it and make it like it's a conversation in a family room on a Sunday afternoon watching the game."[24]

The most controversial change FOX made to NFL game coverage was the addition of a continuous onscreen clock and score graphic. The "FOX box," as it came to be known, was an innovation David Hill had first added to the live coverage of soccer on Sky Sports in the United Kingdom. The live clock and score graphic actually made its debut on American television during the FIFA World Cup '94 soccer telecasts on ABC and ESPN. But when it was introduced on the first FOX NFL preseason game in August 1994, some fans felt their world had been turned upside down. "If you'd go back to our very first broadcast with the FOX box, you would have thought we desecrated the Taj Mahal," said Ed Goren. "I came back after our first broadcast and had a voice mail from an irate 49ers fan who pointed out we ruined his experience watching the game and, 'If you don't get rid of it, I'll come down there and get rid of it for you.'"[25]

FOX Sports had been producing NFL games for three seasons when its first opportunity arrived to televise a Super Bowl at the end of the 1996 season at the Superdome in New Orleans for Super Bowl XXXI. The "FOX box" would make its Super debut, and sticking with its "best lead-in" philosophy, FOX scheduled its pregame show to start at 1:00 p.m. EST and run for a previously unheard-of five hours. People asked, "what are you going to do for five hours," but David Hill said that producer Scott Ackerson's show had so much information that it would have been impossible to find a spare two seconds. Hill said the ratings proved that fans would watch. With ratings that showed more people were watching during each progressive hour, the trend for Super Bowl pregame shows across all networks quickly became "more is better."

The Green Bay Packers defeated the New England Patriots 35–21 in Super Bowl XXXI, returning the Vince Lombardi Trophy to "Titletown" for the first time since 1968. Brett Favre threw touchdown passes of fifty-four and eighty-one yards, and game MVP Desmond Howard returned an Adam Vinatieri kickoff ninety-nine yards. But the biggest winner may have been the FOX Network. "This was for the broadcast network and for all our affiliates," said David Hill. "This proved to the world that FOX Sports was as good, if not better than any of the other networks, with the way we handled it, the professionalism, the way we looked, and more importantly, the way we treated the advertisers and showcased our commercial sponsors. From the very opening to the end credits, it was a huge responsibility because this effectively was the FOX network's coming of age."[26]

The continuous clock and score display would soon be adopted by every network that televised football, whether in a corner box format or as a "dashboard" across the bottom of the screen. The information it provided gave every play a frame of reference by clearly identifying which team was leading, how many points the other team had to score to draw even, and how much time they had to make it happen. That helped develop storylines as to which players and teams were better at comebacks and added drama to fourth-quarter comebacks and two-point conversion tries.

The FOX incursion that left CBS with no NFL regular season or Super Bowl games created a tremendous ripple effect. Automatically the value of NFL television rights hit record heights. Networks had to decide if they could thrive without the NFL as part of their programming schedule. If not, the price to either retain the rights or get back into the game would be far more expensive than ever. Consider the morale and the fear for job security among the NBC Sports group as they prepared for Super Bowl XXXII in January 1998, when they got the news that their contract to continue broadcasting AFC games had been awarded to CBS for the next four years for a rights fee of $500 million per year. NBC had declined to bid after having televised AFL then AFC games since 1964, claiming that it was no longer profitable to carry NFL games. The CBS offer was more than double what NBC had been paying the NFL in its most recent rights deal. The 1997 season that ended with the January 1998 Super Bowl in San Diego between the Broncos and the Packers would be the last NFL game on NBC for the foreseeable future.

Rights Fees Reach the Billions

At the same time, the NFL announced that it had accepted FOX's bid of $550 million per year to continue as the NFC broadcaster for four more years. Between just the two networks, CBS and FOX, the NFL would collect more than $1 billion per year. The very next day, Tuesday, January 13, 1998, the NFL finalized its two other national television contracts by accepting $4.4 billion from ABC for eight more years of *Monday Night Football* and $4.8 billion from ESPN for eight full seasons of *Sunday Night Football*. For the previous eight years, the NFL had split the Sunday night schedule into eight games for ESPN and eight on TNT. ABC's $4.4 billion and ESPN's $4.8 billion would both be paid by their parent, The Walt Disney Company, which had acquired Capital Cities ABC in 1995.

The move from shorter term contracts to eight-year deals brought some welcome stability to the NFL and its television partners. For the league's millions of TV viewers, they brought a renewed sense of familiarity as to where to tune each season for games on Sundays and Mondays. But with the end of the eight-year contracts that would expire after the 2005 regular season came another round of upheaval. In April 2005, NBC agreed to pay the NFL $600 million per year beginning in 2006 for the *Sunday Night Football* package that had been airing on ESPN, plus two Super Bowls in 2009 and 2012. During its years without the NFL, NBC had seen its viewership decline among men and among all adults aged eighteen to forty-nine. During the same time period, CBS had used its NFL telecasts to help promote other programs like *Survivor* and *CSI: Crime Scene Investigation* to male viewers.

In April 2005, the Walt Disney Company renewed its NFL contract for another eight years for $1.1 billion per year, but moved *Monday Night Football* from ABC, after thirty-six consecutive years, to its sibling network ESPN. ABC's rights deal included every third Super Bowl. ESPN's did not include any Super Bowls. The three-network rotation as of 2006 would be CBS, FOX, and NBC. For Dick Ebersol, the chairman of NBC Universal Sports Group who negotiated NBC's return to the NFL family, it was a bittersweet victory. He had been with Roone Arledge at ABC when the original *Monday Night Football* deal had been made with Pete Rozelle. "I can't help thinking over and over," Ebersol told Richard Sandomir of the *New York Times*, "about being Roone's assistant in late 1969, and walking twice to '21' while he had lunch with Pete, to bring him information he wanted as he was making the deal. My thoughts were all about Roone and what his sadness would be to see something that was his dream ending. Roone was ABC personified."[27]

The major economic reason behind moving *Monday Night Football* from ABC to ESPN was ESPN's dual stream of revenue. ABC's primary stream was and still is advertising sales, but ESPN earns most of its income from the monthly subscriber fees it charges each cable, satellite, and video delivery system that carries ESPN. The second stream—accounting for roughly 30 percent of network revenue—is the billions of dollars that ESPN collects for all the commercials it runs on its multiple networks. In 2006, the total number of ESPN subscribers had reached ninety-two million, from whom it collected close to $3 per home per month. That gave ESPN a baseline of more than $250 million in revenue per month ($3 billion per year). The number of cable subscribers has fallen below seventy-five million, but ESPN's monthly fee has risen to approximately $9 per home per month, so that side of the dual stream currently generates approximately $675 million a month. "Renewing *Monday Night Football* did not make financial sense for ABC," said George Bodenheimer, then president of ABC Sports and ESPN, "but it made great financial sense for ESPN."[28]

The new contract allowed ESPN to use NFL content in its shows 365 days each year and put "NFL" in the titles of several programs, which would guarantee larger audiences. Another advantage was the cable network had twenty-four hours each day to devote to sports. On ABC, a Monday night game was allotted a three-and-a-half hour time slot. It was preceded by local affiliate programming and early prime-time ABC entertainment shows and was followed by each local station's late-night news show. ESPN could devote all day to promoting, broadcasting, and then analyzing the game, selling advertising to companies that were targeting a male demographic in twelve hours of programming, not just three or four.

First and Ten

Every play in every game became more interesting when the yellow "first and ten" line technology was added to NFL telecasts in 1998. It was created by Sportvision, a Chicago-based group of computer and data experts who brought their idea along with a demo tape to ESPN in Bristol, Connecticut, in the spring of 1998. They offered ESPN an exclusive one-year agreement if the network would allocate funds to help them finish the research and development work needed to get the system broadcast-ready. ESPN management agreed and testing of "first and ten" began during the preseason games that summer. ESPN used a second truck so that the production team could record a test video of the game that used "first and ten" but had not been broadcast to viewers. Fred Gaudelli, who was producing ESPN's NFL games, remembers going into the test truck after the game: "From what I saw that night I knew immediately this was going to be a home run." When ESPN showed the video to Commissioner Paul Tagliabue and NFL director of broadcasting Dennis Lewin, they had the same reaction.[29]

"First and ten" debuted to a nationwide audience on Sunday night, September 27, 1998, as the Baltimore Ravens hosted the Cincinnati Bengals. Viewers for the first time could see when a ball carrier or receiver crossed the line to gain for a first down. "It's one of the few things, maybe the only innovation I can remember that ever got universal acclaim from everyone, writers, viewers, the league, our competition," said Gaudelli. "There was never any criticism."

FOX had the rights to Super Bowl XXXIII, following the 1998 season, and its producers dearly wanted to include "first and ten," which quickly became a sensation that made NFL telecasts without it pale in comparison. When FOX inquired about getting permission to use the technology in the Super Bowl, Fred Gaudelli remembers the ESPN response: "Give us $1 million to offset our investment in the R&D, and we'll drop our exclusivity. We'll make it non-exclusive." Fox declined the offer, which allowed ESPN alone to use "first and ten" in the 1999 season of *Sunday Night Football* and make its Super Bowl premiere on co-owned ABC at Super Bowl XXXIV at the Georgia Dome on January 30, 2000. The following season, with the exclusivity rights having expired, every network that had broadcast rights to NFL games added "first and ten."

Let's Check the Replay

The story of a Super Bowl, or any game for that matter, can hinge on the outcome of just one or two plays. The increased emphasis that the league has placed on using replays for officiating has made it even more crucial for the networks to provide the definitive angles to look at a play so that the story can be told correctly. Instant replay was first used during the CBS broadcast of the Army–Navy game on December 7, 1963. The game featured Navy's junior quarterback Roger Staubach in the final regular season game of his Heisman Trophy–winning season. CBS director Tony Verna took the videotape machine he used for replays at that game in Philadelphia to the 1964 Cotton Bowl in Dallas, where Staubach and the Midshipmen played the number-one ranked Texas Longhorns on

New Year's Day. That's where his play-by-play announcer Pat Summerall coined the term "instant replay." By the time the Super Bowl began in 1967, replays were a fixture in virtually all sports broadcasts.

NFL owners approved the use of replays by officials to decide close or questionable plays for the 1986 season. The focus on providing every possible angle intensified for broadcasters after the coach's challenge system was introduced in 1999. More camera positions have been added to help decide contested calls, and in 2015, ESPN put cameras inside the pylons that mark the four corners of both end zones for its NFL *Monday Night Football* and prime-time Saturday night college football games. These cameras, which give fixed views down the goal line, the end line, and both sidelines, provide answers for viewers and officials: Did the ball break the plane of the goal line? Were the ball carrier or receiver's feet both in bounds when he had possession of the ball? When did his knee touch the ground? Including the thirty-two miniature cameras housed inside the eight end zone pylons, the total number of cameras used to cover a Super Bowl by CBS, NBC, and FOX is now in the range of seventy-five to more than ninety, depending on each director's preference. With each camera recording to a hard disk replay device, providing the definitive look to get the story right has become a far greater certainty than when Super Bowl I was covered by only a dozen cameras.

"In the history of football on television, the four most important innovations that have improved a producer's storytelling abilities have been instant replay, 'first and ten,' the constant score bug, and SkyCam," said NBC's Fred Gaudelli. The SkyCam system, suspended from cables strung above the football field, is the most recent innovation. It started giving viewers at home a perspective they had never seen beginning with the 2002 NFL season on ESPN. "It gave you a camera on the field at the perfect height," said Gaudelli. "You could see the quarterback's view of the field, how the defenses he faced were set up, how receivers would break free and how blitzes fired through." SkyCam made its Super Bowl debut following that 2002 season, at Super Bowl XXXVII on ABC, the first Super Bowl that Fred Gaudelli produced. When ABC's *Monday Night Football* ended in 2005, he joined NBC as the lead producer of

NBC *Sunday Night Football* and produced all of NBC's Super Bowl telecasts through 2022.

A Network to Call Its Own

For its entire history, the NFL had relied on its media partners to distribute live games and all other NFL content to the viewing public. That changed on November 4, 2003, with the launch of the NFL Network. This new network and the websites owned by the league gave the NFL a direct connection to fans. It did not need to rely on third parties to tell its stories, profile its players and coaches, analyze and promote its games. The league could tell its own stories and control the narrative on its own network. The NFL had devised the ultimate "surround programming" for the Super Bowl and all its other games and events: twenty-four hours a day, 365 days a year of self-directed storytelling.

The first president and chief executive officer of the NFL Network was Steve Bornstein, who had been ESPN's president from 1990 to 1999. Leading up to the launch, he said the NFL Network's mission would be "to deliver programming that honors the NFL's rich tradition and captures the excitement that turns on millions of fans. We will use a lot of innovation to bring our audience the most technologically advanced content possible."[30] New content included the NFL scouting combine, which was first televised by the NFL Network in 2005. The network began the *Thursday Night Football* series of games in 2006, then partnered with broadcast networks for distribution. The league's strategy was to attract millions of prime-time viewers and replicate its successes on Monday and Sunday nights. Fifteen years later, the league made a huge profit by selling its *Thursday Night Football* rights to Amazon Prime for eleven years at $1 billion per year. More importantly, beginning in 2022, this extended NFL programming and promotion to a live streaming service for the first time.

NFL Network started its own coverage of the NFL draft in 2010, in direct competition with ESPN, which had developed the first draft television coverage in 1980 and had provided exclusive telecasts for thirty years. The league continued to create new content and new events that would fill NFL Network programming schedules with NFL coverage and stories that would keep the league front and center in fans' minds throughout the year. The NFL's International Series began in 2007, with teams playing regular season games in Mexico, the United Kingdom, Japan, as of 2023 in Germany and for 2024, Brazil, bringing the total international games to eight per season as of 2025. The league created its own annual awards show, *NFL Honors*, in 2012, and started taking the NFL draft on the road in 2015 to generate added excitement in local NFL markets. NFL Network became the perfect platform for new documentary series from NFL Films such as *A Football Life* and *The Timeline*. For the Super Bowl, NFL Network took the crown from ESPN and became the new king of surround programming. The network routinely produces eighty-five or more hours of live shows from the site of the Super Bowl every year, each segment providing an opportunity to promote the NFL's number-one property.

A Colossus That Stands Alone

The league, its network, and its broadcast partners together built a property that is unrivaled in the history of sport. The concern—voiced more than forty years ago by the NFL's Val Pinchbeck to Chet Simmons of ESPN that the league needed to find ways to keep fans connected during the months between the last play of the Super Bowl in January until the first plays of the regular season in September—has long since been put to bed. There is more NFL coverage and content that produces more revenue than Pete Rozelle or Lamar Hunt could have ever imagined.

Compare the $44.1 million in annual rights fees the 1970 contract provided with 2020, when the NFL collected $7.55 billion in media rights fees. During half a century, the value of the NFL's rights fees grew by a factor of 170. For every $1,000 the NFL received in media revenue in 1970, the league received $170,000 in the year 2020. Taking the rate of inflation into account over the same period, NFL media rights still increased by a multiplier of more than 160.

The NFL's latest media rights contracts negotiated for the 2021 season pushed the league's broadcasting revenue to more than $12 billion per year, including digital streaming of *Thursday Night Football* on Prime and on YouTube TV for the Sunday Ticket package. With digital video distribution having grown so large, more bidders compete for the packages, meaning increased revenue for the NFL. The league commands such large mass media audiences compared to any other league or sport that one network programmer said, "Basically, all they have to do is put a number down on the paper, and we'll sign it."

Every year since 1984, the Super Bowl has been the most-watched television program of the year in the United States. The previous year, the final episode of the *M*A*S*H* television series was seen by more than 105 million viewers on CBS, beating the Super Bowl by twenty-four million. For four consecutive decades, no awards show, drama, comedy, or single news event has attracted a larger audience than the Super Bowl. It is an unmatched entertainment colossus, a partnership of power and prestige shared by the NFL and its media partners across an ever-widening set of distribution platforms.

CHAPTER 11

It's an Entertainment Extravaganza *and* a Football Game

THE SUPER BOWL IS THE MOST-WATCHED SPORTING EVENT OF THE year, and the half-hour halftime segment is the most-watched entertainment event of the year. During the twenty-first century, the halftime show became the highest-rated portion of the entire Super Bowl telecast, attracting a larger audience than any of the football action. The most-watched entertainment show in the history of American television was the halftime performance starring Usher during Super Bowl LVIII in 2024. It peaked at 129.3 million viewers per minute. Compare that to the next highest-rated entertainment show each year, the annual Academy Awards, which averages in the range of 20 million viewers. The Super Bowl's massive reach has had a dramatic effect on music industry sales and the fortunes of artists who perform during halftime or who sing the national anthem or "America the Beautiful" before the game. The impact is felt in the movie industry as well. Studios that promote their upcoming releases with commercials during the Super Bowl build awareness and anticipation among a potential moviegoing audience. And there is a direct effect on entertainment television. The Super Bowl provides the network that airs the event the perfect platform from which to promote its new programs, which often include new series premieres scheduled to begin right after the game. This Super Bowl "halo effect" has made instant hits out of several new series and breathed new life into others.

A Spectacle of Super Sights and Sounds

All-consuming events like the Super Bowl take people away from their everyday lives, transporting them from their troubles and concerns to a diversion that provides entertainment, amusement, and pleasure. The very word "sport" has its origins in the French "desporter," which literally means "to carry away." It has the same root as our words "porter," "portable," and "transport."

Adding more entertainment value to the Super Bowl helps broaden the NFL's fan base and enhances existing fans' experience on multiple levels. Many viewers are intrigued and drawn to the Super Bowl's cultural and lifestyle elements, which include pregame and halftime performances the commercials, even the spectators who might include global superstar Taylor Swift, as much as or more than competition itself. These people are less concerned with the results or outcome of the game than they are in the spectacle. On the flip side, avid football fans are introduced to new cultural experiences and entertainers whom they see integrated into the entertainment fabric of the NFL's biggest event.

"Our goal from the first was to make this more than a game, to make it an event," former commissioner Pete Rozelle told the *Los Angeles Times* several years after his retirement. "That was because of the initial perception that the champion of the American Football League wouldn't be competitive with the National Football League champion. So we wanted an event, even if it wasn't a competitive game. We wanted people to have some fun."[1]

To that end, the NFL hired the former director of entertainment at Disneyland, Tommy Walker, to produce a halftime show for the first Super Bowl. Walker had been the band director at the University of Southern California when Walt Disney became aware of his creative productions for USC football halftimes. As a student at USC in 1947, Walker had been the Trojans' drum major and the football team's kicker for points after touchdown. He had to change into his football uniform after the band performed before the game, back into his band uniform for halftime, and then put on his football jersey for the second half. Disney brought him onboard to stage the opening ceremonies for Disneyland in 1955. Many of the iconic Disney flourishes like fireworks above Cinderella's castle were Walker creations. For the first Super Bowl, he assembled a show titled "Super Sights and Sounds" that featured jazz trumpeter Al Hirt, marching bands from Grambling College and the University of Arizona, a two-hundred-person chorus, the release of three hundred doves and ten thousand balloons. The centerpiece, though, was a pair of "rocket men."[2]

The US space program had captured almost every American's imagination in the 1960s. Two months before the first Super Bowl in January 1967, the last of NASA's Gemini missions practiced docking maneuvers in space, and astronaut Edwin "Buzz" Aldrin, who two years later would walk on the moon, performed an "extravehicular activity" outside the spacecraft for two-and-a-half hours in preparation for the upcoming Apollo moon flights. Tommy Walker capitalized on the "space craze" by hiring two jetpack pilots from Bell AeroSystems who had put on a demonstration at Disneyland the previous year. He had them dressed in replica football jerseys, one with "AFL" emblazoned on his chest, the other with "NFL," and then he hid them inside giant foam footballs for halftime. With the marching bands playing on the field, the two "rocket men" took off from inside their football launch pads, soared high over the field, each completing a circle that brought them back to the turf at the fifty yard line, where they walked toward each other and shook hands to symbolize the joining of the two professional football leagues. There was a roar of approval from the nearly sixty-two thousand fans at the Los Angeles Coliseum. They had never seen anything like it.

The entertainment at the next two Super Bowls, both held at the Orange Bowl in Miami, was short on spectacle, connecting the game more to the traditions of the New Year's Day college bowl games than to the future. The marching band from Grambling made a return performance at Super Bowl II, and in 1969 for Super Bowl III, the Florida A&M marching band was joined by seven high school bands from the Miami area. An announcer also read quotes from the late president John F. Kennedy and Martin Luther King Jr., who had been assassinated the previous year, then invited the crowd to sing "The Battle Hymn of the Republic."

Moving to Tulane Stadium in New Orleans helped reinvigorate half-time entertainment for Super Bowl IV in January 1970. For the first time a host city focused on its culture and heritage with a "Tribute to Mardi Gras" show that was produced by Tommy Walker, who had made such an impression at the first Super Bowl. The spectacle included costumed actors re-creating the Battle of New Orleans with cannons, rifles, and lots of smoke, a Mardi Gras parade, a jazz funeral featuring the Onward and Olympia brass bands, and a two-story Mississippi River steamboat parade float, its decks lined with young women dressed as Southern belles. There was music from New Orleans native Al Hirt and singer Marguerite Piazza, trumpeter Doc Severinsen, who was the bandleader for *The Tonight Show Starring Johnny Carson*, jazz great Lionel Hampton, and the Southern University band. In an interview with United Press International several years later, Walker said that his goal was always "to lighten up America in an exciting way." He believed that "special events will have a growing role as civic entertainment."

Tommy Walker, who in his career picked up the nicknames "Mr. Spectacular" and "The Wizard of Ahs," returned to the Los Angeles Memorial Coliseum for his third and final halftime production at Super Bowl VII in January 1973. His theme was "Happiness is . . ." with per-formances by the University of Michigan marching band and television and recording star Andy Williams. The band formed the letters "*NFL*" in the middle of the field as motorized football helmets the size of giant golf carts drove in circles on either side. There was a helmet for every NFL team with a seated cheerleader aboard doing Rockette-style high kicks. When the stadium public address announcer said, "Happiness is discovering America from coast to coast," the band formed an outline of the US map as eight students carried a sixteen-foot model jetliner "around the country," a chorus sang "This Land Is Your Land," and NBC rolled video clips of scenic shots from the Statue of Liberty to the Grand Canyon. For good measure, Walker added the release of another flock of doves and red balloons that suspended aloft a large red heart banner. Walker died in 1986 at the age of sixty-three, a few months after selling his company, Tommy Walker Productions, to Radio City Music Hall Productions, where he had assumed the position as executive producer for special events. His formula for producing spectaculars that filled a stage the size of a football field established a template for Super Bowl halftime shows that would last almost twenty years. But it also set a trap for the NFL as the world changed dramatically over those two decades and the formula did not.[3]

Popular Culture Makes a Generational Shift

Parallels can be drawn between the presentation of multiple, varied acts in each Super Bowl halftime and the variety shows that had become a staple of American television in the 1950s and 1960s. In one hour of *The Ed Sullivan Show*, a Sunday night mainstay on CBS from 1948 until 1971, viewers could see singers, dancers, comedians, scenes from Broadway musicals or operas, bands, choruses, jugglers, and ventriloquists. *The Ed Sullivan Show* introduced Elvis Presley to a national television audience in 1956 and the Beatles in 1964. One-hour variety shows were a prime-time presence on all three commercial TV networks virtually every night of the week well into the 1970s, with hosts that included Dean Martin, Jackie Gleason, Carol Burnett, Judy Garland, comedian Red Skelton, singers Andy Williams, Sonny and Cher, Glen Campbell, and John Denver, among others. By offering a variety of acts, these shows hoped to provide something for everyone, to offend no one, and to appeal to the widest possible audience, which was precisely the goal of the NFL.

American popular culture was making a generational shift that began during the tumultuous 1960s. The generation that had come of age in the 1940s and 1950s had a very different world view than did the baby boomers, whose formative years were shaped by the upheaval of the civil rights movement, the sadness, uncertainty, and discord of the Vietnam War, and the shock of assassinations. New entertainment options began to emerge in the 1970s that would change the industry forever and offer Americans more choices. The universally upbeat and optimistic variety shows began to drop from the network television schedules, replaced by edgier comedies and dramas that addressed controversial topics and ideas. Among the new ratings winners were *All in the Family*, *M*A*S*H*, *Kojak*, and *Sanford and Son*. The optimism of the pre–Vietnam War era hadn't faded completely. Garry Marshall's nostalgic comedies *Happy*

Days and *Laverne and Shirley* were also at the top of the ratings. *Saturday Night Live* debuted on NBC in 1975, and unlike the variety shows, its goal was to offend, satirize, and poke fun at people for the enjoyment of its young adult target audience, not for the broadest possible range of demographics.

The NFL chose to stay on course with Super Bowl halftime shows that would reflect the league's optimism for America and put the country's most positive and least controversial face forward. For Super Bowl X in 1976 at Miami's Orange Bowl, the NFL presented a tribute to America's bicentennial titled "200 Years and Still a Baby" that featured Up with People, a song-and-dance troupe of more than four hundred eighteen- to twenty-five-year-old performers from around the world. Up with People was founded in 1965 by J. Blanton Belk, who was the national director of what was called the moral re-armament movement. The group was established to provide youth an alternative to the antiwar movement. They opened the halftime show with their "Up with People" theme song, followed by two songs written exclusively for the group, before they sang and danced their way into the show's centerpiece, a medley of American music that opened with "The Charleston" and "The Wabash Cannonball," and moved through "Rock around the Clock" and John Denver's "Take Me Home, Country Roads." For the finale, the four hundred members of Up with People formed an outline of the Liberty Bell as they sang "Philadelphia Freedom," then morphed into a map of the United States for "America the Beautiful."[4]

The NFL was so impressed that they invited Up with People back for three more halftimes. In 1980 for Super Bowl XIV, they did a "Salute to the Big Band Era" of the 1930s and 1940s, and two years later they returned with "A Salute to the '60s and Motown" under the lights of the Pontiac Silverdome. The Silverdome was the home of the Detroit Lions, but not one Motown artist was invited to perform in the Motown salute. Up with People made its final Super Bowl halftime appearance in 1986 at the Superdome in New Orleans with a show entitled "Beat of the Future" for Super Bowl XX. Ebullient but hopelessly bland, "Up with People" was clearly out of step during a decade in which the music scene and sales were dominated by Michael Jackson, Madonna, Prince, Phil Collins,

Whitney Houston, and Bruce Springsteen. Commissioner Pete Rozelle had had his fill of the clean-cut, peppy troupe. The day after Super Bowl XX, he began his staff meeting by declaring, "There are three words that I don't ever want to hear again: Up with People."

The first halftime of the post–Up with People era was splashier but just as clean-cut. The Walt Disney Company produced a "Salute to Hollywood's 100th Anniversary" for Super Bowl XXI at the Rose Bowl in Pasadena, which was liberally populated with Disney cartoon characters in a variety of costumes. New ground was broken in 1988 for the Super Bowl in San Diego, when Chubby Checker became the first popular artist of the rock 'n' roll era to perform at halftime. His recording of "The Twist" had started a dance craze when it hit number one in 1960. The halftime show was produced by Radio City Music Hall and featured the Rockettes along with eighty-eight grand pianos in a show called "Something Grand."

It would be another three years before a contemporary singing group headlined halftime. The New Kids on the Block were featured in a Disney-produced show, "A Small World Salute to 25 years of the Super Bowl" in Tampa for Super Bowl XXV. The fans at the stadium saw the show, but the television audience on ABC did not. Eleven days before the game, on January 16, 1991, President George H. W. Bush announced the start of what would be called Operation Desert Storm, a military operation to expel the Iraqi forces that were occupying Kuwait. Instead of staying with the in-stadium entertainment, ABC News switched live to anchorman Peter Jennings in New York who announced that "we're going to take a few minutes at the beginning of halftime here to get as much up to date as we can with a number of developments in the war today." The halftime show was recorded and played back by ABC after the game, which ended with Buffalo Bills kicker Scott Norwood missing a forty-seven-yard field goal attempt with eight seconds left to secure a 20–19 victory for the New York Giants.

FOX gives the NFL a Wake-up Call

The trap that had been set for the NFL when it adopted the formula for halftime spectaculars that filled the field with marching bands, singers, dancers, pageantry, and "salutes to the past" was sprung in 1992 by the upstart FOX Network. The network was only five years old and still a distant fourth in the ratings, but it had a young, urban audience and was making inroads by capturing the culture of the moment. Comparing the programming on FOX to what the NFL was presenting for halftime entertainment, marketing executives from FOX and PepsiCo's Frito-Lay division hatched an idea to air a live episode of *In Living Color* to lure viewers away from the CBS Super Bowl telecast at halftime.

"I was very confident that we would steal the show," said *In Living Color* creator Keenen Ivory Wayans. "We knew we'd have football fans, and they may not have seen the show. We decided to combine making fun of football and using the characters from the show. There was a lot of improvisation." The cast of the show knew that the NFL's halftime show was primed for a takeover, and Frito-Lay agreed to sponsor the live FOX program.

Weeks in advance FOX began a heavy promotional campaign, inviting people to "be sure to tune in to *In Living Color* when the Super Bowl reached halftime. It worked. More than twenty million viewers switched from the CBS coverage to their local FOX stations. Washington had built a 17–0 lead over Buffalo, and the NFL's "Winter Magic" show from the Metrodome in Minneapolis featured dancers dressed like snowflakes and Olympic champion figure skaters Dorothy Hamill and Brian Boitano performing on an elevated plastic ice rink. The music was provided by Gloria Estefan from the popular Miami Sound Machine, but Jim Steeg, who was the NFL's senior vice president for special events, said the show "wasn't driven by the talent. It was more about a spectacle or spectacular. We were trying to figure out how you could celebrate the North and its elements."

The millions who tuned out from CBS's show saw *In Living Color*'s opening sketch with Keenan and Damon Wayans ostensibly rummaging through the Bills deserted locker room while the players are on the field. They find Thurman Thomas's wallet and joke about how high the limits might be on his gold credit card. All the while, a countdown clock in the corner of the screen tracked the time so that football fans could return to the game for the start of the third quarter. The segment that stole the show was an off-color and silly edition of "Men on Football," that would very likely be deemed inappropriate for primetime television today. Damon Wayans and David Alan Grier played culture critics who analyzed football by delivering as many sexual innuendos and double entendres as possible. Affecting effeminate voices, they chatted about why they had been football fans for years: "What other game boasts such great names as Dick Butkus?" "Or my favorite, Bob Griese." "Now isn't he a tight end?" "He *was*." Grier said later, "Honestly, some of the sketches were probably too risqué. But we had a delay, and if the censors wanted to press the delay button, they'd push it. We were trying to make people flip the channel." The Nielsen ratings showed just how many had made the "flip." That *In Living Color* episode reached a total audience of 28.9 million viewers.[5]

Halftime Becomes a Rock Concert

The NFL immediately went on offense and changed direction. "This isn't going to ever happen again," said Jim Steeg. "We went on the aggressive and selected Radio City to [produce] the halftime show the next year in Pasadena." He said he never remembered Commissioner Rozelle asking what he was going to do, but by March 1992, he and his team had identified who they wanted as the headliner for Super Bowl XXVII at the Rose Bowl. They set a meeting with Michael Jackson's agent.[6]

Jackson was a dynamic performer and the best-selling recording artist of the 1980s. His *Thriller* album, released in 1982, spent thirty-seven weeks in the number-one spot on *Billboard* magazine's charts, and it remained in the top ten for more than a year and a half, a total of eighty weeks. Jackson's *Bad* album came out in 1987, and five of its tracks all hit number one on the best-selling singles charts. The "King of Pop" released his *Dangerous* album in November 1991 and would begin his Dangerous World Tour in June 1992. It started in Munich and made thirty-one stops in Europe that summer and fall, then moved to Tokyo for eight concerts in December. Jackson would be back in the United States in January 1993 and available for the Super Bowl.

However, Jackson's agent had to be sold on doing a halftime show. The Super Bowl had never put the spotlight on just one star, but instead had always woven them into a theme with other bands and performers. Since leaving the Jackson Five in 1984, Michael Jackson had shared his stage with no one. And he paid little attention to NFL football. "Michael wasn't too aware of the Super Bowl. He wasn't too aware of how big this was," recalled Arlen Kantarian, the show's executive producer for Radio City. In one meeting, Kantarian remembered Jackson asking, "Why don't we call it the *Thriller Bowl?*" One number helped seal the deal: 160. That's the number of countries in which the Super Bowl would be televised, many of which were on the itinerary for the resumption of the Dangerous World Tour, which was scheduled to hit the road again in August 1993 with stops in Bangkok, Singapore, Taipei, Moscow, Tel Aviv, Istanbul, and South America. Jackson's appearance in the Super Bowl show would help sell tickets for his concert tour.[7]

Michael brought his own band and dancers to the Rose Bowl to perform on a twelve-ton stage that came in twenty-six separate pieces. The NFL hired 275 stagehands who assembled it in six minutes. On Sunday, January 31, 1993, the halftime show began with James Earl Jones, the voice of Darth Vader, introducing Jackson on the public address system. The crowd began to roar, 3,500 cheering children ran onto the field to surround the elevated stage, and Jackson made his entrance by popping up through the floor, propelled eight feet into the air by a machine called the "toaster," which he was using on the Dangerous tour. Wearing a navy and gold military jacket and aviator sunglasses, Jackson held a rigid pose for a minute and a half as the anticipation and the crowd noise rose to a crescendo. The star had told producer Don Mischer, "Don't cue the music to start, or anything else, until I break my wrist. I'm gonna feel it. I'm gonna feel it." When he did, Jackson broke into a set that started with his megahit "Billie Jean" from the *Thriller* album. The stadium erupted, and the Super Bowl halftime show would never be the same.

That Super Bowl at the Rose Bowl was a 52–17 blowout as the Dallas Cowboys handed the Buffalo Bills their third straight championship loss, but the television audience soared to almost ninety-one million viewers per minute, a jump of 14.3 percent over the previous year. Never again did the television ratings numbers fall to the level of the "pre–rock concert" era. Clearly the King of Pop at halftime made a huge difference, and he set the bar so high that the NFL struggled to outdo itself for the rest of the 1990s.

The year after Michael Jackson's halftime, country performers Clint Black, Tanya Tucker, Travis Tritt, and The Judds took the stage for "Rockin' Country Sunday." Then in 1995, Disney produced a cumbersome "Indiana Jones and the Temple of the Forbidden Eye" show that featured the curious combination of Tony Bennett, Patti LaBelle, Arturo Sandoval, and the Miami Sound Machine, plus flaming skydivers, snakes, skulls, a giant rolling boulder, a stolen Vince Lombardi Trophy stunt, and a finale that included audience participation with light sticks. When Diana Ross took the stage in 1996 to celebrate the thirtieth anniversary of the Super Bowl, the spotlight focused only on her, and the rock concert aura of Michael Jackson's show returned.

The World Changed Forever

Several months before Super Bowl XXXVI in 2002, the NFL had booked Janet Jackson as the halftime headliner and the Bee Gees to perform before the game at the Louisiana Superdome. But on September 11, 2001, the world changed. The horrific terror attacks on American soil changed everyone's perspective, including how the NFL looked at the meaning of halftime at the Super Bowl for the millions who would be watching at home and around the world. The league and that year's broadcaster, FOX, were determined to present a somber salute and an unparalleled spectacular. "It was 'OK, all the plans are out the window; we've got to start over,'" said David Hill, FOX Sports president. "We knew we had to come up with something that would fit the mood of the country."[8]

The task of finding a replacement for Janet Jackson was put in the hands of John Collins, who at the time was the NFL's top marketing executive. On Wednesday, October 24, 2001, just six weeks after New York was devastated by the attacks on the World Trade Center's Twin Towers, Collins had attended a performance by U2 at Madison Square Garden. During one of the band's encores that night, the names of the nearly three thousand people killed on 9/11 scrolled slowly across the domed roof of the arena. "At first people didn't know what was going on," Collins remembered, "and then you heard, 'Oh, my God!' as they realized. People were reading the names of victims they'd known. It was a heavy moment, an amazing moment." Two days later the NFL signed U2 for the halftime of Super Bowl XXXVI, which would be played one week later than originally scheduled because the league had chosen not to play any games on the weekend following the terrorist attacks in September. There were some reservations at the NFL offices about an Irish band commemorating an American tragedy, but the league's chief operating officer at the time, Roger Goodell, endorsed John Collins's choice. Bono, the lead singer of U2, was passionate about doing the tribute. He explained to NFL executives that the purpose of the solemn roll call would be to shift the focus from the statistics, the number of dead, and return it to the individuals.[9]

The fans gathered in New Orleans on February 3, 2002, and an audience approaching ninety million worldwide witnessed the most powerful halftime in Super Bowl history. As Bono belted out "Where the Streets Have No Name," the names of every person killed in the 9/11 attacks slowly scrolled skyward on towering, illuminated columns of fabric. And in what was for many a most fitting conclusion to a game that in so many ways had evoked the spirit of America, the New England Patriots were the victors 20–17 over the St. Louis Rams. The team had chosen to be introduced before the game, not as individuals as was the custom, but simply as "the Patriots."

The Wardrobe Malfunction Returns Halftime to Vintage Rock 'n' Roll

When Janet Jackson was originally booked as the halftime headliner for Super Bowl XXXVI, she was riding high. Her single "All for You" had spent seven weeks at number one on the Billboard Hot 100, and she was in the middle of a concert tour that began in July 2001 and was scheduled to conclude in February 2002, right after the Super Bowl. Jackson's upbeat and theatrical All for You Tour took her to sixty-eight cities in North America and four in Japan in support of her album of the same title. When she was booked to perform two years later for the halftime show at Super Bowl XXXVIII, she was not touring, and her string of ten career number-one hits that began in 1986 had come to an end with "All for You."

CBS was the designated broadcaster for the Super Bowl that would be played February 1, 2004, at Reliant Stadium in Houston. The NFL hired MTV, which along with CBS was co-owned by Viacom, to stage the show. MTV producers were given a wide berth to create a halftime that would feature Janet Jackson with artists P. Diddy, Nelly, Kid Rock, and a surprise appearance by rising star Justin Timberlake. The finale of the show was a duet with Jackson, who was thirty-seven years old, and Timberlake, who had just turned twenty-three the day before the game, singing "Rock Your Body." The song concluded with the lyric, "Bet I'll have you naked by the end of this song," at which point Timberlake pulled away a piece of Janet Jackson's leather top, exposing her bare right breast for half a second.[10]

The aftermath of the "wardrobe malfunction" was immediate and considerable. The NFL moving forward would take much more control and exercise greater oversight over the content and production of Super Bowl halftimes. MTV was banned from ever producing another halftime, Janet Jackson's career suffered with far more of the blame unfairly falling on her than on Timberlake or the show's producers, and the NFL entered a prolonged era of vintage rock 'n' roll headliners who would perform their hits from the past and not venture anywhere close to the risqué line that had been crossed in 2004.

The first was sixty-three-year-old Paul McCartney at halftime of Super Bowl XXXIX in Jacksonville, followed in 2006 by the Rolling Stones, who were still immensely popular but who hadn't had a number-one hit since 1978. Prince headlined an unforgettable halftime show in 2007, performing his 1984 hit "Purple Rain" in the pouring rain at Dolphins Stadium in Miami, and one year later Tom Petty and the Heartbreakers took the stage for Super Bowl XLI in Glendale, Arizona. The vintage rock era concluded with Bruce Springsteen and the E Street Band bringing down the house at Raymond James Stadium in Tampa in 2009, and the Who performing on a circular stage in an elaborate synchronized light show for the halftime of Super Bowl XLIV on February 7, 2010, back in Miami.

Keeping Pace with Twenty-First-Century Culture

Super Bowl halftimes in the twenty-first century had irretrievably taken on the identity of rock concerts featuring artists with mass popular appeal whose performances would attract millions of fans more interested in the entertainment, not football. The actual performances average only twelve minutes out of each thirty-minute Super Bowl halftime. It takes nine minutes after the end of the first half to set up the staging, and after the twelve-minute concert is over, eight minutes are allotted to remove all the set pieces from the field. That leaves one minute for the teams to assemble for the start of the second half.

A trend toward more current artists began in 2011 with the halftime show for Super Bowl XLV at the brand-new Cowboys Stadium in Texas starring the Black-Eyed Peas, Usher, and Slash. It was the first year that the NFL's new senior vice president for programming and production, Mark Quenzel, was put in charge of Super Bowl halftimes. "We believe that football in general and music are an intersection of cultures," said Quenzel. "We believe that our fans, and there are many of them who enjoy music and they enjoy the NFL, and we try to merge those cultures. Obviously the most visible example of that is the Super Bowl, and certainly Super Bowl halftime."[11]

The NFL begins the process of selecting a halftime performer more than a year in advance, reaching out to those who would appeal to the broad demographic of viewers who range in age from eight to eighty-plus. And they field offers from performers who reach out directly to the league to express their interest in stepping onto the Super Bowl stage. Finding the right match is crucial because, "It is the merging of two gigantic brands all the time," said Mark Quenzel. "It's the NFL brand and it's the artist's brand. The idea is to try and make sure that both brands are represented in the way we want ours to be represented and the way the artist does." Timing is an important part of the selection process. Artists that are "in cycle," meaning that they will be touring or releasing new music right after the Super Bowl, tend to make the best candidates.

The NFL does not pay the halftime headliners. It never has. The league covers the costs of staging the halftimes, but there is no fee for the performers. The payoff for them is the exposure, so an artist "in cycle" reaps the greatest benefit from the promotion to a huge audience that the Super Bowl provides. For example, immediately following their halftime show at Super Bowl LIV in Miami in 2020, Jennifer Lopez saw an 800 percent increase in her music sales, and Shakira got a bump of 925 percent. The biggest beneficiary of Super Bowl exposure in the decade of 2011 through 2020 was Lady Gaga, whose music sales soared by 1,009 percent after her halftime show in 2017 at NRG Stadium in Houston. Katy Perry's Super Bowl halftime show in 2015 helped her launch a new cosmetics line, and her music sales increased by 146 percent.

An average of 129.3 million viewers per minute watched Usher's performance at Super Bowl LVIII in February 2024. Compare that to the average of 123.7 million per minute who watched the football segments of the telecast. Almost six million more people tuned in to see the entertainment than the contest in which the Kansas City Chiefs defeated the San Francisco 49ers 25–22 in overtime.

"When I started, the goal of the Super Bowl halftime was to really maintain somewhere in the range of 95 percent of the audience that was there at the end of the first half," said the NFL's Mark Quenzel. It has now surpassed 100 percent of the game viewership every year.

To Honor America

"The Star-Spangled Banner" was officially designated as the national anthem of the United States on March 3, 1931, when President Herbert Hoover signed into law a bill that had been passed by both houses of Congress. The bill was originally proposed in 1929 by a Maryland congressman whose goal was to promote Baltimore's patriotic history. The song was written in 1814 by Francis Scott Key during the British siege of Fort McHenry in Baltimore harbor, near the end of the War of 1812. When "The Star-Spangled Banner" became the national anthem, the National Football League had been playing games for a decade.

Performing the anthem before sporting events has long been a tradition in the United States, but in the 1930s it was not routinely performed at NFL games. That changed after the nation was plunged into World War II following the Japanese attack on Pearl Harbor, Hawaii, on December 7, 1941. NFL teams adopted the anthem as part of every pregame beginning with the 1942 season to show support for the American servicemen and women fighting overseas. When the war came to an end in August 1945, NFL Commissioner Elmer Layden announced that he would instruct all teams to make the playing of "The Star-Spangled Banner" a permanent part of every NFL game beginning with the 1945 season. "The playing of the National Anthem should be as much a part of every game as the kickoff," said Layden. "We must not drop it simply because the war is over. We should never forget what it stands for."[12]

The NFL embraced "The Star-Spangled Banner" as it connected its identity with the attributes and ideals that represent America. The birth of the Super Bowl in 1967 provided the league with a stage of unprecedented size and scale upon which to show the patriotism it shared with its devoted fans. A choir from UCLA sang the national anthem preceding the game at the Los Angeles Coliseum, accompanied by the Pride of Arizona and the Michigan Marching Band. The following year at the Orange Bowl in Miami, the Grambling State Marching Band performed the anthem before the game without a choir and did the halftime show. Instrumental versions of "The Star-Spangled Banner" were presented at each of the next three Super Bowls, all by renowned trumpet players: jazz great Al Hirt from New Orleans did the honors at Super Bowl III in 1969; Lloyd Geisler, who was first trumpet for the National Symphony in Washington, DC, played at Super Bowl IV; and Tommy Loy, the regular trumpeter for Dallas Cowboys games performed the anthem at Super Bowl V (which his Cowboys lost to the Baltimore Colts 16–13). "We wuz robbed," said Loy after the game.

It was not until Super Bowl VIII in Houston in 1974 that the NFL saw the opportunity to add star power to the performance of the national anthem. They chose Charley Pride, who had won the Country Music Association Entertainer of the Year award in 1971 and a Grammy in 1972 for Best Male Country Vocal. In the history of the CMA awards from their inception in 1969 through 2023, Charley Pride is the only African American ever to win Entertainer of the Year. Over the course of his career, Pride had twenty-nine number-one country singles, including his biggest hit, "Kiss an Angel Good Mornin'" in 1971. Charley Pride played professional baseball with the Memphis Red Sox of the Negro American League and several other minor league teams across the country in the 1950s long before he began his singing career. The first time he ever sang before a crowd was to perform the national anthem at ballparks before he took the field to either pitch or play the outfield.

The only Super Bowl at which "The Star-Spangled Banner" was not performed during the game's more than half century was in 1977, when the NFL chose to honor America with the singing of "America the Beautiful" at Super Bowl XI. The stirring lyrics, "O beautiful for spacious skies/For amber waves of grain/For purple mountain majesties/Above the fruited plain!" had been written in 1893 by Katharine Lee Bates, a thirty-three-year-old English literature instructor from Wellesley College. She was with a group climbing Pike's Peak in Colorado during the summer of 1893. "It was then and there," she told the *Boston Evening Transcript* in 1904, "as I was looking out over the sea-like expanse of fertile country spreading away so far under those ample skies, that the opening lines of the hymn floated into my mind."

The artist chosen to sing "America the Beautiful" in 1977 was Vikki Carr, a Grammy nominee who had released seventeen albums, had sung at the White House, and was seen regularly on the television variety shows of the era. Born Florencia Bisenta de Casillas Martinez Cardona in El Paso, Texas, she recorded in both Spanish and English, earning gold and platinum albums in the United States, Mexico, Chile, Puerto Rico, Venezuela, Costa Rica, Colombia, and Ecuador. In the 1970s, Vikki Carr was national chairwoman of the Christmas Seal Drive to fight lung disease. She has since been inducted into the Latino Legends Hall of Fame and was honored with the National Hispanic Media Coalition Impact Lifetime Achievement Award.

The NFL returned to "The Star-Spangled Banner" for Super Bowl XII and for every game since, but the league had begun to shine a brighter light on its pregame anthems and had taken a step toward reaching a more international audience.

Moving the Super Bowl pregame and anthem performances up to the next level was one of Jim Steeg's first goals when he joined the NFL in 1979, at age twenty-nine, as the director of special events.

He remembered walking into Commissioner Pete Rozelle's office in 1981 and saying, "I'd like to try for Diana Ross." Rozelle's response was, "Go ahead, kid, but you've got no shot."[13] Steeg succeeded in landing Diana Ross, one of the biggest stars of her generation, to sing the national anthem for Super Bowl XVI at the Pontiac Silverdome, which was just outside her hometown of Detroit. When she was introduced by the stadium's public address announcer, Ross asked the 81,270 people in attendance, "Can we sing our national anthem with authority? Sing with me." She proceeded to sing the anthem a cappella, her only accompaniment the voices of the crowd joining her in unison. The game between the San Francisco 49ers and the Cincinnati Bengals was seen on CBS by an average of 85,240,000 viewers per minute, all of whom witnessed the Super Bowl suddenly rachet up its star power. In subsequent years, Diana Ross was followed by pop superstars Barry Manilow, Neil Diamond, Billy Joel, and Whitney Houston. When you consider that the group at the NFL's New York offices that was booking rock stars to sing the anthem were the same people still scheduling Up with People and salutes to "Superstars of the Silver Screen" for halftime, you can see how powerful the inertia must have been to stick with the formula that had endured for decades and had indelibly defined what an on-field spectacular at the Super Bowl was supposed to be.

Whitney Houston's performance at Super Bowl XXV on January 27, 1991, is still ranked by many observers as the greatest ever. The patriotic message of "The Star-Spangled Banner" was magnified by the fact that American forces had been dispatched to the Middle East less than two weeks earlier to battle Saddam Hussein's Iraqi army. As she stepped to the microphone wearing a white tracksuit because of the chilly temperatures in Tampa that evening, the public address announcer said, "And now to honor America, especially the brave men and women serving our nation in the Persian Gulf and throughout the world, please join in the singing of our nation anthem." Whitney Houston's voice seemed to come from deep within her soul, and she transformed the song dating back to 1814 into a powerful beacon of hope for 1991. She and music director Rickey Minor literally transformed the anthem from its traditional 3/4 time signature to 4/4 time. "What we tried to do was to put it in 4/4 meter," said Minor. "We wanted to give her a chance to phrase it in such a way that she would be able to take her time and really express the meaning."

The music and Whitney Houston's vocal had been prerecorded because of the difficulty in hearing onself when singing in a cavernous stadium, but the impact was not diminished in the least. As Houston finished with "and the home of the brave," she raised first her right arm then her left above her head and belted out the final word, holding it for a dramatic eight seconds. The crowd erupted, and F-16 fighter jets from Tampa's MacDill Air Force Base screamed by overhead.[14]

Two years later in January 1993, Super Bowl XXVII at the Rose Bowl in Pasadena came within minutes of not having a performer for the national anthem at all. In retrospect, it was a star-crossed game. This Super Bowl was originally scheduled to be played in Phoenix, but after a 1990 referendum to join virtually every other state in adopting the Martin Luther King Jr. holiday was rejected by Arizona voters, the NFL moved the game to the Rose Bowl. It was also the Super Bowl at which Michael Jackson's electric performance transformed halftime shows forever. Garth Brooks, the CMA Entertainer of the Year in both 1991 and 1992, was booked to sing "The Star-Spangled Banner." He would win the CMA award for an unprecedented third consecutive year in 1993.

Brooks had agreed to sing the anthem if, in return, NBC would air his "We Shall Be Free" music video earlier in its pregame show. NBC had consented to Brooks's request, but an hour before the game, a network representative told the country music star that it would not air the video because he had failed to meet the deadline for delivery of the tape. Brooks was in his dressing room at the Rose Bowl and started to take off his boots, telling the NBC official that if his conditions weren't met, he wouldn't be performing. The NFL and NBC began to scramble, even approaching Jon Bon Jovi, who was attending the game as a fan, to ask if he would sing in place of Brooks.

"We Shall Be Free" was the first single released from Garth Brooks's *The Chase* album, which debuted in September 1992 at number one on the Billboard multigenre charts. Its message of acceptance and inclusiveness had struck some people, including several at the NFL and at NBC, as taking a greater political stand than they would have preferred. The lines at the end of Brooks's lyrics that spoke of everyone's freedom to choose who they love proved to be problematic because at the time the AIDS epidemic was inexorably linked to homosexuality. Garth Brooks said he was inspired to write the song by the Los Angeles riots of April 1992, which erupted after the acquittal of the police officers who had been charged with the savage beating of Rodney King. He and his band had been leaving the Academy of Country Music Awards in Los Angeles when they saw buildings burning throughout the city. "It was pretty scary for all of us, especially a bunch of guys from Oklahoma," said Brooks in a 1996 radio interview.[15]

NBC did have the "We Shall Be Free" tape, and when Garth Brooks saw it appear on the television in his dressing room, he pulled his boots back on, and fifteen minutes later sung an inspired rendition of "The Star-Spangled Banner" to the crowd of 98,374 fans in Pasadena and more than ninety million watching on NBC. Brooks held his trademark cowboy hat in his left hand and actress Marlee Matlin stood at his right, signing the words for the hearing impaired. The delay in getting "We Shall Be Free" into the telecast pushed the kickoff back by two minutes. It didn't matter to the Dallas Cowboys, who thrashed the Buffalo Bills 52–17.

Only two artists have ever sung the national anthem at the Super Bowl more than once. Billy Joel had the honor at Super Bowl XXIII in 1989, then returned eighteen years later to sing it in 2007 at Super Bowl XLI. Both games were played in Miami. Aaron Neville performed the anthem solo at Super Bowl XXIV in 1990, then joined Aretha Franklin and Dr. John in Detroit at Super Bowl XL in 2006.

A span of twenty-four years elapsed after Vikki Carr sang "America the Beautiful" before the song would return to join the national anthem in a Super Bowl pregame show. At Super Bowl XXXV in Tampa on January 28, 2001, the legendary Ray Charles delivered perhaps the most soulful rendition ever of this hymn to America. Standing at a microphone flanked by three backup singers, Charles, who was then seventy years old, embraced "America the Beautiful," adding phrases that personalized the song as his own testament to the land of his birth: "He crowned thy good, yes he did, with brotherhood," and, "America, oh I love you America, God shed his grace on thee."

As a tribute to Ray Charles, who died in 2004, the NFL brought five-time Grammy Award winner Alicia Keys to Jacksonville to sing "America the Beautiful" before Super Bowl XXXIX. Starting at her piano, she was surrounded by nearly one hundred students from Ray Charles's alma mater, the Florida School for the Deaf and Blind in nearby St. Augustine. They sang and signed the lyrics together as Alicia Keys stepped forward on the stage and was accompanied by a recording of Ray Charles performing "America the Beautiful." With Charles on the huge stadium video screen, they sang in harmony to a rousing finish. It was wise that the NFL booked the combined choirs from the US Armed Forces for the national anthem that year so that no one artist had to take the stage after that showstopping performance.

It was becoming apparent that the addition of "America the Beautiful" did not diminish the importance of the national anthem at the Super Bowl, but rather added to the expressed love of country and the patriotic fervor that the NFL wants the Super Bowl to represent. Beginning with Faith Hill in 2009, "America the Beautiful" became an annual part of Super Bowl pregames. The artists selected by the league each year since have tended to be up-and-coming stars or those with a primarily domestic following compared to the global superstars that headline the halftime concerts. The NFL's Mark Quenzel said the goal is to balance the national anthem and "America the Beautiful." He used Super Bowl LIII in 2019 as an example. "We've got Gladys Knight doing the national anthem, which is fabulous, legendary. She's from Atlanta, just a generational talent. And these two young sisters named Chloe and Halle singing 'America the Beautiful' represent the future of music."

In 2021, following the social upheaval ignited by the killing of George Floyd by Minneapolis police, the NFL added "Lift Every Voice and Sing" to the annual pregame presentations. That year it was a prerecorded performance by Alicia Keyes, and since 2023 it has joined "America the Beautiful" and "The Star-Spangled Banner" as part of the live Super Bowl pregame. The lyrics to "Lift Every Voice and Sing" were written in 1900 by James Weldon Johnson as a poem commemorating the death of Abraham Lincoln and expressed the hopeful appeal of Black Americans for liberty. His brother John set the words to music five years later. The song was adopted by the NAACP as its anthem in 1919, and it rose to prominence in the civil rights movement of the 1950s and 1960s.

The Super Bowl Halo

The Super Bowl has grown into such a powerful entertainment entity that it has also proven itself to be a vehicle for the effective promotion of nonsports entertainment programs and products, as well as for sports. When their turn comes every year, each of the broadcast networks in the rotation develops strategies to create interest and awareness for new comedy or drama series that will soon premiere, as well to grow the viewing audiences for their current programs. Very often the promotional strategy includes a special event such as the launch of a new direct-to-consumer service or an upcoming sports event such as the Olympics on NBC. The established network rotation would have had NBC televising the Super Bowl in early 2021 followed by CBS in 2022. NBC, however, negotiated a swap with CBS so that it could broadcast Super Bowl LVI on February 6, 2022, which would coincide with the opening of the Beijing Winter Olympic Games that same weekend. The Super Bowl, the first one at the new SoFi Stadium in Los Angeles, served as a major platform from which NBC stimulated interest in and viewership for its Olympic programming, which continued through Sunday, February 20, 2022, and drew a total of 150 million viewers.

The shows with the greatest potential for benefitting from the massive exposure generated by the Super Bowl are those scheduled to air immediately following the game on the network airing the telecast. They can expect the kind of ratings boost that will guarantee a successful series launch or bring renewed life to an established program. For example, NBC premiered the second season of *The Voice* on February 5, 2012, following its Super Bowl XLVI telecast in which the New York Giants spoiled the New England Patriots bid for a perfect 19–0 season. An average of more than 111 million viewers watched the game, and 37.6 million stayed tuned for *The Voice*. As a result, the show became one of NBC's biggest hits for the remainder of the decade. The broadcast networks use valuable time during commercial breaks to promote their upcoming shows. With thirty-second commercials selling for more than several million dollars each, using the time for promotions instead of selling it to advertisers is a major investment in the success of the network's programming.

When CBS scheduled a live episode of *The Late Show with Stephen Colbert* to follow its broadcast of Super Bowl 50 on February 7, 2016, it promoted Colbert's guests Tina Fey, Will Ferrell, Margot Robbie, Keegan Michael Key, and Jordan Peele. Colbert had taken over the show from David Letterman the previous year, and the post–Super Bowl slot helped expose his brand of entertainment to 20.6 million viewers. That was eight times as many as were watching the regular Monday through Friday programs. The powerful Super Bowl coattails helped Colbert build momentum, and within two years *The Late Show* had taken the late-night ratings lead from NBC's *The Tonight Show with Jimmy Fallon*.

The all-time coattails leader is the *Friends* episode that followed Super Bowl XXX on NBC in 1996. More than half of the 94.1 million viewers who watched the Super Bowl stayed tuned to watch the regular cast and their special guest stars Brooke Shields, Chris Isaak, Julia Roberts, Jean-Claude Van Damme, Fred Willard, and Dan Castellaneta. *Friends* was doing well in its second season, but gaining 52.9 million viewers from the Super Bowl halo helped propel the series to eight more successful seasons on NBC.

The halo, however, does not always guarantee a ratings winner. Following its telecast of Super Bowl LI in February 2017, FOX awarded the coveted slot to *24: Legacy*, a reboot of its *24* franchise, which had been a hit for a decade. Its star, Kiefer Sutherland, was gone, replaced by Corey Hawkins in the lead role as Eric Carter, a former army ranger whose team gets tangled in a terrorist assassination plot. FOX promoted the show heavily during the thrilling comeback win by the New England Patriots over the Atlanta Falcons, but only 17.6 million viewers stayed tuned to watch *24: Legacy* out of more than 111 million who watched the Patriots erase the Falcons 28–3 third quarter lead; *24: Legacy* just didn't connect with viewers, and it was canceled in June 2017.

The promotional power that the Super Bowl has demonstrated for television entertainment programs extends to the motion picture industry. Each year several studios buy commercial time in the Super Bowl to excite fans with their movie trailers and kick off a promotional campaign for the upcoming release of new films. With an audience averaging more than one hundred million people in the United States, a studio would need to entice only 5 percent of the viewers to buy a ticket to make a sizeable impact at the box office. Five million people paying $15 to $20 each would generate $75 to $100 million in revenue. That's an excellent return on the $7 million or so spent to buy a commercial.

In Super Bowl LII on February 4, 2018, six movies were advertised during the game. One, *The Cloverfield Paradox* on Netflix, was released that day, with the intention of encouraging Netflix subscribers to watch the movie after the game and to generate new subscribers by showing people in non-Netflix homes what they were missing. Paramount on the other hand bought time in the Super Bowl to promote *Mission Impossible: Fallout*, which would not hit US theaters until July 27. Six months between a television commercial and a consumer's first opportunity to make a purchase is a long time, but Paramount used the Super Bowl to launch its campaign to the largest audience possible then build from there until the premiere. In five months—from July 27 until the end of 2018—*Mission Impossible: Fallout* took in $200 million at the box office, making it the eighth most successful film of the year. Marvel Studios' *Avengers: Infinity War* also advertised in Super Bowl LII in advance of its release on April 27, 2018. Its box office total for the year hit $678.8 million, which sent it all the way to the number-two position for the year (behind *Black Panther*, which hit $700 million and did not buy time in the Super Bowl). The six movies that did use the Super Bowl as a promotional platform raked in a total of almost $1.8 billion in North American receipts.[16]

Not every film that is advertised in the Super Bowl is guaranteed to succeed, but the telecast's promotional power is on display every year. In Super Bowl LIII in 2019, Marvel Studios returned with an ad for *Avengers: End Game*, which was due to be released on April 26. It rocketed to number one for the year, with a total box office of $858 million, not counting international sales. In 2019, however, only three theatrical releases bought time in the Super Bowl, reflecting the public's move to online video consumption. Netflix, Amazon's Prime Video, and Hulu stepped in to promote their digital offerings. Regardless of how or where Americans consume their entertainment, the Super Bowl has proven that it is the best place to reach a huge audience across all demographics and stimulate interest and the intent to buy.

The Super Bowl in the Movies

The Super Bowl has never needed promotion from the movies to increase its reach, but in 1975 Los Angeles Rams owner Carroll Rosenbloom convinced his fellow NFL owners that having the game featured in a major motion picture would be good for the league and add to the prestige of its annual showcase event. Rosenbloom was on the board of Warner Brothers, which was planning to produce a film entitled *Black Sunday*, starring Robert Shaw, Bruce Dern, and Marthe Keller. The movie is based on a novel by Thomas Harris in which a terrorist organization plots an attack on the Super Bowl using the Goodyear blimp. They enlist a psychologically scarred Vietnam veteran, played by Dern, who is an active blimp pilot. Robert Shaw is the law enforcement agent trying to thwart the attack. What should have raised a red flag for the NFL was the fact that the terrorist group in the script was patterned after Black September, the Palestinian splinter group responsible for the deadly attack on the 1972 Olympics in Munich. The director Warner Brothers signed was John Frankenheimer, who won acclaim in the 1960s with *Birdman of Alcatraz*, *The Manchurian Candidate*, and *Seven Days in May*.

The NFL allowed Frankenheimer to shoot several scenes at Super Bowl X in Miami's Orange Bowl in January 1976, including plays on the field between the Pittsburgh Steelers and the Dallas Cowboys. NFL Commissioner Pete Rozelle and Dolphins owner Joe Robbie appeared in cameo roles as themselves, and at one point Robert Shaw's character dashes into the CBS truck, where executive producer Robert Wussler repels his intrusion and sends him packing. One scene in the script called for Shaw to run across the field, but the NFL refused, so instead he sprinted along the sideline behind the benches and then around the end zone while the game was underway. The access granted the *Black Sunday* film crew was a first for the NFL, and it would never be repeated.

When the movie came out in April 1977, people in theaters across the country saw thousands of Super Bowl fans being injured and fleeing for their lives as the blimp crashes into the stands. The last thing that the NFL would ever want associated with its biggest event and celebration would be fear and the risk of death. From then on, access to the Super Bowl itself has been strictly limited. Other movies have used the Super Bowl as part of their stories, notably *Two-Minute Warning* in 1976, *Heaven Can Wait* in 1978, and *Ace Ventura: Pet Detective*, starring Jim Carrey and Dan Marino from 1994, but they all had to stage their football and stadium scenes elsewhere.

The NFL's goal of using a major motion picture to add prestige to the Super Bowl did not work out, but attendance did not suffer. The first Super Bowl after the release of *Black Sunday* was played January 15, 1978, before a packed house of 76,400 at the Louisiana Superdome, which was 1,900 patrons above capacity, and the game has been a consistent sell-out ever since.

The one goal set by Pete Rozelle that was realized perhaps to a greater extent than any other was for the Super Bowl to become "more than a game, to make it an event." Surveys now show that a majority of Americans consider the Super Bowl to be more of a social event or an entertainment spectacle than a sporting event. And that perception is even greater among millennials than in the general population. It is the centerpiece of a day that millions of Americans treat as a holiday and a telecast that features elite entertainment before the game, a dazzling twelve-minute concert of contemporary music at halftime, the most-watched festival of short films that come disguised as commercials, trailers that offer glimpses of scenes from upcoming films and television programs—and the most anticipated football game of the year.

CHAPTER 12

The Drive to Super Bowl 100

THE SUPER BOWL HAS CHANGED SO MUCH IN ITS FIRST HALF-CENTURY that virtually the only thing that has remained the same is the game itself. Projecting forward to the year 2066, in what ways will the event as we now know it have changed for Super Bowl 100? Where will it be played? In the United States or in some foreign capital that has become a hotbed for American gridiron football? How will we see and experience the game and all its surrounding entertainment? Will the NFL use "100" instead of the Roman numeral "C?" (The league abandoned Roman numerals in 2016 for Super Bowl 50 because the digits made a stronger statement on the logo than a simple "L" would have).

The Super Bowl—and all sports—are now played in an era of technology that did not exist when the first "AFL versus NFL World Championship" took place in 1967. The internet, streaming video services, commercial satellite delivery of programming, cable television, dedicated sports networks, enhanced audio, virtual, and augmented reality, and three-dimensional graphics and advanced analytics all had yet to arrive. You would need to be a gifted futurist to guess what tools and technology will be commonly used in 2066 and to predict peoples' preferences for their personal and collective entertainment four decades from now. As Yogi Berra once said, "It's tough to make predictions, especially about the future," but there are some signs we can follow as we look toward Super Bowl 100.

Will American Football Still Be Played in 2066?

The safe, correct answer here is "yes." Many people look at the data that show a decline in the number of youth and high school football teams and players in the United States and forecast doom for the NFL. They point to the fact that from the 2011 season to the 2022 season there were almost seventy-five thousand (74,421) fewer high school athletes playing eleven-man football in the U.S. That's a drop of 6.7 percent in eleven years, which in part can be attributed to increased parental concern for the safety of their children, particularly from potential head injuries and the chilling prospect of CTE and long-term disability. The COVID pandemic that interrupted and canceled seasons, disbanded teams, and left would-be players inactive was also partly to blame. And the alternative activities that these students sought out, including the vast array of new video games and mobile apps available, diverted thousands from pursuing team sports. The decline in participation, if projected forward another four decades, would shrink scholastic football dramatically. During the same eleven years, 556 schools dropped football in its eleven-man format. However, the total number of high schools fielding football teams remained virtually unchanged during that time period at 15,393, because more schools offered the game in either its eight- or nine-man formats. The passion for football apparently remained very much alive in towns large and small, but in many places, it was no longer possible to field teams of eleven players per side.[1]

Two other points to consider regarding the relative importance of high school participation for the continued survival of professional football: First, the lack of high school mixed martial arts teams didn't hurt the rapid growth of the Ultimate Fighting Championship (UFC). At the beginning of the 2020s, only 230 US high schools had martial arts teams for boys and only thirty-four schools offered the sport for young women. Yet UFC is an international phenomenon, attracting millions of fans to its live events, pay-per-views, and shows on television.

Second is the risk-versus-reward factor. A large percentage of young people who are skilled in contact sports will take the offer to make millions of dollars per year competing in the NFL, UFC, or any other league, even if they do run the risk of injury. The Bureau of Labor Statistics reports that the average American worker aged twenty-four or younger earns less than $40,000 per year.[2] For even a short period of time, that pales in comparison to a multimillion-dollar contract that carries with it the risk of personal injury.

Make no mistake, the number of youth and high school participants in football is important. College and professional sports need a base of players who have learned and excelled at the game from which to select their future stars. Playing a sport as a youngster is one of the prime indicators of future fandom. If someone played a sport growing up, they are very likely to remain a fan for life. A decline in youth participation very often means there will be fewer young people following a sport and the average age of fans and viewers will increase. The average age of people who now identify as NFL fans has risen to forty-four, and the average age of television viewers watching NFL games has increased to fifty-four. This is problematic for sports that are mass marketed and depend upon large audiences, because the sweet spot for television advertisers is the eighteen to thirty-four age bracket.[3] That's the age when most people are willing to sample new or different products, making them more susceptible to media advertising than older adults who have already decided which beers, cars, or other products they will continue to buy throughout their lifetimes.

Therefore, even though the NFL has the largest fan base in the United States, estimated at around 180 million, and attendance at games has exceeded prepandemic levels, the demographics show a predominantly older audience. Fewer and fewer young people watch linear television like the traditional broadcast or cable networks where NFL games including the Super Bowl are usually seen. They are growing up as video streamers, with the freedom to select the programs they want to see when they want to watch. They are not destined to become cable subscribers. And surveys show that the percentage of school-age children who are avid sports fans is lower than ever. A generation that cares less about sports than their parents and lives in homes where cable and broadcast television have been replaced by streaming services with few or any live games would indeed pose a threat to all professional sports in America.

Streaming television is rapidly displacing broadcast and cable. In 2022, the total consumption of video programming on streaming services surpassed broadcast and cable for the first time, and the trend will not be reversed. The challenge for the NFL and all professional leagues in the coming years will be finding effective ways to reach younger fans on platforms or in environments where their passions intersect with sports. These include sports content on streaming services, on social media, or in video games, all available universally on every device. The move in 2022 to start streaming NFL *Thursday Night Football* games on Amazon's Prime Video and the first Super Bowl simulcast on Nickelodeon in 2024 are examples of the early efforts being made to add youngsters to the fan base. "We are continually looking for ways to deliver our games to fans wherever they watch whether on television or on digital platforms," said Brian Rolapp, the chief media and business officer for the NFL.[4] These steps are undoubtedly the first in what will become a stampede toward a dramatically different delivery of NFL programming.

Will the Super Bowl broadcast on a streaming service in the future? Absolutely, but almost certainly not exclusively. New communications technology not yet invented could provide a variety of options that will appeal to younger viewers, more mature age groups, or both. It will surely become a multiplatform program available to the widest possible audience in numbers and demographics.

What Will Fans See in 2066?

In 2066, expect the game itself to be faster. The pauses that now delay a return to action because of the "official review" of close plays will end. By 2066, the referee looking "under the hood" at replays will be a distant memory. Electronic mapping of every cubic inch of every stadium will allow for instant 360-degree scanning of every play on every axis. Programmed algorithms for every eventuality will automatically provide answers to questions about whether a penalty occurred or if a player's feet were in bounds when he got control of the ball. The "first and ten" line won't be just for TV viewers. It will be superimposed on the field for everyone in the stadium to see: players, spectators, and officials. As a result, decisions as to whether a first down has or has not been achieved also will be automatic. The game in 2066 will still need officials on the field, but more to decide a player's intent when he committed an infraction or when coaches deserve to be ejected for sideline comments than to signal penalties or first downs.

The game will also be safer. To survive and thrive deep into the twenty-first century, safety is an imperative for professional football. New impact-resistant fabrics, pads, and helmets with embedded digital sensors and transmitters will become the norm, providing players far greater protection from injury than they currently enjoy. The NFL initiated its 1st and Future competition in 2021, awarding grants to independent research firms that develop products or systems to improve safety and performance. In its first year, a group at Cornell University received funding for sensors in the form of stretchable materials that use light to detect muscle fatigue and respiration, which can be woven into textiles or stitched into helmets. Another winning firm is using advanced computational modeling and biomimicry, which is the practice of adopting traits found in nature, to create safer headgear. They study the horns of bighorn sheep and the beaks of woodpeckers to learn how these creatures survive powerful forces to their heads. Four decades from now, innovations such as these and countless others will make football at all levels less dangerous for its participants, and fewer stoppages of play to aid injured players will also serve to speed up the game.

Regardless of which platforms televise Super Bowl 100, the show will likely include much of the same storytelling about the players, their teams, the effort, and the games that got them to the championship that we currently see in NFL games. But beyond the basics, technologies yet to be developed will again lead the way. Consider the elements that were part of the most recent Super Bowl you watched that had not been dreamed of or invented back in 1967 for Super Bowl I.

- The Telestrator for analysts to explain visually how and why plays succeeded or failed
- The first-and-ten line showing exactly the point at which the ball secures a first down

- Super slow-motion replays
- Microphones on referees and players
- Cameras suspended over the field that follow the game action
- Highly maneuverable drone cameras in the sky rather than a blimp
- Three-dimensional graphics and animations
- Advanced live-tracking statistics
- The half-hour halftime featuring a rock concert
- On-field live trophy presentations
- Four-hour pregame shows from multiple locations, including each team's locker room
- Multiple network simulcasts in twenty-five-plus languages, feeding the game live around the globe

Innovations now in development will most certainly continue the pattern of debuting in Super Bowl telecasts and then being incorporated into regular season games in each successive decade. Super Bowl LXI (that's 61 for the Roman-numerically challenged) in February 2027 is likely to represent a new milestone in media coverage of the event. That will be the first time that ESPN and ABC combine to present a Super Bowl. Watch for the ultimate "megacast" of all time. We can expect a different version of the game on each network in the ESPN/ABC family, plus:

- A "statcast" with every analytical statistic imaginable (and some unimaginable)
- A Peyton and Eli "Manning-cast"
- An ESPNBet channel using the network's newly acquired sportsbook to track every wager and prop bet after every play.
- A kids-only presentation that focuses on the fun, making each play feel like "kids' play"

- A discrete telecast from a dedicated set of cameras, such as all SkyCam and drone cams or all low-angle field-level cameras
- A live mobile ESPN+ app, and any number of variations still to be determined

By 2066, virtual imagery technology will have reached the point where the NFL will sell virtual tickets to each Super Bowl after seats at the game itself have sold out. With the exception of the pandemic year of 2021, every year since 1969 has been a sellout. Fans who want to experience "being there," without flying to the host city or paying for hotel rooms, will be able to see and hear everything that the fan in that actual seat enjoys. They will buy a virtual ticket to the seat of their choice, put on the latest edition of three-dimensional, 360-degree headset and goggles, and see it all from their favorite sofas. An option would be available to hear the call of the game from either the English-language world feed broadcasters, the announcing team from that year's broadcast/streaming rightsholder, or any of twenty-five or more languages. The price of these virtual seats will be set according to the desirability of the location in the stadium. By selling the same seats twice or more, the NFL will increase its revenue from ticket sales, and more fans will rave about the experience to their friends.

For me, the ideal Super Bowl production for the viewer at home would include all the sounds as they happen, such as player-and-coach interactions on the field and along the sidelines, which are recorded each year at the game by NFL Films crews for use in their edited shows. These live conversations, cheers, jeers, and exultations would add so many more layers of authenticity, character, and subplots to the action on the field. Analysts in the booth would no longer feel pressure to speculate as to how different strategies and tactics were being used. We would hear how and why firsthand, directly from the coaches and players, and sometimes in language not appropriate for a G-rated telecast. The major roadblock to including all this available audio, of course, is the NFL's fear of obscenities being overheard during live presentations that are meant for the widest possible audience, including children and people of varying sensitivities. My solution: create yet another variant, a "Super

Bowl Uncensored" channel that would require an online access code in an attempt to require parental approval. Such a channel would probably be one of the most popular because fans would feel like insiders, privy to the discussions and decision-making before plays and all the colorful reactions afterward.

The Gambling Solution

Virtually since its inaugural game in 1967, more people have bet more money on the Super Bowl than any other single sporting event each year. The legalization of sports gambling, which began in the United States in 2018, is already at work changing the demographics of NFL fans. As more states have adopted sports gambling legislation, the number of Americans placing bets on the Super Bowl has more than doubled, and the total amount they have wagered has quadrupled. Research by the American Gaming Association shows that 45 percent of the group it calls "core" gamblers—people who have actively bet on games—are in the twenty-three to thirty-four age bracket. And 93 percent of them are interested in gambling on NFL games.[5] Young people who have money riding on the outcome of games are more engaged and they watch telecasts for longer periods of time. Their presence in greater numbers will undoubtedly decrease the average age of both NFL fans and viewers as we move toward Super Bowl 100.

It is a paradox that gambling would represent a solution for some of the NFL's ills, because for nearly its entire first century, gambling was seen as a major problem for the NFL. The league punished players who made bets and tried to distance itself as widely as possible from sportsbooks, casinos, and the entire gambling industry. The networks televising NFL games prohibited their commentators from talking about point spreads or making reference to any other gambling propositions during games for fear that their valuable rights contracts with the NFL could be jeopardized. In 1976, after ten Super Bowls, CBS Sports acknowledged the extent of wagering interest on NFL games by adding Jimmy "the Greek" Snyder to its *NFL Today* pregame show. He was not allowed to mention point spreads, so he would predict the final scores for each Sunday's games then explain the factors that went into his forecast. In so doing, Snyder clearly provided the spread. For example, if he said the winner of a certain game would score twenty-four points and the loser's score would be twenty-one, it was easy to deduce that the betting spread was three points.

These restrictions began to change after the May 2018 ruling by the US Supreme Court that the 1992 law intended to protect professional and amateur sports from gambling interests (the Professional and Amateur Sports Protection Act) was unconstitutional. Less than six years later, by the time Super Bowl LVIII was played in February 2024, thirty-eight states and the District of Columbia had approved various forms of regulated sports wagering. Seeing this trend as irreversible and as an opportunity to begin a new revenue stream, the NFL on April 15, 2021, officially reversed its stand on gambling and announced its first-ever US sportsbook partnerships. Caesars Entertainment, DraftKings, and FanDuel all reached agreements to become official sports betting partners of the NFL. These multiyear agreements gave all three partners the exclusive ability to leverage NFL marks within the sports betting category and activate around retail and online sports betting. They also encouraged fans to engage in NFL-themed free-to-play games.[6]

As the number of states that approve sports gambling reaches a plateau, the annual increases in the number of gamblers and the amount wagered on the Super Bowl will become more predictable and less dramatic. However, as gambling itself becomes more commonplace among a larger percentage of the American population over the next few decades, significant changes could lie ahead for the NFL and the Super Bowl itself.

By 2066—and probably long before that milestone Super Bowl 100—we should expect to see widespread mobile betting and kiosks set up at multiple locations in the host city, including bars and restaurants, so that more than just the ticketed fans can get in on the action. Those with tickets who get into the stadium will more than likely be able to place a variety of bets before and during the action using the latest generation of mobile devices. The live video entities, networks, streaming services, and any new distribution technologies providing Super Bowl preview content and game coverage will steadily increase their coverage of the variables that affect gambling lines to meet the growing demand from their viewers.

In the coming years, the proliferation of sports betting and its promotion will produce billions of dollars in profits for the NFL, its gambling partners, and the states that establish legalized wagering operations. It will also gradually alter the demographics of the fans who follow the sport and their motivations for watching or attending the Super Bowl and regular season games. As the characteristics of fandom itself change, some fans who gamble will change their perceptions of players as being responsible for their financial losses, if for example a player drops a pass or misses a kick that would have changed the outcome against the spread. These incidents requiring expanded NFL security measures and player protection are also bound to multiply.

The success of all current and future sports betting is based on product integrity. If someone placing their money on any game even suspects that the outcomes will not be fairly decided on the field of play, they will stop betting on that sport. The wave of increasingly accessible sports gambling and its public acceptance will, however, surely prove irresistible to some individuals inside the game, so expect to see the NFL's vigilance in policing its players, personnel, and partners intensify at a rate commensurate with the expansion of sports wagering itself. The stakes could not be higher for the NFL.

An Audience without Borders

The success of the NFL's International Series of regular season matchups that began in 2007 has raised the question of whether the league will ever establish a franchise overseas. The answer is "Yes, absolutely." League officials have stated that there is a logical time frame from a business perspective to establish the first international expansion team in London. Will a Super Bowl ever be played outside the United States? It's possible, but this answer is only a definite "Maybe."

The NFL began experimenting with exhibition and preseason games in Canada during the pre–Super Bowl era and then in Mexico in 1978. The first preseason NFL game outside North America was in August 1976 at the Tokyo stadium where the Yomiuri Giants baseball team played. The St. Louis Cardinals defeated the San Diego Chargers 20–10. Seeing enthusiastic fans turning out in large numbers, the league created its American Bowl series in 1986. Preseason games were played until 2005 in several countries including Mexico, Canada, Japan, Great Britain, Spain, Ireland, Sweden, and Australia. The largest crowd ever to see an NFL game anywhere was at the preseason matchup between the Dallas Cowboys and the Houston Oilers at Azteca Stadium in Mexico City on August 15, 1994. That attendance record of 112,376 still stands.

The first attempt at playing a full season of games beyond the borders of the United States was the World League of American Football (WLAF), which started as a spring developmental league in 1991. It had ten teams, four of them international: the London Monarchs, Barcelona Dragons, Frankfurt Galaxy, and the Montreal Machine. During its first year, the other six teams were based in the United States. After stops and starts, dwindling crowds, and never turning a profit, the WLAF was rebranded as NFL Europa in 1998. The US- and Montreal-based teams were gone, replaced by three more clubs in Germany and one in the Netherlands. The league limped along for almost another decade until June 2007.

It had always been a minor-league product with a few players going on to NFL careers, but Europa team rosters lacked the drawing power of marquee stars. And watching the Monarchs versus the Dragons was never going to approach the excitement or the high-caliber competition of the Packers versus the Cowboys, no matter where it was played. That is precisely what new commissioner Roger Goodell provided when the league launched its international series of regular season games just a few months after NFL Europa folded. The New York Giants played the Miami Dolphins at London's Wembley Stadium on October 28, 2007. "The time is right to re-focus the NFL's strategy on initiatives with global impact, including worldwide media coverage of our sport and the staging of live regular-season NFL games," said Mark Waller, senior vice president of NFL International at the time. "We will continue to build our international fan base by taking advantage of technology and customized digital media that make the NFL more accessible on a global scale than ever before and through the regular-season game experience," said Waller. "NFL Europa has created thousands of passionate fans who have supported that league and our sport for many years, and we look forward to building on this foundation as we begin this new phase of our international development."[7]

In 2022, after having played thirty regular season games in London, virtually every one of them an instant sellout, the NFL expanded the International Series to include Germany. "We are very pleased to welcome Munich and Frankfurt to the NFL family and excited to reward our fans in Germany for their passion by bringing them the excitement of regular season NFL football," said Commissioner Goodell. In announcing these games before Super Bowl LVI in Los Angeles, Goodell said that the league was exploring "broader areas of collaboration" with the Bundesliga soccer league. Frankfurt's sports councilor Mark Josef hinted at the possibility of more than just occasional NFL games. "American football was and still is at home in Frankfurt," he said. "The NFL is not just coming to Frankfurt for a game. With its sustainable engagement in our community, we are sure to achieve a great boost for sports in Frankfurt." NFL surveys have reported that the league has more than thirty million fans in Europe, 13.8 million of them in Germany. The NFL already has close to thirty international media rights deals from Australia to Africa and Brazil to Bulgaria. The first international game in Brazil will be played in Sao Paolo in the fall of 2024. Playing more regular season games in more places is bound to continue expanding the list.[8]

To engage these fans and connect them more closely with individual teams, the NFL announced the beginning of its International Home Markets program in December 2021. Eighteen teams were granted marketing areas in eight countries as part of a long-term, strategic effort to enable clubs to build their global brands and drive NFL fan growth internationally. "NFL fandom begins with our clubs," said Christopher Halpin, NFL executive vice president, chief strategy and growth officer, on the occasion of the launch. In its second year, the initiative, renamed the Global Markets Program, expanded to twenty-one teams operating in fourteen different countries. They each have five-year terms in which to market their brands, engage fans, and activate promotions and commercialization. "We know that global fandom is accelerated through direct engagement with our clubs and players, and we are excited to see the continued impact of this program to reach and engage more fans and grow our sport at every level globally," said NFL Executive Vice President Peter O'Reilly.[9]

The first year that an NFL team is based in a city outside the United States, the possibility will exist for a playoff or conference championship game to be played on foreign soil. But awarding a Super Bowl to any city outside the fifty states would be highly problematic. Only sixteen US-based teams have hosted Super Bowls, which means that half the teams, their owners, and their respective cities have never had that honor bestowed on them. Along with the prestige, of course, would come the opportunity for local businesses and nonprofit organizations to reap the multimillion dollar benefits associated with playing host to the biggest one-day sporting event in the world. Imagine the outcry from the congressional representatives and senators from those cities and states. They would surely summon the commissioner to appear before hearings on Capitol Hill to explain why their constituents were to be denied these considerable benefits and why the Super Bowl, an institution that so overwhelming represents America, was being moved offshore.

A Smaller World Will Mean a Bigger NFL

One factor that will accelerate the placement of NFL teams in Europe, and perhaps even in Asia, is the return of supersonic commercial air travel. Testing and construction are already well underway on aircraft that by the end of this decade will each carry sixty-five to eighty passengers at close to twice the speed of sound. American Airlines, United, and Japan Airlines have already placed orders for more than one hundred Overture jets from Boom Technologies of Englewood, Colorado. The planes will fly at approximately 1,300 miles per hour, shrinking the flying time from London to New York to three and a half hours. A production facility being built in Greensboro, North Carolina, will have the capacity to build thirty-three of the supersonic jets each year. The return of commercial supersonic travel will arrive a quarter century after the Concorde SST last flew in 2003. For forty years, its flights between London and

New York took only four hours, but the planes were retired due to costly inefficiencies.[10]

NASA has also teamed with Lockheed Martin to build a supersonic passenger jet. The X-59 will reduce the loud sonic boom caused when a plane surpasses the speed of sound to what is described as "a gentle bump." The first X-59 aircraft was completed in 2023, and ground testing began at Lockheed's Skunk Works facility in Palmdale, California. The plane is designed to achieve speeds of 925 miles per hour, which would cut flying time in half between any two airports, foreign or domestic.[11]

The advent of a new supersonic age will make it possible for an NFL team, with its entire fifty-three-man roster and a contingent of coaches, to fly from East Coast cities to London in four hours and from San Francisco to Tokyo in six hours. By drastically reducing flight times, these new aircraft will make international travel far more feasible and thereby dramatically increase the likelihood of expansion franchises across both oceans. But I don't expect that anyone, team members or fans, will have to book a supersonic flight for a Super Bowl in Europe, or elsewhere outside American borders, any time soon.

An Unrivaled Entertainment Colossus

In its early years, the Super Bowl was one TV show on one Sunday afternoon in the winter. It became a primetime show beginning with Super Bowl X in 1976. Its audience and success continued to grow, but it was still one night only. The move to expand American mass media coverage to more than one day began in 2012 with the first *NFL Honors*, televised live on the Saturday night before Super Bowl XLVI in Indianapolis. The show, which has been moved to Thursday night each year, features the announcement of the season's MVP and other major awards. A third night of live sports entertainment was added to Super Bowl week when the game observed its fiftieth birthday in 2016. The league transformed its annual Super Bowl Media Day into Super Bowl Opening Night. What had been a Wednesday afternoon event that gave credentialed media representatives an opportunity to ask questions of both teams' players and coaches became a Monday night prime-time show with live music and staged entertainment.

During its first fifty years, the Super Bowl expanded from one to three days of live, heavily sponsored television. During its second half-century, the move to take over American mass media during Super Bowl Week and attract millions more viewers around the globe will continue until there is a major Super Bowl–themed live media entertainment event not just on Monday, Thursday, and Sunday, but on every day of the week. Consider these possibilities:

- *The Super Bowl Superstars of Music.* Three simultaneous concerts, all streaming live around the world on separate channels. One would be in the Super Bowl host city, and the other two at the home stadiums of the teams that are competing. This would make for something very special to engage the fans back home in the two AFC and NFC championship-winning cities as well as at the site of the Super Bowl. Proceeds would benefit charities selected by the NFL teams in all three cities.

- *The Madden Interactive Super Bowl.* Instead of having the Super Bowl simulated in advance thousands of times by EA Sports computers, this would be a live interactive esports special with a million or more gamers playing the EA Sports Super Bowl simulation. Their results would register in real time on live streams in several countries with the predicted Super Bowl winner being announced at the end of the show. (The video game debuted in 1988, so by 2066 it would be in its seventy-ninth year. It still may be named "Madden" by then, or it may have been updated and renamed for the greatest coach-turned-broadcaster with the biggest personality of the 2030–2055 era.)

- *The Pro Football Hall of Fame Announcement Special.* The announcement of the year's new class of inductees is currently part of *NFL Honors*, but working with the Pro Football Hall of Fame, NFL Films could produce a one-hour live special featuring introductions of each inductee along with video segments highlighting their career achievements in the style of the NFL's *A Football Life* series.

- *The NFL's Salute to Service.* This event would profile American service units that are making a difference at home and abroad, cutting live to wherever they are stationed for quick interviews with commanders and corporals alike. And the definition of "service" would be expanded to nonprofit organizations in the host city that each year receive funding from the local Super Bowl Host Committee. These groups are at work all year long, helping those in need, improving education and opportunity, and enhancing the environment of their regions and states. The *Salute to Service* event could conclude with the NFL commissioner appearing live to present a $1 million NFL Foundation grant to a deserving charity followed by a patriotic fireworks show.

- *The Super Bowl Super Chefs: Tastes of the World.* Each country with an NFL franchise (by 2066 that should total at least four or five) would send several great chefs to the Super Bowl host city. At a huge food festival lasting at least three or four nights, these visiting chefs and the best from the host region would cook their best recipes for thousands of visitors. The first night of the festival, the live *Super Chef* show would be televised in each country represented via multiple streams, either live or on a delay depending upon time zones. Each stream would be hosted by one of the famous food critics/hosts of the era (the Guy Fieri, Gordon Ramsay, and Giada DeLaurentiis of the day). Viewers using interactive remotes could rate each dish: (1) I'd Love It, (2) I'd Try It, or (3) I'd Pass It By. At the end of the show, the audience picks for each nation would be tabulated and the winning chefs celebrated. Currently there's an annual *Taste of the NFL*, which is a one-night fundraiser with a few hundred guests that benefits local organizations that feed the hungry. The *Super Chefs* show could multiply the impact many times over and extend its reach to serve people in need around the world.

If the NFL were to develop all five of these event suggestions, Super Bowl Week would have to be expanded to eight days—not at all beyond the realm of possibility.

The Super Bowl Has Changed America

The Super Bowl has changed what was just another wintry Sunday into America's unofficial holiday, bigger than most of our official US holidays. As such, it has become an important part of how millions of people connect with each other: at parties and gatherings and in conversations about the game, its teams, the stars on the field, or the performances at halftime, as well as the commercials. It has become the biggest entertainment event of the year, attracting huge audiences and massive media attention, broadcast and social.

The Super Bowl has long been, and will continue to be, the most important advertising event of the year. Super Bowl commercials reach more than one hundred million viewers at a time, and millions more in online replays. Our introduction to many new products and services that we will buy for years to come is in one of these commercials.

How we spend billions of dollars of our disposable income is affected by the Super Bowl. More money is wagered on the game than on any other event all year long. The purchases of new televisions, lounge furniture, and food and drink skyrocket in the days leading up to every Super Bowl. When you calculate the economic impact of the Super Bowl, it is larger than the annual gross domestic product of many small nations.

The Super Bowl has dramatically changed the cities that host the game. Millions of dollars are spent on infrastructure improvements. Local vendors, schools, and charitable organizations see an influx of revenue and donations. The myriad of activities surrounding the Super Bowl and all the effort needed to stage the event represent development opportunities for youth, volunteers, and the enhancement of cultural resources. Many first-time visitors will plan return visits because they were impressed with the city and its environs. Perhaps most importantly, hosting a Super Bowl puts a city into an elite club, elevating its national and international reputation. For example, there are fifty-two cities in the United States with larger populations than New Orleans, including Charlotte, Nashville, and Kansas City, all of which are home to NFL franchises. But, having hosted ten Super Bowls and counting, New Orleans's reputation as a great city and a fun destination has benefitted tremendously from its resulting media exposure.

In this book, I have detailed how the Super Bowl's impact has been social, cultural, economic, political, and international. The Super Bowl has become a symbol that represents America to the rest of the world. The ultimate game of a truly American sport that is based on the forceful conquering of territory, the Super Bowl rewards courage, strength, determination, and resilience. It is "American optimism on full display for the world to see," in all its glorious celebration, success, and excess.

Looking ahead to the second half-century of the Super Bowl, the NFL said that it was "staking our claim that the next 50 years is only going to get better—for the NFL, our fans, and America." The challenges to be faced by this nation and its institutions in the decades to come will no doubt cause frustrating setbacks, troubles both foreseen and unforeseen. But with the optimism that all adversity can be overcome with strength of character, strength of will, and innovative problem solving, the NFL and the United States alike have the opportunity to celebrate victories large and small season by season, year by year.

NOTES

CHAPTER 1

1. George Stanley Halas, *Halas by Halas: The Autobiography of George Halas* (New York: McGraw-Hill, 1979), 30–32.

2. Gary Brown, "Remembering Pro Football's Ralph Hay: League Founder Called Canton Home," Canton Repository, 2019, www.cantonrep.com/story/news/local/canton/2019/09/08/remembering-pro-football-s-ralph/3462090007/ (accessed 13 Oct. 2019).

3. Jim Thorpe History, Oklahoma Sports Hall of Fame, https://oklahomasportshalloffame.org/jim-thorpe-museum (accessed 13 Oct. 2019).

4. Oorang Indians, Pro Football Hall of Fame, www.profootballhof.com/football-history/oorang-indians/ (accessed 14 Oct. 2019).

5. Christopher Klein, "The Birth of the National Football League," 2014, www.history.com/news/the-birth-of-the-national-football-league (accessed 16 Oct. 2019).

6. "Joining the NFL," www.packers.com/history/ (accessed 16 Oct. 2019).

7. Gary Reinmuth, "Red Grange: Greatness and Humility," *Chicago Tribune*, 29 Jan. 1991, www.chicagotribune.com/news/ct-xpm-1991-01-29-9101090327-story.html (accessed 17 Oct. 2019).

8. Dave Anderson, "Sports of the Times; When Grange Put the Pros in New York," *New York Times*, 26 Nov. 2000, www.nytimes.com/2000/11/26/sports/sports-of-the-times-when-grange-put-the-pros-in-new-york.html (accessed 17 Oct. 2019).

9. Pro Football Hall of Fame, "Chronology of Professional Football," www.profootballhof.com/football-history/chronology-of-professional-football/ (accessed 18 Oct. 2019).

10. Associated Press, "This Day in Sports," 17 Dec. 1933, "When the Bears Were Young Lions," *New York Times*, https://archive.nytimes.com/www.nytimes.com/packages/html/sports/year_in_sports/12.17.html?scp=3&sq=the%2520rivals&st=cse (accessed 19 Oct. 2019).

11. Jim Campbell, "Pro Football's First TV Game," *Football Digest*, 1981, https://profootballresearchers.org/archives/Website_Files/Coffin_Corner/03-03-062.pdf (accessed 20 Oct. 2019).

12. Woodrow Strode Jr. and Pamela Strode, "Strode Road: The Extraordinary Life of Woody Strode," 1946 Halley Harding Speech, www.youtube.com/watch?v=9pfsypXi6oc (accessed 2 Nov. 2019).

13. Kenneth R. Crippen and Matt Reaser, eds., *The All-America Football Conference: Players, Coaches, Records, Games and Awards 1946–1949* (Jefferson, NC: McFarland, 2018), 41–50.

14. Michael MacCambridge, *America's* Game*: The Epic Story of How Pro Football Captured a Nation* (New York: Anchor Books 2005), 110–15.

15. Louis Effrat, "Colts Beat Giants, Win in Overtime," *New York Times*, 29 Dec. 1958, 1, 25.

16. MacCambridge, *America's Game*, 120–24.

17. David Debolt, "Oakland Raiders: What Was the Team's First Mascot?" *East Bay Times*, 29 March 2017, www.eastbaytimes.com/2017/03/29/oakland-raiders-what-was -the-teams-first-mascot/ (accessed 4 Nov. 2019).

18. Al Michaels, "The History of the NFL on Television," interview by David Plaut, NFL Films transcript, 29 Sept. 1997.

19. Richard Sandomir, "Rozelle's NFL Legacy: Television, Marketing and Money," *New York Times*, 8 Dec. 1996, 64.

20. *United States v. National Football League*, 196 F. Supp. 445 (E.D. Pa. 1961), 20 July 1961, Civ. A. No. 12808, https://law.justia.com/cases/federal/district-courts/FSupp/196 /445/1690845/ (accessed 7 July 2019).

21. William N. Wallace, "Pete Rozelle Dies at 70; Led N.F.L.'s Growth Years," *New York Times*, 8 Dec. 1996, 62.

CHAPTER 2

1. Michael MacCambridge, *America's Game: The Epic Story of How Pro Football Captured a Nation* (New York: Anchor Books, 2005), 112, 113.

2. Roone Arledge, "The History of the NFL on Television," interview by David Swain, NFL Films transcript, 23 Sept. 1997.

3. *American Football League v. National Football League*, 205 F. Supp. 60 (D. Md. 1962), 21 May 1962, Civ. No. 12559, https://law.justia.com/cases/federal/district-courts/FSupp /205/60/2181427/, (accessed 9 July 2019).

4. *Los Angeles Rams Football Club v. Cannon*, 185 F. Supp. 717 (S.D. Cal. 1960), 20 June 1960, No. 32–60 WB (accessed 11 July 2019).

5. "Full Color Football: The History of the American Football League," NFL Films, episode 1, 16 Sept. 2009.

6. Mark Kriegel, *Namath: A Biography* (New York: Penguin, 2005), 141.

7. Don Weiss and Chuck Day, *The Making of the Super Bowl: The Inside Story of the World's Greatest Sporting Event* (New York: McGraw-Hill, 2003), 51.

8. MacCambridge, *America's Game*, 223.

9. Weiss and Day, *The Making of the Super Bowl*, 42.

10. MacCambridge, *America's Game*, 228–30.

11. Floyd Little, interview with the author, 30 April 2016.

CHAPTER 3

1. Lamar Hunt, "The History of the NFL on Television," interview by David Swain, 2 Oct. 1997, NFL Films transcript.

2. Michael MacCambridge, *America's Game: The Epic Story of How Pro Football Captured a Nation* (New York: Anchor Books, 2005), 237.

3. MacCambridge, *America's Game*, 229.

4. MacCambridge, *America's Game*, 229.

5. Don Weiss and Chuck Day, *The Making of the Super Bowl: The Inside Story of the World's Greatest Sporting Event* (New York: McGraw-Hill, 2003), 98.

6. Weiss and Day, *The Making of the Super Bowl*, 107.

7. Gene Wojciechowski, "Q&A with Pete Rozelle," *Los Angeles Times*, 24 Jan. 1993.

8. Chet Simmons, "The History of the NFL on Television," interview by David Swain, 12 Sept. 1997, NFL Films transcript.

9. William Fitts, interview with the author, 4 Jan. 2011.

10. Weiss and Day, *The Making of the Super Bowl*, 126–27.

11. Curt Gowdy, "The History of the NFL on Television," interview by David Plaut, 19 Sept. 1997, NFL Films transcript.

12. William N. Wallace, "Green Bay Wins Football Title: National League Champions Beat Kansas City, 35–10 in Super Bowl Game," *New York Times*, 16 Jan. 1967, 1, 32(N).

CHAPTER 4

1. Dave Anderson, "Jets Upset Colts by 16–7 for Title in the Super Bowl," *New York Times*, 13 Jan. 1969, 1, 32(N).

2. Mark Kriegel, *Namath: A Biography* (New York: Penguin, 2005), 262.

3. Michael MacCambridge, *America's Game: The Epic Story of How Pro Football Captured a Nation* (New York: Anchor Books, 2005), 253.

4. Super Bowl III transcript, NBC telecast, 12 Jan. 1969.

5. Kriegel, *Namath*, 262.

6. William N. Wallace, "Green Bay Wins Football Title: National League Champions Beat Kansas City, 35–10 in Super Bowl Game," *New York Times*, 16 Jan. 1969, 1, 32(N).

7. Tex Maule, "Say It's So, Joe," *Sports Illustrated*, 20 Jan. 1969.

8. David Brooks, *The Road to Character* (New York: Random House, 2015), 221.

9. Jimmy Breslin, "Namath All Night," *New Yorker*, 7 April 1969, https://nymag.com/news/sports/50144/ (accessed 8 Aug. 2020).

10. "Marlin Briscoe, African American Pioneer," Pro Football Hall of Fame, 1 Jan. 2005.

11. Jason Reid, "Willie Thrower: A Perfect Name for a Trailblazing Quarterback: His Contributions to the Game Go Well beyond His Short NFL Career," *The Undefeated*, 10 Oct. 2017.

12. Cliff Brunt, "Former Broncos' Marlin Briscoe—the 1st Black Starting QB—Reflects on Changes in Game, Society," *Denver Post*, 25 Sept. 2018.

13. Maury Z. Levy, "The Playboy Interview: Terry Bradshaw," *Playboy*, March 1980.

14. Frank Litsky, "John McKay, U.S.C. and Buccaneers Coach, Dies at 77," *New York Times*, 11 June 2001.

15. William C. Rhoden, "Third and a Mile: The Trials and Triumphs of the Black Quarterback," ESPN Films documentary, 2007.

16. Jill Lieber, "Well Armed Pioneer," *Sports Illustrated*, 1 Feb. 1988, https://vault.si .com/vault/1988/02/01/702669-toc (accessed 3 Feb. 2019).

17. Mike Bianchi, "Dumbest Question Was Never Asked," *Orlando Sentinel*, 30 Jan. 2007.

18. Rhoden, "Third and a Mile."

19. Roger B. Brown, "NFL's Black Quarterback Barrier Finally Topples," *Chicago Tribune*, 12 Oct. 1997.

20. Dave Anderson, "Sports of the Times: Bus Ride to History," *New York Times*, 2 Feb. 1988.

21. Anderson, "Sports of the Times."

22. Greg Garber, "Williams' Super Bowl Start Opened Door to Dreams," ESPN.com, 31 Jan. 2007.

23. Garber, "Williams' Super Bowl Start Opened Door to Dreams."

24. Greg Garber, "Doug Williams Embraces History," ESPN.com, 29 Jan. 2013.

CHAPTER 5

1. NFL's vision statement for Super Bowl 50 in 2016, shared with the author by an NFL official.

2. Ira Berkow, "Once Again It's the Star-Spangled Super Bowl," *New York Times*, 27 Jan. 1991, www.nytimes.com/1991/01/27/sports/sports-of-the-times-once-again-it-s -the-star-spangled-super-bowl.html (accessed 10 Aug. 2020).

3. Michael Schottey, "The Flag and the Shield: The Long Alliance between the NFL and US Military," Bleacher Report, 26 May 2014, https://bleacherreport.com /articles/2029052-the-flag-and-the-shield-the-long-alliance-between-the-nfl-and-the -us-military (10 Aug. 2020).

4. "Red Sox Beat Cubs in Initial Battle of World's Series," *New York Times*, 6 Sept. 1918, 14(N).

5. Don Babwin, "1918 World Series Started the U.S. Love Affair with National Anthem," *Chicago Tribune*, 3 July 2017.

6. Len Travers, *Encyclopedia of American Holidays and National Days* (Westport, CT: Greenwood Press, 2006), 33.

7. Associated Press, "Dawson Receives Hail from Chief," *New York Times*, 12 Jan. 1970, 52(N).

8. NFL video, "President Obama Invites the Super Bowl Champion Broncos to the White House," YouTube, 10 Feb. 2016.

9. Steve Wyche, "Colin Kaepernick Explains Why He Sat during National Anthem," NFL.com, 27 Aug. 2016.

10. Roger Goodell, NFL Communications press release, 23 Sept. 2017.

11. Robert Kraft, New England Patriots press release, 23 Sept. 2017.

12. DeMaurice Smith, NFLPA press release, 23 Sept. 2017.

13. Gerald Eskenazi, "Super Bowl XXV; Tagliabue Calls Game 'Winter 4th of July,'" *New York Times*, 26 Jan. 1991.

14. Lee Simmons, "How the NFL Turned the Super Bowl into a Money Machine: A Sports Management Expert Explains the Economic Impact of America's Largest Sporting Event," *Stanford Graduate School of Business Insights*, 2 Feb. 2016.

15. Ronald Reagan, *The White House Diaries*, 20 Jan. 1985, Presidential Foundation and Institute.

16. Rhiannon Walker, "When Arizona Lost the Super Bowl Because the State Didn't Recognize Martin Luther King Jr. Day," The Undefeated, 2 March 2017.

17. Fernanda Santos, "Arizona Governor Vetoes Bill on Refusal of Service to Gays," *New York Times*, 26 Feb. 2014.

18. Michael Silver. "9/11 Forced Ex-NFL Commish to Make Decision of Lifetime," Yahoo News, 7 Sept. 2011, https://news.yahoo.com/911-forced-ex-nfl-commish-to-make-decision-of-lifetime.html (accessed 15 Aug. 2020).

19. Harry S. Truman, "Special Message to the Congress: The President's First Economic Report," January 8, 1947, The American Presidency Project, UC Santa Barbara, www.presidency.ucsb.edu/documents/special-message-the-congress-the-presidents-first-economic-report#:~:text=Nor%20have%20our%20prospects%20ever,do%20the%20job%20at%20hand (accessed 16 Aug. 2020).

20. Department of Homeland Security Major Event Security Cases, "The Super Bowl: How DHS Secures the Biggest Party on the Planet," www.dhs.gov/major-event-security-cases (accessed 16 Aug. 2020).

21. Shaheem Reid, "Janet, Justin, MTV Apologize for Super Bowl Flash," MTV News, 1 Feb. 2004.

22. Michael Waters, "Super Bowl Flashback: The Forgotten Details of Janet Jackson's 'Nipplegate,'" *Hollywood Reporter*, 1 Feb. 2018, www.hollywoodreporter.com/news/hollywood-flashback-what-happened-justin-timberlake-janet-jacksons-2004-super-bowl-halftime-show-1080688 (accessed 18 Aug. 2020).

23. Broadcast Decency Enforcement Act of 2005, 109th Congress (2005–2006).

24. John H. Cushman Jr., "Supreme Court Rejects F.C.C. Appeal in Janet Jackson Case," *New York Times*, 29 June 2012.

CHAPTER 6

1. Elise Harris, "Pope Francis Has a Special Message for the Super Bowl," Catholic News Agency, 5 Feb. 2017.

2. "Heinz Launches Petition to Make Day after Super Bowl a Holiday," Change.org, 3 Feb. 2017, www.change.org/l/us/heinz-launches-petition-to-make-day-after-super-bowl-a-holiday (accessed 10 Jan 2018).

3. Burson, Cohn and Wolfe/PSB Research, "Millennials Crave More Excitement from Super Bowl Experience, According to Sixth Annual BCW Super Bowl Survey," 29 Jan. 2019.

4. Andrea Quintero, "How NFL Fans Used Wi-Fi at Super Bowl LVII and Why It Matters," Extreme Networks, 24 Feb. 2023, www.extremenetworks.com/resources/blogs/how-nfl-fans-used-wi-fi-at-super-bowl-lvii-and-why-it-matters (accessed 28 Feb 2023).

5. Robert B. Cialdini and Robert J. Borden, "Basking in Reflected Glory: Three (Football) Field Studies," *The Journal of Personality and Social Psychology* 34, no. 3 (1976): 366–75.

6. Nathan A. Heflick, "Suicide Rates over the Holidays: Unravelling the Truth about Holiday Suicide Rates," *Psychology Today*, 25 Dec. 2013.

7. Ken Ringle, "Debunking the 'Day of Dread' for Women," *Washington Post*, 31 Jan. 1993.

8. Automobile Club of Southern California, "More DUI Crashes Occur on Super Bowl Sundays," 26 Jan. 2015.

9. Tex Maule, "Players Are Not Just People: The NFL Suspends Its Golden Boy," *Sports Illustrated*, 29 April 1963.

10. "NFL Commissioner Roger Goodell Issues Statement on Gambling," NFL Communications, 21 May 2018.

11. Dave Zirin, "Athletes Aren't Roulette Chips: Bill Bradley Speaks out on Gambling in Sports," *The Nation*, 12 June 2018.

12. Katie Cox and Derrik Thomas, "Five Years Later, Super Bowl Legacy Still Impacts Indianapolis," The Indychannel.com, 3 Feb. 2017.

13. Brian Cronin, "Did the New York Giants Originate the Gatorade Shower?" *Los Angeles Times*, 14 Sept. 2011.

CHAPTER 7

1. "Consumers Say They'll Spend an Average $81 on Super Bowl," National Retail Federation, 24 Jan. 2019, https://nrf.com/media-center/press-releases/consumers-say-theyll-spend-average-81-super-bowl (accessed 27 Jan. 2019).

2. "Spending for the Big Game," National Retail Federation, 24 Jan. 2024, https://nrf.com/research-insights/holiday-data-and-trends/super-bowl (accessed 31 Jan 2024).

3. Megan Cerullo, "Americans Buy Pricey TVs to Watch the Super Bowl—Then Return Them," CBS News Moneywatch, 30 Jan. 2019.

4. Sandra Cook, "Keeping Score: Capitalizing on Super Bowl LI: The Stage Is Set for America's Biggest Party," DowntownHouston.org, 1 Dec. 2016.

5. Daniel Kaplan, "League to Choose Super Bowl Sites through Single-City Negotiations," *Sports Business Journal*, 29 Jan. 2018.

6. Tim Tucker, "Inside Atlanta's Super Bowl Bid: NFL Sought, Got a Lot," *Atlanta Journal Constitution*, 3 June 2016.

7. Mike Kaszuba and Rochelle Olson, "NFL Had a Long, Pricey and Secret Super Bowl Wish List for Minneapolis," *Minneapolis Star Tribune*, 9 June 2014.

8. Kenneth McGill and Jon Gray, "The Economic Impact of Super Bowl LII on Minneapolis and Minnesota, Post-Event Full Report," *Rockport Analytics*, May 2018.

9. Jon Banister, "The Reason behind The NFL's 'Blatantly Dishonest' Super Bowl Economic Impact Studies," *Bisnow*, 4 Feb. 2017.

10. Brandon Bielich, "Super Bowl Survey: Will We See a Spike in Absenteeism?" The Workforce Institute, 7 Feb. 2023, https://workforceinstitute.org/super-bowl-survey-will-we-see-a-spike-in-absenteeism/ (accessed 8 Feb. 2023).

11. Emma Burleigh, "The Super Bowl Flu Will Soon Hit Millions of Employees—And It Could Cost Businesses More Than $6 Billion," *Fortune*, 9 Feb. 2024

Chapter 8

1. Michael Oriard, *Brand NFL: Making and Selling America's Favorite Sport* (Chapel Hill: University of North Carolina Press, 2010), 45–46.

2. "NFL Launching Women's Clothing Line," Foxsports.com, 28 Sept. 2010, www.foxsports.com/stories/nfl/nfl-launching-womens-clothing-line (accessed 10 Dec. 2012).

3. Roger Goodell, "Communicating the NFL Brand," NFL Identity Guidelines. 2010.

4. John Madden, "The History of the NFL on Television," interview by David Swain, NFL Films, 18 Sept. 1997.

5. "Industry Demographics," The Fantasy Sports and Gaming Association 2023 report, https://thefsga.org/industry-demographics/ (accessed 11 Aug. 2023).

6. NFL Communications press release, "Electronic Arts, the NFL and the NFLPA Announce a Groundbreaking Multi-Year Global Partnership," 28 May 2020.

7. Adam Harter, interview with the author, 16 Nov. 2021.

8. Richard Sandomir, "Not Quite Saying 'Super Bowl,' but Cashing in on It," *New York Times*, 6 Feb. 2010.

9. Bill Brubaker, "Judge Blocks Coors," *Washington Post*, 6 Aug. 1999.

10. Marcus Baram, "NFL Sacks Church Super Bowl Parties: Dozens of Churches Have Cancelled Bowl Parties That Could Violate NFL Policy," ABCNews.com, 2 Feb. 2008.

11. Emily Kaplan, "Paid to Give Concussions," *Sports Illustrated*, 9 Dec. 2015.

12. Mark Fainaru-Wada, "Bob Costas, Unplugged: From NBC and Broadcast Icon to Dropped from the Super Bowl," ESPN.com, 10 Feb. 2019.

13. University of Boston School of Medicine, "New Study of 111 Deceased Former NFL Players Finds 99 Percent Had CTE," 26 July 2017.

14. "Poll: Three-Quarters of Football Fans See Head Injuries as Major Problem," 6 Sept. 2017, UMass-Lowell, www.uml.edu/News/press-releases/2017/NFLPoll09062017.aspx (accessed 10 Sept. 2018).

15. Roger Goodell, "NFL Commitment to Player Health and Safety: A Letter from Commissioner Roger Goodell," PlaySmartPlaySafe.com, 14 Sept. 2016.

16. Mark Murray, "Poll: Nearly Half of Parents Would Discourage Football Due to Concussions," NBCNews.com, 2 Feb. 2018.

17. Thomas George, "Prosecutor Drops Charges of Murder in Deal with Lewis," *New York Times*, 6 June 2000.

18. Malcolm Gladwell, *Blink: The Power of Thinking without Thinking* (New York: Little, Brown, 2012), 24.

Chapter 9

1. Aaron Taube, "How the Greatest Super Bowl Ad Ever—Apple's '1984'—Almost Didn't Make It to Air," *Business Insider*, 22 Jan. 2014, www.businessinsider.com/apple-super-bowl-retrospective-2014-1 (accessed 10 Jan. 2016).

2. Sports Media Watch, "Super Bowl Ratings History (1967–present)," www.sportsmediawatch.com/super-bowl-ratings-historical-viewership-chart-cbs-nbc-fox-abc/ (accessed 14 Feb. 2023).

3. "Average Cost of Super Bowl Ads Breakdown by Year," SuperBowl-Ads.com, www.superbowl-ads.com/cost-of-super-bowl-advertising-breakdown-by-year/ (accessed 24 Feb. 2023).

4. David Kenyon, "Super Bowl Ads 2020: Analyzing Value and Cost of Top Commercials," *Bleacher Report*, 1 Feb. 2020.

5. Stuart Elliott, "The Media Business: Advertising; Even with a Blowout on the Field, Companies Buying Super Bowl Spots See a Victory," *New York Times*, 27 Jan. 1995.

6. Nielsen Media Research and Insights, "Super Bowl Viewership Transcends Platforms and Devices," Feb. 2023, www.nielsen.com/insights/2023/super-bowl-viewership -transcends-platforms-and-devices/ (accessed 4 March 2023).

7. *Wall Street Journal*, "A Master of Super Bowl Commercials Explains How to Create Iconic Ads," YouTube, 29 Jan. 2019, www.youtube.com/watch?v=ESbZRyQw_6Y (accessed 24 Feb. 2019).

8. Nat Ives, "Budweiser 'Puppy Love' Named the Best Super Bowl Ad Meter Winner of All Time," *AdAge*, 31 Jan. 2018.

9. Clifton B. Parker, "Do Super Bowl Ads Really Work? Not All Big Game TV Commercials Drive Enough Sales to Offset the Ad's Cost," *Stanford Graduate School of Business Insights*, 29 Jan. 2015.

10. "A-B Ends 34-Year Run as Super Bowl's Exclusive Alcohol Advertiser," *Sports Business Journal*, 17 June 2022.

11. Chris Nashawaty, "Bud Bowl: The Novel Idea That Forever Changed Super Bowl Commercials," SI.com, 2 Nov. 2015.

12. Nashawaty, "Bud Bowl."

13. Alice Gomstyn, "Banned Super Bowl Commercials: Are Advertisers Seeking out Controversy on Purpose?" ABC News, 1 Feb. 2010, https://abcnews.go.com/ Business/super-bowl-ads-tim-tebow-men-kissing-publicity-commercials-banned/story ?id=9720930 (accessed 15 June 2020).

14. Delaney Strunk, "The Biggest Rivalry in Atlanta on Super Bowl Weekend Has Nothing to Do with Football," CNN.com, 29 Jan. 2019, www.cnn.com/2019/01/29/ media/super-bowl-2019-coke-pepsi-trnd/index.html (accessed 3 Feb. 2019).

CHAPTER 10

1. Dick Ebersol, "The History of the NFL on Television," interview by David Swain, NFL Films transcript, 6 Oct. 1997.

2. Ray Scott, "75 Seasons: The Story of the NFL," interview by Jonathan Hock, NFL Films transcript, 6 Sept. 1996.

3. "Vinnie, Vidi, Vici," *Time*, 12 Dec. 1962, 56–61.

4. Michael MacCambridge, *America's Game: The Epic Story of How Pro Football Captured a Nation* (New York: Anchor Books, 2005), 240.

5. Jerry Izenberg, interview with the author, 20 July 2019.

6. Izenberg, interview with the author.

7. Michael MacCambridge, *America's Game: The Epic Story of How Pro Football Captured a Nation* (New York: Anchor Books, 2005), 256–58.

8. William N. Wallace. "Pro Football Gets 4-Year TV Pact," *New York Times*, 27 Jan. 1970.

9. Dick Ebersol, "The History of the NFL on Television," interview by David Swain, NFL Films transcript, 6 Oct. 1997.

10. Roone Arledge, "The History of the NFL on Television," interview by David Swain, NFL Films transcript, 23 Sept. 1997.

11. Arledge, "The History of the NFL on Television."

12. Tony Kornheiser, "Super Bowl a Cultural Phenomenon in Prime Time," *New York Times*, 9 Jan. 1978.

13. Chet Simmons, "The History of the NFL on Television," interview by David Swain, NFL Films transcript, 12 Sept. 1997.

14. William Fitts, interview by the author, 4 Jan. 2011.

15. Steven Bornstein, "The History of the NFL on Television," interview by David Swain, NFL Films transcript, 7 Oct. 1997.

16. Chet Simmons, "The History of the NFL on Television."

17. Bob Rauscher, interview with the author, 3 March 2020.

18. Steven Bornstein, "The History of the NFL on Television," interview by David Swain, NFL Films transcript, 7 Oct. 1997.

19. Bornstein, "The History of the NFL on Television."

20. John Madden, "The History of the NFL on Television," interview by David Swain, NFL Films transcript, 18 Sept. 1997.

21. Bob Goldsborough, "Leonard Reiffel, Inventor of Telestrator Used to Show NFL Replays, Dies at 89," *Chicago Tribune*, 20 April 2017.

22. Richard Sandomir, "Fox Network Outbids CBS for Rights to Pro Football," *New York Times*, 18 Dec. 1993.

23. David Hill, "The History of the NFL on Television," interview by David Swain, NFL Films transcript, 24 Sept. 1997.

24. James Brown, "The History of the NFL on Television," interview by David Swain, NFL Films transcript, 22 Sept. 1997.

25. Sam Gardner, "Twenty Years Ago, FOX Tackled the Super Bowl for the First Time," FOXSports.com, 5 Feb. 2017.

26. Gardner, "Twenty Years Ago, FOX Tackled the Super Bowl."

27. Richard Sandomir, "Monday Nights Are Changing: N.F.L. off ABC," *New York Times*, 19 April 2005.

28. Sandomir, "Monday Nights Are Changing."

29. Fred Gaudelli, interview by the author, 12 June 2020.

30. Bornstein, "The History of the NFL on Television."

CHAPTER 11

1. Bob Oates, "It's His Baby: Pete Rozelle Brought the Super Bowl into the World, and It Grew up in a Hurry," *Los Angeles Times*, 27 Jan. 1996.

2. Rick Maese, "At First Super Bowl, the Halftime Show Passed with Flying Colors," *Washington Post*, 13 Jan. 2017.

3. Dan Jacobson, "Radio City Hires 'Mr. Spectacular,'" UPI, 17 July 1986.

4. John Helyar, "The Evolution of an Extravaganza," ESPN.com, 29 Jan. 2007, www .espn.com/nfl/playoffs06/news/story?id=2747099 (accessed 30 March 2016).

5. Ericka N. Goodman-Hughey, with reporting by Charlotte Gibson. "How In Living Color Won the 1992 Super Bowl," ESPN.com, 30 Jan. 2020, www.espn.com/espn/story/ _/id/28592073/super-bowl-half-show-never-same-jennifer-lopez-living-color (accessed 24 Feb. 2020).

6. Helyar, "The Evolution of an Extravaganza."

7. Steve Knopper, "Flashback: Michael Jackson Reclaims His Pop Throne at Super Bowl XXVII," *Rolling Stone*, 31 Jan. 2018, www.rollingstone.com/music/music-features/ flashback-michael-jackson-reclaims-his-pop-throne-at-super-bowl-xxvii-129576/.

8. Helyar, "The Evolution of an Extravaganza."

9. Austin Murphy, "It's Halftime," *Sports Illustrated Longform*, undated, www.si.com/ longform/halftime/ (accessed 4 April 2020).

10. Marin Cogan, "In the Beginning There Was a Nipple," ESPN.com, 28 Jan. 2014, www.espn.com/espn/feature/story/_/id/10333439/wardrobe-malfunction-beginning -there-was-nipple (accessed 10 Dec. 2014).

11. Mark Quenzel, interview by the author, 31 Jan. 2019.

12. "Pro Football Pass for the President," *New York Times*, 8 Aug. 1945, 19(N).

13. Helyar, "The Evolution of an Extravaganza."

14. Chris Cuomo and Andrew Paparella, "Whitney Houston's Star-Spangled Secret," ABCNews.com, 16 Feb. 2012.

15. Tom Rivers, "The Garth Brooks Story," Westwood One Entertainment, 4 July 1996.

16. Donovan Kidd, "Highest Grossing Movies of 2018," IMDB.com, www.imdb.com /list/ls064494766/ (accessed 15 March 2019).

CHAPTER 12

1. National Federation of State High School Associations, High School Participation Survey Archive, www.nfhs.org/sports-resource-content/high-school-participation -survey-archive/ (accessed 7 July 2023).

2. US Bureau of Labor Statistics, "Usual Weekly Earnings of Wage and Salary Workers, Fourth Quarter 2023," 18 July 2023, www.bls.gov/news.release/archives/wkyeng _07182023.pdf (accessed 18 July 2023).

3. Associated Press, "NFL Regular-Season Ratings down 3% over Last Season," 13 Jan. 2023, ESPN.com (accessed 23 Jan. 2023).

4. Ed Sherman, "Amazon to Make 'Thursday Night Football' Streaming Debut," NFL.com, 28 Sept. 2017, www.nfl.com/news/amazon-to-make-thursday-night-football -streaming-debut-0ap3000000852728 (accessed 14 Nov. 2017).

5. American Gaming Association, "Five Years Post PASPA: Consumer Sports Betting Trends," 9 May 2023, www.americangaming.org/resources/five-years-post-paspa -consumer-sports-betting-trends/ (accessed 13 June 2023).

6. NFL Communications, "NFL Announces Tri-Exclusive Official Sports Betting Partners," NFL.com, 15 April 2021, www.nfl.com/news/nfl-announces-tri-exclusive -sports-betting-partners (accessed 16 April 2021).

7. NFL Communications, "NFL Europa Closes," NFL.com, 3 Aug. 2007, www.nfl.com/news/nfl-europa-closes (accessed 5 Jan. 2014).

8. NFL Communications, "Munich to Stage First-Ever Regular Season Game in Germany, Frankfurt Also to Host Future Games," NFL.com, 9 Feb. 2022.

9. NFL Communications, "NFL Announces International Home Marketing Area Teams and Markets," NFL.com, 15 Dec. 2021.

10. Michael Verdon, "Boom's New Supersonic Jet Just Got Closer to Hitting the Air," *The Robb Report*, 26 June 2023.

11. Sasha Ellis and Amiee Lomax, "NASA's X-59 Moves Closer to Runway," NASA.gov, 5 July 2023, www.nasa.gov/aeroresearch/nasa-x-59-moves-closer-to-runway.

INDEX

ABOUT THE AUTHOR

Dennis Deninger is an Emmy Award–winning former television producer, author, and innovative educator. He has produced live sports television from six continents and across the United States. He spent twenty-five years at ESPN leading production teams and creating new programming for studio, live events, and digital video platforms.

He is a professor at Syracuse University's Falk College of Sport, where he has been recognized for excellence in teaching. He was the founding director of the sports communications graduate program at the Newhouse School of Public Communications and has created several new graduate and undergraduate level courses including the Super Bowl and Society at Syracuse, his alma mater.

Dennis Deninger covered his first Super Bowl as head of production for ESPN Digital. As a professor at Syracuse University, he created the only college course in the United States that focuses on the impact the Super Bowl has had on American life, "The Super Bowl and Society." It is the most popular (and one of the most difficult) courses offered by the Falk College of Sport.

For more than a decade, Deninger has been researching the Super Bowl and connecting with his sources at the NFL and the networks that televise the game. For Super Bowl LIII in Atlanta, he launched a program that takes a small group of Syracuse University student reporters to cover Super Bowl week as credentialed members of the press on Radio Row. It has continued for every Super Bowl since, including the pandemic year of 2021 in Tampa.

Deninger's comments and analysis on the Super Bowl and other sports broadcasting topics have been quoted in national and international media including the *New York Times, Forbes, USA Today,* ABC News, NBC News, CNN, Associated Press, Reuters, *Wall Street Journal, Christian Science Monitor, Financial Times, International Business Times, Guardian, Sporting News,* NewsNation, and NFL Network.

Dennis Deninger is also the author of *Live Sports Media: The What, How and Why of Sports Broadcasting* and *Sports on Television.*